Lecture Notes in Computer Science 9584

Commenced Publication in 1973
Founding and Former Series Editors:
Gerhard Goos, Juris Hartmanis, and Jan van Leeuwen

More information about this series at http://www.springer.com/series/7409

Zhiguo Gong · Dickson K.W. Chiu
Di Zou (Eds.)

Current Developments in Web Based Learning

ICWL 2015 International Workshops, KMEL, IWUM, LA
Guangzhou, China, November 5–8, 2015
Revised Selected Papers

Springer

Editors
Zhiguo Gong
University of Macau
Macau
China

Dickson K.W. Chiu
The University of Hong Kong
Hong Kong
China

Di Zou
The Hong Kong Polytechnic University
Hong Kong
China

ISSN 0302-9743 ISSN 1611-3349 (electronic)
Lecture Notes in Computer Science
ISBN 978-3-319-32864-5 ISBN 978-3-319-32865-2 (eBook)
DOI 10.1007/978-3-319-32865-2

Library of Congress Control Number: 2016946960

LNCS Sublibrary: SL3 – Information Systems and Applications, incl. Internet/Web, and HCI

Printed on acid-free paper

This Springer imprint is published by Springer Nature
The registered company is Springer International Publishing AG Switzerland

Preface to ICWL 2015 Workshops

Since its inception in 2002, the International Conference on Web-Based Learning (ICWL) has become an important forum for the exchange and dissemination of Web-based learning techniques among researchers, educators, and practitioners from around the world. In 2015, ICWL was held in Guangzhou, China. This volume comprises papers from three workshops KMEL 2015 IWUM 2015 and LA 2015 that were selected from several workshop proposals associated with the main conference ICWL 2015.

As the events collocated with the main conference, the ICWL 2015 workshops concentrated on novel ideas and new technologies and developments in areas related to Web-based learning. We thank the workshop chairs for putting great effort into soliciting, reviewing, and selecting papers through a rigorous review process and extensive communication. A total of 20 papers from various countries were finally accepted and are included in this volume.

We would like to thank the ICWL organizers for their arrangements and coordination of the presentation sessions of the workshops. We also thank all the authors for their contributions.

November 2015

Zhiguo Gong
Yiwei Cao

The 5th International Symposium on Knowledge Management and E-Learning (KMEL 2015)

Program Chairs

Dickson K.W. Chiu	Faculty of Education, The University of Hong Kong, Hong Kong, SAR China
Maggie M. Wang	Faculty of Education, The University of Hong Kong, Hong Kong, SAR China

Program Committee Members

Patricia A. Abbott	Johns Hopkins University, USA
Elizabeth Borycki	University of Victoria, Canada
Michael Chau	The University of Hong Kong, Hong Kong, SAR China
Irene Y.L. Chen	National Changhua University of Education, Taiwan
Lei Chen	Hong Kong University of Science and Technology, Hong Kong, SAR China
Kuan-Chung Chen	National University of Tainan, Taiwan
Xiaochun Cheng	Middlesex University, UK
Chi-hung Chi	Tsing Hua University, China
Alexandra I. Cristea	University of Warwick, UK
Liya Ding	Macau University of Science and Technology, SAR China
Xun Ge	University of Oklahoma, USA
Sabine Graf	Athabasca University, Canada
David Guralnick	Kaleidoscope Learning, New York, USA
Heinz Ulrich Hoppe	University of Duisburg-Essen, Germany
Haiyang Hu	Zhejiang Gongshang University, China
Wendy W.Y. Hui	University of Nottingham at Ningbo, China
Patrick C.K. Hung	University of Ontario, Institute of Technology, Canada
Hiroshi Igaki	Kobe University, Japan
Tsukasa Ishigaki	National Institute of Advanced Industrial Science and Technology, Japan
Jiyou Jia	Peking University, China
Eleanna Kafeza	Athens University of Economics and Business, Greece
Kengo Katayama	Okayama University of Science, Japan
David M. Kennedy	Lingnan University, Hong Kong, SAR China
Rajiv Khosla	La Trobe University, Australia
Ichiro Kobayashi	Ochanomizu University, Japan
Mario Koeppen	Kyushu Institute of Technology, Japan

Siu Cheung Kong	Hong Kong Institute of Education, Hong Kong, SAR China
P. Radha Krishna	SET Labs - Infosys Technologies Ltd., India
Andre W. Kushniruk	University of Victoria, Canada
Carmen Ka Man Lam	Hong Kong Baptist University, Hong Kong, SAR China
Jean H.Y. Lai	City University of Hong Kong, Hong Kong, SAR China
Raymond Y.K. Lau	City University of Hong Kong, Hong Kong, SAR China
Chien-Sing Lee	Multimedia University, Malaysia
Chei Sian Lee	Nanyang Technological University, Singapore
Ho-fung Leung	Chinese University of Hong Kong, Hong Kong, SAR China
Xiaojing Liu	Indiana University, USA
Pierre Levy	The University of Ottawa, Canada
Tieyan Li	Institute for Infocomm Research (I2R), Singapore
Fu-ren Lin	National Tsing Hua University, Taiwan
Wenyin Liu	City University of Hong Kong, Hong Kong, SAR China
Edwin Lughofer	Fuzzy Logic Laboratorium Linz-Hagenberg, Austria
Zongwei Luo	University of Hong Kong, Hong Kong, SAR China
Yinghua Ma	Shanghai JiaoTong University, China
Huiye Ma	Eindhoven University of Technology, The Netherlands
Akira Maeda	Ritsumeikan University, Japan
Mitsunori Matsushita	Kansai University, Japan
Farid Meziane	Salford University, UK
Marcelo Milrad	Linnaeus University, Sweden
Atsuyuki Morishima	University of Tsukuba, Japan
Anders Morch	University of Oslo, Norway
Jürgen Moormann	Frankfurt School of Finance and Management, Germany
Koichi Moriyama	Osaka University, Japan
Sanaz Mostaghim	University of Karlsruhe, Germany
Yoichi Motomura	National Institute of Advanced Industrial Science, Japan
Kiyoshi Nakabayashi	Chiba Institute of Technology, Japan
Eugenia M.W. NG	Hong Kong Institute of Education, Hong Kong, SAR China
Mark E. Nissen	Naval Postgraduate School, USA
Murali Raman	Multimedia University, Malaysia
Waltraut Ritter	Knowledge Enterprises, Hong Kong, SAR China
Qiyun Wang	Nanyang Technological University, Singapore
Mudasser F. Wyne	National University, USA
Ming-Hsiung Ying	Chung-Hua University, Taiwan
Jianwei Zhang	State University of New York at Albany, USA
Xiaohui Zhao	Unitec Institute of Technology, New Zealand

The First International Workshop on User Modeling for Web-Based Learning (IWUM 2015)

Program Chairs

Di Zou	English Language Centre, The Hong Kong Polytechnic University, SAR China
Fu Lee Wang	Caritas Institute of Higher Education, Hong Kong, SAR China
Haoran Xie	Caritas Institute of Higher Education, Hong Kong, SAR China
Yanghui Rao	School of Mobile Information Engineering, Sun Yat-sen University, China
Yi Cai	School of Software Engineering, South China University of Technology, China

Program Committee

Raymong Y.K. Lau	City University of Hong Kong, Hong Kong, SAR China
Neil Y. Yen	University of Aizu, Japan
Raymong Wong	Hong Kong University of Science and Technology, Hong Kong, SAR China
Yunjun Gao	Zhejiang University, China
Ke Li	Michigan State University, USA
Wong Tak Lam	Hong Kong Institute of Education, Hong Kong, SAR China
Jianfeng Si	Institute for Infocomm Research, Singapore
Xi Tan	Purdue University, USA
Wei Chen	Agricultural Information Institute of CAAS, China
Xudong Mao	Alibaba, China
Ksenia Troshina	The Hong Kong Polytechnic University, Hong Kong, SAR China
Wenyin Liu	City University of Hong Kong, Hong Kong, SAR China
Xun Xiao	Huawei European Research Center, Germany
Shaojie Qiao	Southwest Jiaotong University, China
Jianke Zhu	Zhejiang University, China
Derong Shen	Northeastern University, China
Wenji Ma	Columbia University, USA
Jing Yang	Research Center on Fictitious Economy and Data Science CAS, China
Yuqing Sun	Shangdong University, China
Jian Chen	South China University of Technology, China

Yangqiu Song University of Illinois at Urbana-Champaign, USA
Zhiwen Yu South China University of Technology, China
Shaoxu Song Tsinghua University, China

Web Master

Yufeng Lu School of Mobile Information Engineering, Sun Yat-sen University, China

Contents

Knowledge Management and E-Learning

A Clustering Algorithm Based on Minimum Spanning Tree with E-learning Applications

Siyang Wang[1], Zeping Tang[1], Yanghui Rao[1(✉)], Haoran Xie[2], and Fu Lee Wang[3]

[1] School of Data and Computer Science, Sun Yat-sen University, Guangzhou, China
{sysu_siyang,tzpsmie}@163.com, raoyangh@mail.sysu.edu.cn
[2] Department of Mathematics and Information Technology, The Education University of Hong Kong, New Territories, Hong Kong
hrxie2@gmail.com
[3] Caritas Institute of Higher Education, Tseung Kwan O, Hong Kong
pwang@cihe.edu.hk

Abstract. The rapid development of web-based learning applications has generated large amounts of learning resources. Faced with this situation, clustering is valuable to group modeling and intelligent tutoring. In traditional clustering algorithms, the initial centroid of each cluster is often assigned randomly. Sometimes it is very difficult to get an effective clustering result. In this paper, we propose a new clustering algorithm based on a minimum spanning tree, which includes the elimination and construction processes. In the elimination phase, the Euclidean distance is used to measure the density. Objects with low densities are considered as noise and eliminated. In the construction phase, a minimum spanning tree is constructed to choose the initial centroid based on the degree of freedom. Extensive evaluations using datasets with different properties validate the effectiveness of the proposed clustering algorithm. Furthermore, we study how to employ the clustering algorithms in three different e-learning applications.

Keywords: Clustering · Density · Minimum spanning tree · E-learning

1 Introduction

As a new learning pattern, e-learning has received a lot of attention and been widely applied. Confronting large volume of e-learning resources, it is necessary to cluster similar data and recommend suitable resources to learners. Clustering is the process of assigning objects to groups by the similarity [1]. Clustering is widely used in scientific areas [2]. Taxonomists, social scientists, biologists and

Y. Rao—The research work described in this article has been substantially supported by the Fundamental Research Funds for the Central Universities (Project Number: 46000-31610009).

Z. Gong et al. (Eds.): ICWL 2015 Workshops, LNCS 9584, pp. 3–12, 2016.
DOI: 10.1007/978-3-319-32865-2_1

many others who collect and process real-world data have all contributed to the clustering methodology [3].

Noise objects are prevalent in many real-world datasets. Traditional clustering algorithms (e.g., K-means) assign the initial centroid of each cluster randomly, which may introduce the noise as the representation of clusters, in addition to converge to an unstable result. In this paper, we propose a new scheme to alleviate the problem of instability in clustering. Noise objects are first eliminated by the density. Then, a minimum spanning tree is constructed to estimate the degree of freedom for each object. The object with the largest degree of freedom is considered as the initial centroid.

The paper is structured as follows: In Sect. 2, we introduce some algorithms related to our work. Section 3 describes our scheme. Section 4 presents the experimental results. Section 5 discusses the possible e-learning applications for the proposed algorithm. In Sect. 6, we give our conclusions and future work.

2 Related Work

The development of e-learning systems is very quickly [4]. Specifically, Zou et al. proposed a load-based learner profile for the generation of incidental word learning tasks [5]. The clustering algorithms are extensively applied in community discovery [6,7] and event detection [8], which can be further applied to e-learning. With the rapid development of e-learning resources, learners need an efficient way to get the similar resources. However, there may exists some resources which are useless. To eliminate the noise centroid in clustering, Mimaroglu and Erdil defined two variables, weight and attachment [3]. The first one estimates the similarity between two objects, and the second one is used to rank the quality of each candidate centroid. Luo et al. also proposed a method based on the density to eliminate the "fake" centroid [9], as follows:

Let $X = \{x_1, x_2, \ldots, x_n\}$ be the set of prototypes. $DEN(x_i)$ is the density of prototype x_i. If the value of $DEN(x_i)$ is small, it means x_i locates at a place which has a relative high density, or vice versa. To determine whether x_i is a "fake" centroid, the density of x_i is compared with the average density $ADEN$. If $DEN(x_i)$ is larger than $ADEN$, it will be considered as a "fake" centroid and removed from the centroid set.

3 Methodology

3.1 Eliminate Noise

The existence of noise will produce useless learning resources in e-learning, in addition to disturb the effect of clustering. To solve this problem, we employ the method proposed in [9]. Here are the definitions.

Definition 1. *The density of an object is:*

$$DEN(x_i) = \frac{1}{m} \sum_{y_j \epsilon \varphi(x_i)} d(x_i, y_j),$$

where $\varphi(x_i)$ is the set of m nearest objects of x_i, $d(x_i, y_j)$ is the Euclidean distance between x_i and y_j.

Definition 2. *The average density is:*

$$ADEN = \frac{1}{p}\sum_{i=1}^{p} DEN(x_i),$$

where p is the number of objects.

Lemma 1. *The DEN of some normal objects is larger than ADEN.*

Proof 1. *If all object are normal, i.e., no noise objects, the value of ADEN must between DEN_{max} and DEN_{min}. Thus, some normal objects' DEN must be larger than ADEN.*

According to Lemma 1, we add a constant DEV to $ADEN$. If $DEN(x_i)$ is larger than the sum of $ADEN$ and DEV, it will be considered as a noise object and removed from the dataset.

3.2 Generate the Minimum Spanning Tree

E-learning resources are still abundant after the elimination of noise. We need an efficient way to combine the similar resources together, as follows:

After the elimination of noise, the normal objects are clustered. In this step, we will construct a minimum spanning tree to form a link of all objects. To build the tree, we first calculate the distance between each pair of objects, and then use the Prim's algorithm to build the minimum spanning tree. The steps are shown in Algorithm 1.

Algorithm 1. Algorithm of generating the minimum spanning tree

Input: A weighted connected graph, with a vertex set V and an edge set E;
Output: A set V_{new} and a set E_{new} by which the minimum spanning tree is described

1: initialization: $V_{new} = \{x\}$ (x is the starting point chosen from V), E_{new} = empty;
2: **while** $V_{new} \neq V$ **do**
3: choose edge $< u, v >$ with minimum weight from E ($u \in V_{new}$, $v \notin V_{new}$ and $v \in V$);
4: add v into V_{new} and add $< u, v >$ into E_{new};
5: **end while**

3.3 Merge Objects into Clusters

Based on the generated minimum spanning tree, we get the degree of freedom of each object.

Definition 3. *The degree of freedom of an object x_i is:*

$$df(x_i) = |x_j|(x_i, x_j)\epsilon E|,$$

where E denotes the edges that x_i belongs to.

Table 1. The value of every point

Object	v_1	v_2	v_3	v_4	v_5	v_6
DEN	1.207	1.000	1.207	1.500	1.000	1.500
df	2	2	1	2	2	1

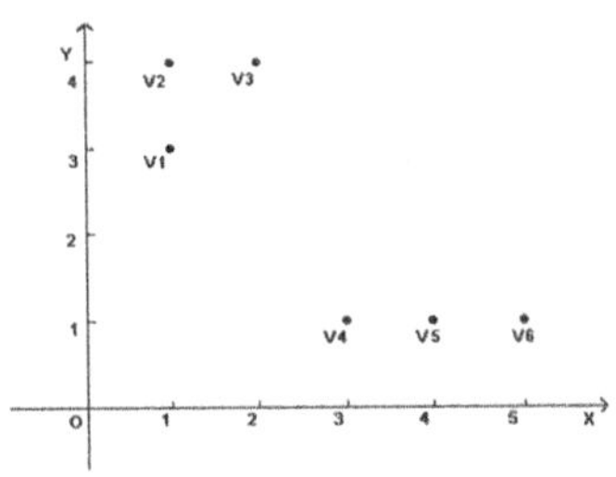

Fig. 1. Data before clustering

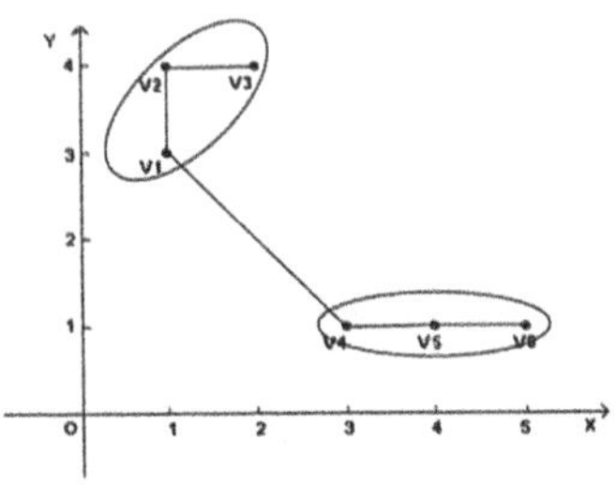

Fig. 2. Data after clustering

A large degree of freedom of an object means that it has many neighbors, and it may be a centroid [3]. We thus sort objects by their degree of freedom in decreasing order. A partitioning method based on minimum spanning tree is described in Algorithm 2.

This algorithm can be illustrated as follows:

(1) For six objects $v_1, v_2, ..., v_6$ as shown in Fig. 1, we set $DEV = 0.5$ and $m = 2$. The results of DEN are presented in Table 1. There is no noise and all objects are reserved;
(2) We construct a minimum spanning tree based on the Prim's algorithm. The resulting edges of the minimum span tree are (v_1,v_2), (v_2,v_3), (v_1,v_4), (v_4,v_5), (v_5,v_6);
(3) The degree of freedom of each object is estimated and presented in Table 1. We sort the value in descending order. The order after sorting is $v_1, v_2, v_4, v_5, v_3, v_6$. Thus, we put v_1 into the first cluster, $Cluster1$;
(4) For the immediate neighbors of v_1 are v_2 and v_3, we put v_2 into $Cluster1$ because $d(v_1, v_2) < d(v_2, v_3)$. v_4 is not included in $Cluster1$ because $d(v_1, v_4) > d(v_4, v_5)$;
(5) For the neighbors of the newly added object, i.e., v_3, we also put it into $Cluster1$ because v_3 does not have any neighbors and the minimum distance between v_3 and its neighbors is $d(v_2, v_3)$. Now, we have $Cluster1 = \{v_1, v_2, v_3\}$.

Algorithm 2. A partitioning method based on minimum spanning tree

Input: D: Date Set
Output: C: Clusters

```
Calculate the Euclidean distance between each pair of objects;
Calculate the Density based on the Euclidean distance;
Calculate the average density ADEN;
for all data do
    if DEN > ADEN + DEV then
        Elimination
    end if
end for
Construct a minimum spanning tree based on the Prim's algorithm;
Calculate and sort the degree of freedom of each vertex in the tree;
cluster = 1;
while there are unmarked data do
    Add ummarked data with the highest degree to an empty queue;
    while queue is not empty do
        V = the top element from the queue;
        queue pop;
        Add V to the present cluster;
        Mark V;
        for all edge< v, w > do
            if w is unmarked then
                weight = weight(v, w);
            end if
            for all edge< w, t > do
                if weight(w, t) ≤ weight then
                    is_max = false;
                    break;
                end if
            end for
            if is_max ≡ true then
                Add w to the queue;
            end if
        end for
    end while
    cluster++;
end while
for every cluster obtained above do
    if the number of objects in the cluster < minNum then
        if distance between the cluster and neighbour cluster < minDis then
            merge the cluster into the neighbor cluster;
        end if
    end if
end for
```

(6) For the three unmarked points v_4, v_5, v_6, we first choose the one with the largest degree of freedom, i.e., v_4. The neighbors of v_4 are v_1 and v_5. As v_1 has been put into $Cluster1$, it is not considered here. We include v_5 into $Cluster2$ because $d(v_4, v_5) = d(v5, v6)$. Then, we consider the neighbors of the newly added object, i.e., v_6. It is also added into $Cluster2$ because it does not have any neighbors, and the minimum distance between v_6 and its neighbors is $d(v_5, v_6)$. All objects have been marked and we finally have two clusters (Fig. 2), i.e., $Cluster1 = \{v_1, v_2, v_3\}$ and $Cluster2 = \{v_4, v_5, v_6\}$.

3.4 Merge Small Clusters by the Distance

In the previous subsection, we have achieved an initial clustering result based on the minimum spanning tree. However, there may exist many small clusters which only contain a few objects. In this case, we further merge these small clusters into large ones. The method of merging small clusters is described in Algorithm 3, where $minNum$ is the minimum number of objects a cluster should have, $minDis$ is the minimum distance between any two clusters. If the number of objects in one cluster is less than $minNum$ and the distance between it with the closest cluster is less than $minDis$, this cluster is merged into the one which is closest to it.

Algorithm 3. Merge small clusters based on the distance

```
for every cluster obtained above do
    if the number of objects in cluster < minNum then
        if distance between the cluster and neighbor cluster < minDis then
            merge the cluster into the neighbor cluster;
        end if
    end if
end for
```

4 Experiments

In this section, we evaluate our scheme of clustering on two different datasets, i.e., Smileface (http://smie2.sysu.edu.cn/~ryh/data/Smileface.zip) and Aggregation

Table 2. Performance of different algorithms on Smileface

Algorithm	Purity	Rand index
K-means	0.7888	0.8423
Average link	0.8075	0.8481
Complete link	0.7811	0.8319
Proposed algorithm	0.9968	0.9973

Table 3. Performance of different algorithms on Aggregation

Algorithm	Purity	Rand index
K-means	0.8997	0.9189
Average link	1	1
Complete link	0.9530	0.9343
Proposed algorithm	0.9570	0.9676

Table 4. Parameter values of the proposed algorithm on Smileface

Parameter	m	DEV	$minNum$	$minDis$
Value	10	0.5	80	0.5

Table 5. Parameter values of the proposed algorithm on Aggregation

Parameter	m	DEV	$minNum$	$minDis$
Value	30	0.5	70	2

(http://cs.joensuu.fi/sipu/datasets/). The K-means, average link and complete link hierarchical clustering algorithms are implemented for comparison. Two quantitative metrics, the purity and the rand index [10] are employed as indicators of performance. Tables 2 and 3 show the results of different algorithms on Smileface and Aggregation, which indicate that our algorithm yields competitive performance with other baselines. The parameter values of our algorithm on Smileface and Aggregation are presented in Tables 4 and 5, respectively.

4.1 The Smileface Dataset

We first test all algorithms on the Smileface dataset, which contains 644 points from four clusters.

The K-means algorithm does well in globular shaped clusters. However, clusters in the Smileface dataset are not the globular shape. We set the value of K

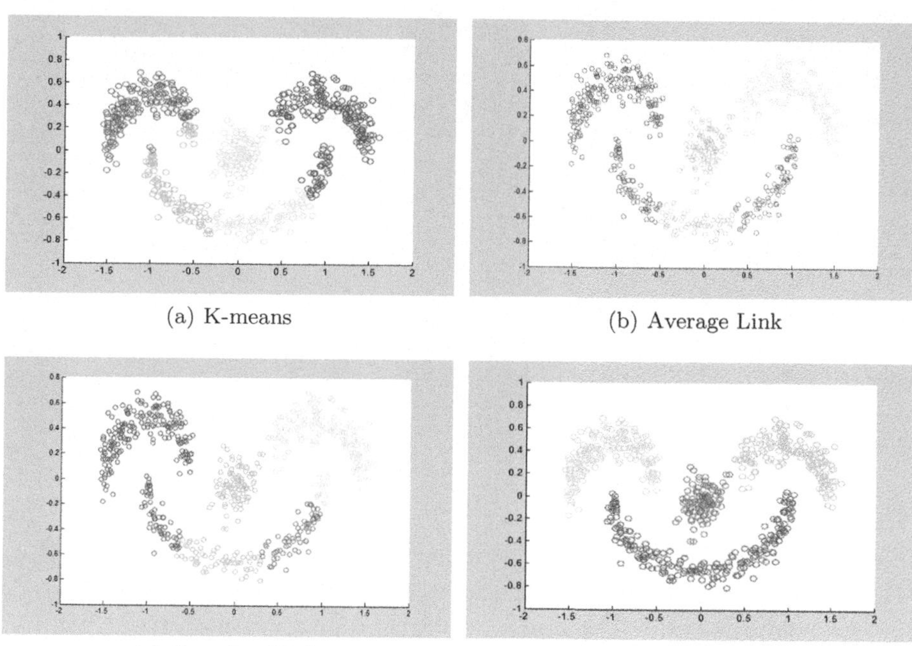

(a) K-means

(b) Average Link

(c) Complete Link

(d) Proposed Algorithm

Fig. 3. Results of different algorithms on Smileface

to 4, and the result is presented in Fig. 3a. The average link and complete link clustering algorithms are both hierarchical clustering algorithms. Figure 3b and c show the final results of them, respectively. We can observe that the 4 clusters are not separated well by these baselines.

The clustering result of our algorithm is presented in Fig. 3d, which shows the robustness of the proposed clustering scheme to outliers. Compared to the other three baselines, the clustering result of our algorithm is more satisfactory.

4.2 The Aggregation Dataset

The Aggregation dataset is also tested by all algorithms. This dataset contains 788 points which are assigned to seven clusters. Compared to Smileface, this dataset is more complex.

The clustering result of K-means is shown in Fig. 4a, from which we can observe that the red cluster contains points originally assigned to three different clusters. Furthermore, two clusters in the right hand side with internal touch are separated into three different clusters. Figure 4b and c show the results of average link and complete link clustering algorithms, respectively. The result of the average link is well but the complete link performs poorly.

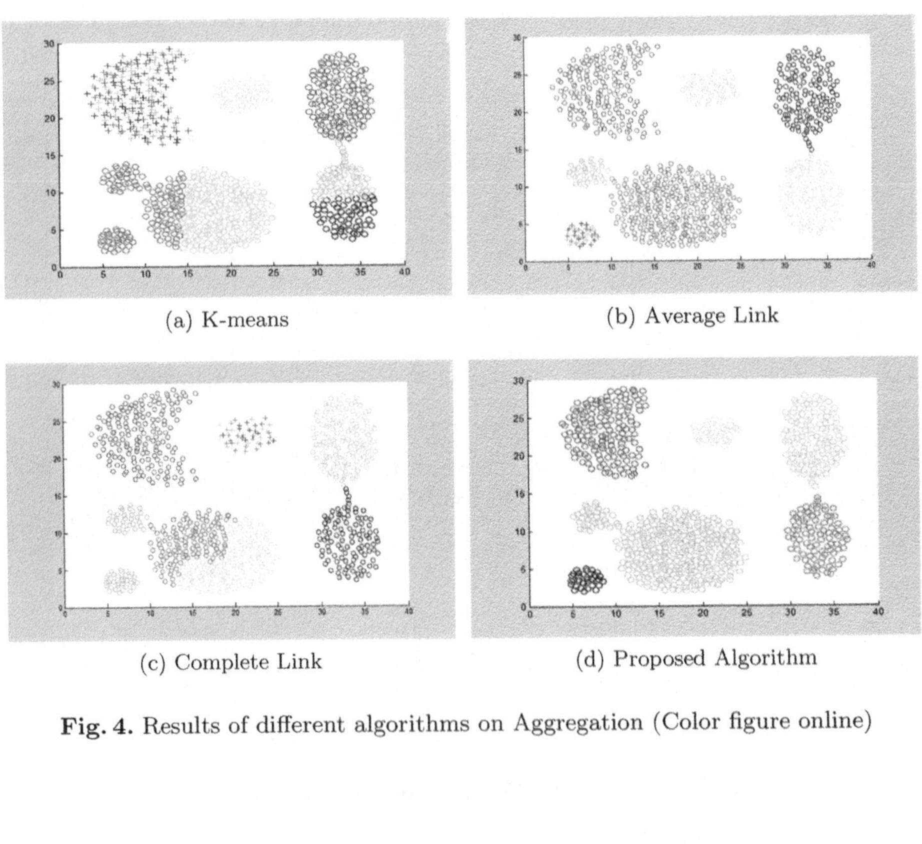

(a) K-means

(b) Average Link

(c) Complete Link

(d) Proposed Algorithm

Fig. 4. Results of different algorithms on Aggregation (Color figure online)

The experimental result of our algorithm is shown in Fig. 4d, which correctly separated two clusters in the right hand side. However, it groups the points in the lower-left corner into two clusters, which deserves our further research.

5 E-learning Applications

In this section, we briefly discuss how to apply the proposed clustering approach in e-learning systems. Generally, we can employ the density-based clustering algorithm in the following three aspects.

- **Learner Classification.** As more than thousands of learners in a single course in popular MOOCs platforms, e.g., Coursera (www.coursera.com) and EdX (www.edx.org), it is quite important to classify the large amount of learners into different groups. The learning effectiveness can be improved by identifying common features in each group. Take the HarvardX-MITx dataset [11] as an example, we can observe that the features of learners with good grades have similar frequency of course video playing. These learners are quite close if we plot their features (e.g., video playing frequency) in a N-dimensional space. Thus, the density-based clustering algorithm can be well explored to distinguish the active and inactive learners in this case.
- **Learning Path Discovery.** Learning path discovery is a typical and useful application in e-learning system. As it is time-consuming and difficult for users to identify their optimize learning paths when they acquire new knowledge in a specific topic. A key process in learning path discovery is to identify whether there is a strong linkage between two knowledge units [12]. To achieve this goal, we can employ our density-based clustering algorithm to see whether two knowledge units is in the same cluster or not rather than the comparison between all pairs of two knowledge units.
- **Resource Recommendation.** In the field of web-based learning, users face a plethora of learning resources available online. Thus, it is valuable to identify suitable learning resources from a potentially overwhelming variety of choices [13]. The goal of our density-based clustering algorithm is to effectively discover the natural grouping(s) of a set of unlabeled objects, which can be applied to recommend both interesting learning resources and people with similar tastes and beliefs to users.

6 Conclusions

In this paper, we propose a clustering algorithm based on the minimum spanning tree. It uses the Euclidean distance as the density to eliminate noise, and builds a minimum spanning tree to connect the objects with short distance together by edges. To evaluate the performance of different methods, we use the K-means, average link and complete link algorithms for comparison. Furthermore, we discuss how to employ the algorithm in three different e-learning applications (i.e., learner classification, learning path discovery and resource recommendation).

The experimental result demonstrates the effectiveness of our method. In our future work, we plan to apply the clustering method to choose the representative documents for sentiment analysis [14], in addition to test our algorithm using a large and high-dimensional dataset.

Acknowledgements. The research work described in this article has been supported by a grant from the Research Grants Council of the Hong Kong Special Administrative Region, China (UGC/FDS11/E06/14).

References

1. Li, C.-Z., Xu, Z.-B., Luo, T.: A heuristic hierarchical clustering based on multiple similarity measurements. Pattern Recogn. Lett. **34**(2), 155–162 (2013)
2. Ben, S., Jin, Z., Yang, J.: Guided fuzzy clustering with multi-prototypes. In: The International Joint Conference on Neural Networks (IJCNN), pp. 2430–2436 (2011)
3. Mimaroglu, S., Erdil, E.: Combining multiple clusterings using similarity graph. Pattern Recogn. **44**(3), 694–703 (2011)
4. Li, Q., Lau, R.W.H., Wah, B., Ashman, H., Leung, E., Li, F., Lee, V.: Guest editors' introduction: emerging internet technologies for e-learning. IEEE Internet Comput. **13**(4), 11–17 (2009)
5. Zou, D., Xie, H., Li, Q., Wang, F.L., Chen, W.: The load-based learner profile for incidental word learning task generation. In: Popescu, E., Lau, R.W.H., Pata, K., Leung, H., Laanpere, M. (eds.) ICWL 2014. LNCS, vol. 8613, pp. 190–200. Springer, Heidelberg (2014)
6. Xie, H.R., Li, Q., Cai, Y.: Community-aware resource profiling for personalized search in folksonomy. J. Comput. Sci. Technol. **27**(3), 599–610 (2012)
7. Xie, H.R., Li, Q., Mao, X.D., Li, X.D., Cai, Y., Rao, Y.H.: Community-aware user profile enrichment in folksonomy. Neural Netw. **58**, 111–121 (2014)
8. Rao, Y.H., Li, Q.: Term weighting schemes for emerging event detection. In: IEEE/WIC/ACM International Conference on Web Intelligence and Intelligent Agent Technology (WI-IAT), pp. 105–112 (2012)
9. Luo, T., Zhong, C., Li, H., Sun, X.: A multi-prototype clustering algorithm based on minimum spanning tree. In: Proceedings of the 7th International Conference on Fuzzy Systems and Knowledge Discovery (FSKD), pp. 1602–1607 (2010)
10. Manning, C.D., Raghavan, P., Schütze, H.: Introduction to Information Retrieval, pp. 356–359 (2008)
11. MITx and HarvardX: Harvardx-MITx person-course academic year 2013 de-identified dataset, version 2.0. http://dx.doi.org/10.7910/DVN/26147
12. Leung, E.W.C., Li, Q.: A dynamic conceptual network mechanism for personalized study plan generation. In: Zhou, W., Nicholson, P., Corbitt, B., Fong, J. (eds.) ICWL 2003. LNCS, vol. 2783, pp. 69–80. Springer, Heidelberg (2003)
13. Manouselis, N., Vuorikari, R., Assche, F.V.: Collaborative recommendation of e-learning resources: an experimental investigation. J. Comput. Assist. Learn. **26**(4), 227–242 (2010)
14. Rao, Y.H., Li, Q., Mao, X.D., Wenyin, L.: Sentiment topic models for social emotion mining. Inf. Sci. **266**, 90–100 (2014)

Analysis of Heart Rate Monitors for Evaluating Student's Mental Working Capacity

Elena Berdnikova, Andrey Lyamin(✉), and Anton Skshidlevsky

ITMO University, St. Petersburg, Russia
{helen, anton}@cde.ifmo.ru, lyamin@mail.ifmo.ru

Abstract. It is necessary to develop smart e-learning systems that can evaluate in real time not only student's knowledge, skills and experience, but also his functional state. The learning load and intensity should not lead to a reduction of student's functional state, including learner's mental working capacity. Student's functional state can be evaluated by analysis of heart rate variability, since heart rhythm responds to all changes in the human body and environment. There are a lot of devices for measuring heart rate variability, which called heart rate monitors. In massive e-learning more accessible monitors should be used but such monitors may not be sufficiently accurate. This paper studies three devices that can be used to estimate student's mental working capacity.

Keywords: e-learning systems · Student's mental working capacity · Heart rate variability analysis · Heart rate monitors

1 Introduction

The sophisticated smart e-learning system should be designed and developed as a smart student-centered biotechnical system with certain features of smart systems (sensing, transmission, big data processing, activation of actuators) and levels of "smartness" (adaptation, sensing, inferring, learning, anticipation, self-organization) [1]. Capabilities of the system depends on kind of learning algorithms and dimension of feedbacks, which are needed to realize adaptive learning as well as to preserve the health of students and to reduce the cost of achieved learning outcomes.

A student is a key component of thee-learning system. He has specific abilities to read, write, infer, learn, retain and use knowledge. The optimization of these activities involves obtaining the maximum learning outcome in the minimum time. However, this process can be effective and optimal under the condition that student's psychophysiological state (student's functional state) is optimal [1, 2]. The functional state is a set of characteristics of physiological and psychophysiological processes in many respects determining the level of activity of functional systems, working capacity and behavior of a person; it determines a student's ability to carry out a specific activity.

The learning load and intensity should not lead to a reduction of student's functional state, including student's mental working capacity (MWC). Hence the e-learning system should make an impact on a student (learning, training, quizzes, etc.) on the

Z. Gong et al. (Eds.): ICWL 2015 Workshops, LNCS 9584, pp. 13–22, 2016.
DOI: 10.1007/978-3-319-32865-2_2

basis of information not only about achieved learning outcomes, but also about the functional state (Fig. 1). In order to evaluate student's MWC the heart rate variability (HRV) analysis can be used. There are a lot of various heart rate monitors for measuring HRV. These monitors will make available various methods of HRV analysis in e-learning: adaptive e-learning, identification of students, smart classrooms, and smart environments for learning [3–7]. In massive e-learning more accessible monitors should be used but such monitors may not be sufficiently accurate. In the paper we study three types of devices that can be used to evaluate student's functional state, including student's MWC: ECG recorder, electrical HR monitor, optical HR monitor. ECG recorder is a more precision device. HR monitors with electrical and optical sensors were examined in comparison with this device.

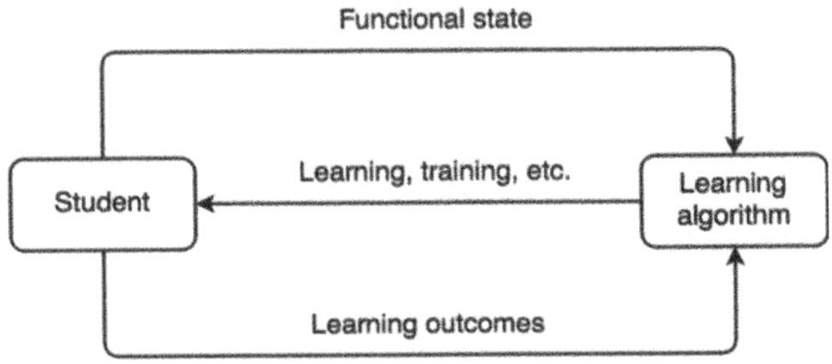

Fig. 1. e-Learning system

2 Student's Mental Working Capacity

In order to predict a reduction of student's MWC, it is necessary to distinguish the following MWC phases and corresponding degrees of regulatory mechanisms' tension:

(1) getting started with a certain tension of regulatory mechanisms;
(2) optimal MWC when the tension level of physiological systems corresponds to MWC;
(3) full productivity with possible initial signs of tiredness but without decrease of MWC;
(4) unstable productivity with clear signs of tiredness and decrease of MWC;
(5) progressive decrease of MWC with fast increase of tiredness and obvious decrease of learning efficiency.

HRV analysis is focused on monitoring of student's regulator mechanisms (a) before, (b) during, and (c) after learning. This method is based on (a) recognition and measurement of RR-intervals (Fig. 2) between the high-amplitude peaks of electrocardiogram (R-peak), (b) construction of time series of RR-intervals between two neighboring peaks, and (c) numerical analysis of obtained R-peak data. The most informative parameters of HRV analysis are (a) Heart Rate (HR), (b) Stress Index (SI), and (c) Index of Centralization (IC) [8].

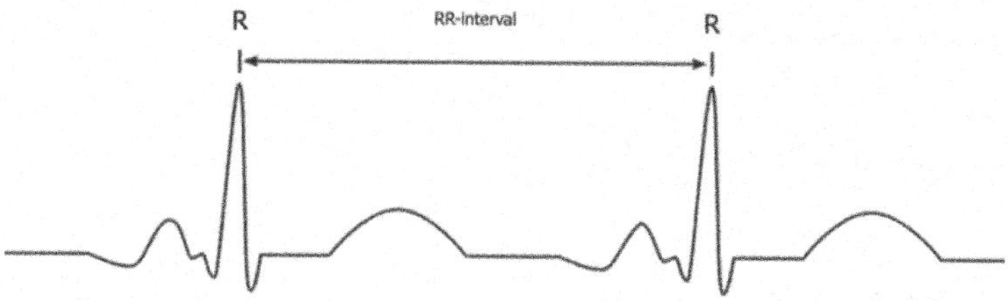

Fig. 2. RR-interval

The SI parameter is calculated based on the RR-intervals histogram:

$$SI = \frac{Amo \times 100\,\%}{2 \times Mo \times MxDMn},$$

where Mo – mode, Amo – mode's amplitude, MxDMn – variation range. The SI parameter is sensitive to increased sympathetic nervous system tone; as a result, a small physical, emotional or mental overload may increase SI values by 1.5–2 times.

The IC parameter is calculated based on the RR-intervals spectrum:

$$IC = \frac{VLF + LF}{HF},$$

where VLF – spectral density of RR-intervals in a very low frequency range, LF – in the range of low frequency, HF – in the high frequency range. It is associated with psycho-emotional stress and brain's functional state. Increasing IC means a rise in central control of heart rhythm.

As shown in [1, 2], parameters of student's psychophysiological state should be actively used in the advanced smart e-learning systems for more usability, higher efficiency of student's learning process, long-time retention of student's knowledge and learning outcomes. Based on obtained specific values of HR, SI, IC for a particular student for a particular learning assignment and range of "normal" values for this type of students the e-learning system will get additional useful criteria to smartly compile an individual learning trajectory for a student. In other words, it will be able to automatically generate an individual sequence of reusable information, learning objects and atoms, learning modules and assignments in order to provide maximum efficiency of student's learning process [9]. For example, each student in the online course gets a set of assignments for a new course topic on the specific level of complexity, and, if necessary, revised assignments for a previous topic in case IC parameter crossed the border (Figs. 3 and 4) [1].

3 Description of Heart Rate Monitors

The study included three devices that differ in types of sensors used and a number of estimated parameters: Varikard 2.51 (ECG recorder), Polar H7 (electrical HR monitor), and Mio Link (optical HR monitor). A comparison of the devices is shown in Table 1.

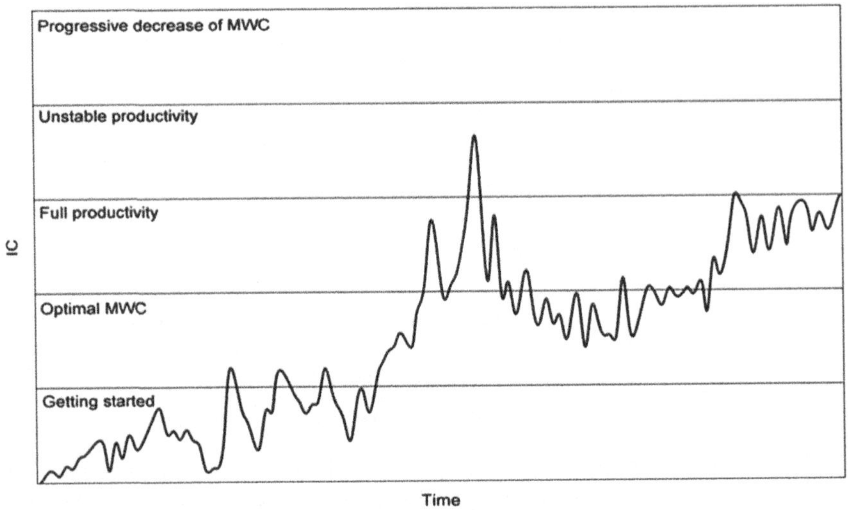

Fig. 3. Index of centralization

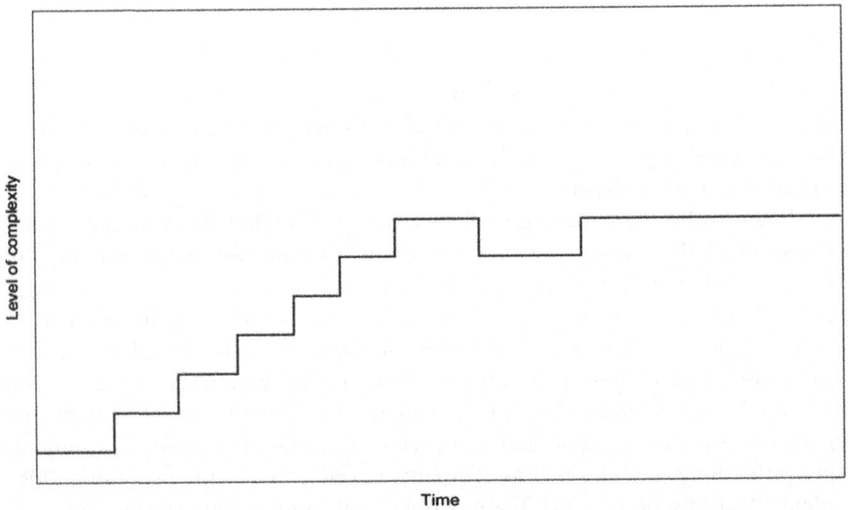

Fig. 4. Level of complexity

Table 1. Comparison of devices

	Varikard 2.51	Polar H7	Mio Link
Type of sensors	Electrical	Electrical	Optical
Connection type	Wired, USB	Wireless, Bluetooth	Wireless, Bluetooth
Data format	Electrocardiogram	Heart rate, BPM	Heart rate, BPM
Frequency data output	1200 Hz	1 Hz	1 Hz
Area of application	Medicine and science	Fitness and sport	Fitness and sport

The complex “Varikard 2.51”, which has been designed for the analysis of HRV, provides 40 various parameters that had been recommended by both Russian and European-American standards [8]. The complex is running under Microsoft Windows graphical operating systems, using the specialized software. It consists of a cardio amplifier associated with a computer via USB. Varikard provides the analysis of records with duration from several minutes to 24 h. At the same time some fragments of records which are needed to analyze HRV can be selected. The standard analysis is performed on the basis of five minute records. For measuring the potential difference electrodes are imposed on various parts of the body (Fig. 5). In order to improve an electrical contact with the electrodes a conducting gel is applied on the skin. The complex allows to obtain the RR-intervals and to carry out calculations of HRV in real time.

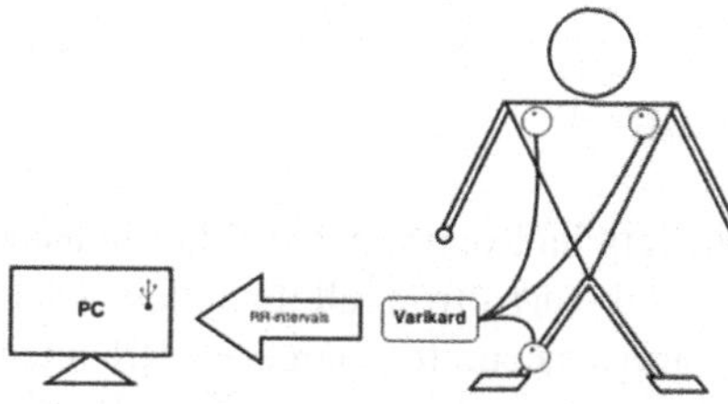

Fig. 5. Varikard 2.51

Polar H7 is the heart rate monitor that measures the electrical signals of the heart muscle. The electrode belt is fastened around the chest and transmits beats per minute (BPM) wirelessly via Bluetooth (Fig. 6).

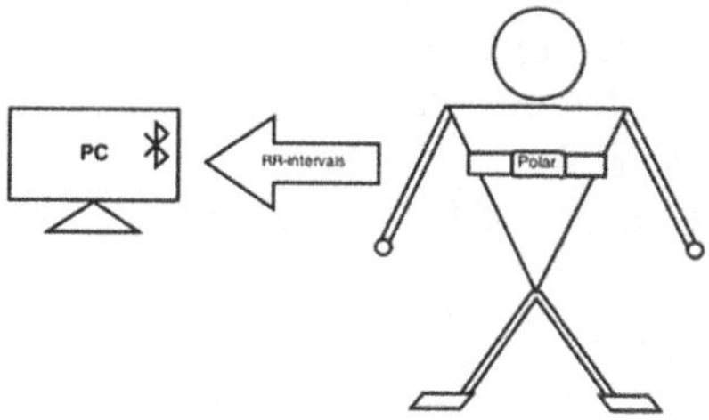

Fig. 6. Polar H7

Mio Link is the heart rate wristband. LED lights and an electro-optical cell sense the volume of blood under the skin. From there, sophisticated algorithms are applied to pulse signal so that heart’s true rhythm can be detected, even while running at performance speeds. BPM are transmitted via Bluetooth to a computer (Fig. 7).

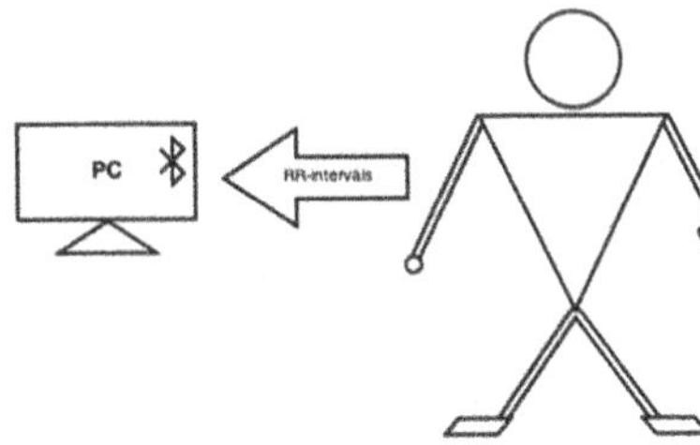

Fig. 7. Mio Link

Polar H7 and Mio Link heart rate monitors are compatible with Bluetooth smart devices that support heart rate service. These devices are used in fitness and sport in conjunction with exercise machines and fitness trackers.

4 Experimental Results

In the experiment nine subjects had participated. The timestamps and RR-intervals in milliseconds were received and stored from all three devices at the same time. Varikard 2.51 is considered as the most accurate source of RR-intervals. The obtained data shows that Polar H7 has slightly smoothed series of RR-intervals, and Mio Link has considerably smoothed series of RR-intervals in comparison with Varikard 2.51. And there is a time delay during transmission of the data from Polar H7 and Mio Link to a computer. For Polar H7 the time delay is 1 s, and for Mio Link – 6 s. In the experiment the data from all three devices were synchronized in time, i.e. the time delays of the devices were eliminated. For each subject and device the following parameters were calculated by using the data received during 300 s:

- Sample size – number of RR-intervals;
- Minimum – minimum value of RR-interval;
- Maximum – maximum value of RR-interval;
- Mean – mean of RR-intervals;
- Deviation– standard deviation of RR-intervals;
- SI – Stress Index;
- IC – Index of Centralization.

The calculations for some subject are shown in Table 2.

Two-sample t-test has shown that means of RR-intervals from the various devices for one subject are equal at the significance level at least 24 %. The mean probabilities, under the null hypothesis, of observing a value as extreme or more extreme of the test statistic are shown in Table 3.

The distribution of RR-intervals for the various devices corresponds to the normal distribution, but the form of the distribution for the various devices is slightly different (Fig. 8). Polar H7 and Mio Link provide a narrower range of RR-intervals, thereby showing a smaller standard deviation. To compare the distributions of RR-intervals a two-sample Kolmogorov-Smirnov test has been performed for all subjects under the

Table 2. Calculations of HRV

	Varikard 2.51	Polar H7	Mio Link
Sample size	327	300	300
Minimum	619	779	789
Maximum	1125	1090	1071
Mean	910	920	915
Deviation	91	64	53
SI	28	67	107
IC	2	8	12

Table 3. Two-sample t-test

	Varikard 2.51	Polar H7	Mio Link
Varikard 2.51	1.00	0.28	0.24
Polar H7	0.28	1.00	0.44
Mio Link	0.24	0.44	1.00

null hypothesis that the intervals of the various devices from the same continuous distribution. The mean probabilities of observing a value as extreme or more extreme of the test statistic are depicted in Table 4. The significance level was not less than 17 %.

Table 4. Two-sample Kolmogorov-Smirnov test

	Varikard 2.51	Polar H7	Mio Link
Varikard 2.51	1.00	0.66	0.17
Polar H7	0.66	1.00	0.23
Mio Link	0.17	0.23	1.00

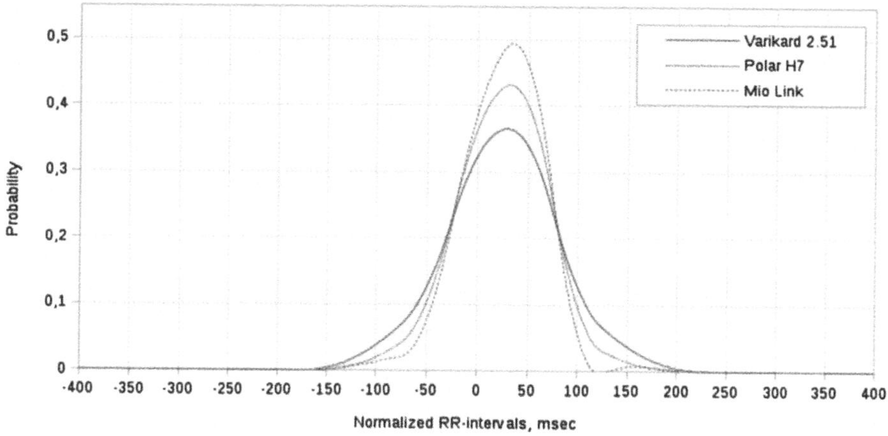

Fig. 8. Aggregated distributions of RR-intervals

Spectral analysis shows differences in the frequency characteristics of the output data for the various devices (Fig. 9). PolarH7 and Mio Link attenuate the signal in the high frequency range.

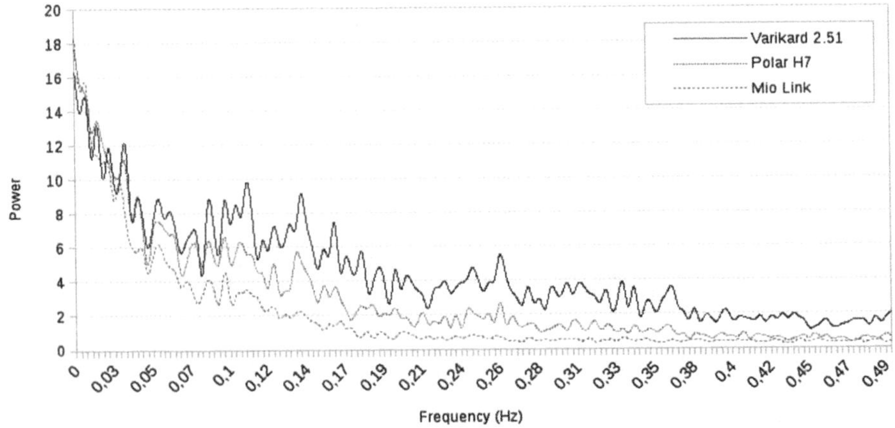

Fig. 9. Aggregated power spectral density

The comparative analysis of the dynamics in the indexes SI and IC which are calculated on the basis of the data from the various devices has shown a correlation between the indexes, although their values can vary considerably in numerical terms (Figs. 10 and 11).

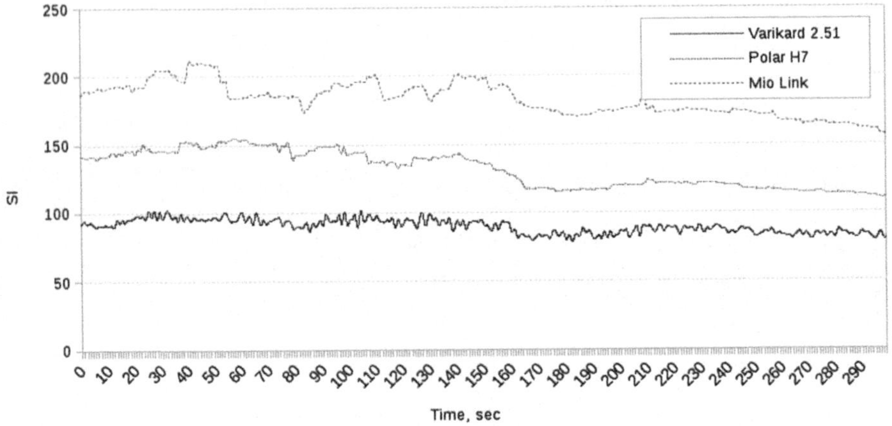

Fig. 10. Aggregated stress index

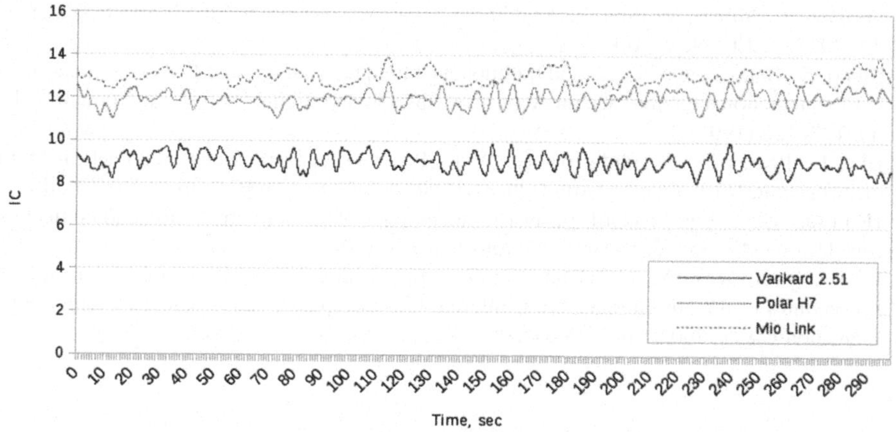

Fig. 11. Aggregated index of centralization

5 Conclusion

Based on the results of this study it can be concluded that the SI and IC that are calculated on the data from the various heart rate devices cannot be used at the same time. However, for the problem of measuring heart rate variability to provide biofeedback in the e-learning systems such devices as Polar H7 and Mio Link can be used. For this purpose, measuring background values of the indexes and then monitoring changes in values of the indexes over time with the same device are needed.

Acknowledgement. This paper is supported by Government of Russian Federation (grant 074-U01).

References

1. Uskov, V., Lyamin, A., Lisitsyna, L., Sekar, B.: Smart e-learning as a student-centered biotechnical system. In: Vincenti, G., Bucciero, A., Vaz de Carvalho, C. (eds.) eLEOT 2014. LNICST, vol. 138, pp. 167–175. Springer, Heidelberg (2014)
2. Lisitsyna, L., Lyamin, A., Skshidlevsky, A.: Estimation of student functional state in learning management system by heart rate variability method. In: Neves-Silva, R., Tsihrintzis, G.A., Uskov, V., Howlett, R.J., Jain, L.C. (eds.) Smart Digital Futures 2014 - Frontiers in Artificial Intelligence and Applications, vol. 262, pp. 726–731. IOS Press (2014)
3. Wu, W., Lee, J.: Improvement of HRV methodology for positive/negative emotion assessment. In: Proceedings of the 5th International Conference on Collaborative Computing: Networking, Applications and Worksharing, Washington, pp. 1–6 (2009)
4. Maraes, V., Carreiro, D., Barbosa, N.: Study of heart rate variability of university trained at rest and exercise. In: 2013 Pan American Health Care Exchanges (PAHCE), Medellin, pp. 1–5 (2013)

5. Denison, T., Morris, M., Sun, F.: Building a bionic nervous system. IEEE Spectr. **52**(2), 32–39 (2015). IEEE, New York
6. Silipo, R., Banolan, G.: Neural and traditional techniques in diagnostic ECG classification. In: IEEE International Conference on Acoustics, Speech, and Signal Processing, Munich, vol. 1, pp. 123–126 (1997)
7. Biel, L., Pettersson, O., Philipson, L., Wide, P.: ECG analysis: a new approach in human identification. IEEE Trans. Instrum. Measur. **50**(3), 808–812 (2001). IEEE, New York
8. Heart rate variability. standards of measurement, physiological interpretation and clinical use. Eur. Heart J. **17**, 354–381 (1996). Oxford University Press
9. Uskov, V., Uskova, M.: Reusable learning objects approach to web-based education. In: Proceedings of the 5th International Conference on Computers and Advanced Technology in Education CATE-2002, 20–22 May 2002, Cancun, Mexico, pp. 165-170 (2002)

Pedagogical Principles of the Implementation of Social Networks at Schools

Blanka Klimova and Petra Poulova(✉)

University of Hradec Kralove, Rokitanskeho 62, Hradec Kralove, Czech Republic
{blanka.klimova,petra.poulova}@uhk.cz

Abstract. At present technologies have already penetrated in all spheres of human life. All fully employed people cannot imagine their work without a computer nowadays. In addition, more and more people also use social network sites on a regular daily basis, either for private and/or business purposes. In this study the authors attempt to firstly define a concept of social network sites as well as explore their types. Secondly, the authors of this article discuss pedagogy behind the creation of a social network from all stakeholders' point of view. Thirdly, they set a few pedagogical principles, including the universal principles set already by Jan Amos Comenius in the 17th century. Finally, they emphasize the potential of educational social networks in students' motivation to learn.

Keywords: Education · Social networks · Pedagogy · Implementation

1 Introduction

Maslow's theory [1] claims that man in order to meet his basic needs, such as a need to survive and a need to be safe, also needs to meet a need of respect, appreciation and self-fulfillment. Therefore when the first online social media and networks appeared, a socially oriented man started to be interested in them [2].

There are many definitions of social networks nowadays. They are usually perceived as a place of meeting people, sharing experiences and information. Mutual interaction among people is expected. Furthermore, there are various kinds of social network sites. Some are typical for family relationships, friends, topics, other focus on making new friends (cf. [3]). This means that the first and foremost purpose of social networks (SNs) is grouping people according to their interests. It only depends on an individual what information s/he wants to search for and share on SNs. Moreover, with the help of SNs, user can express his feelings, chat with friends, or make new friendships. The main idea of SNs consists in the activities of their members (cf. [4]). Social networks or social network sites (SNSs) can be defined as those which possess the three key elements [5]: (1) they have a user-built public or semi-public profile; (2) they enable a link with other users in the system; and (3) they enable to view a list of links and the links made by other users within the system.

Z. Gong et al. (Eds.): ICWL 2015 Workshops, LNCS 9584, pp. 23–30, 2016.
DOI: 10.1007/978-3-319-32865-2_3

Fig. 1. A historical development of SNSs [24]

Thus, Boyd and Ellison define SNs as web-based services that allow individuals to construct a public or semi-public profile within a bounded system; articulate a list of other users with whom they share a connection; and view and traverse their list of connections and those by other within the system.

SNSs have existed before the origination of the Internet itself. The concept of SNSs was described for the first time by professor Barnes who was exploring researching relations among fishermen in one village in Norway. Thanks to this research, he discovered that these fishermen created a kind of relational net, in fact a social network. That means that each person is part of some social network, be it a member of class or a user of the Internet social network [3]. Figure 1 below illustrates the historical development of social networks in the world.

The most common SNSs worldwide include Facebook, Twitter and Skype [6]. In the Czech Republic these are Lide.cz (people.cz) and Spoluzaci.cz (schoolmates.cz).

2 SNSs and Their Types

There are different types of SNSs which can be split into several main categories according to their main purpose. Thus, SNSs can be divided as follows [7]:

- SNSs aimed at social connections through which a user maintain his/her contacts with family members or friends. These SNSs include, for example, Facebook, Twitter, Google, or MySpace.
- SNSs targeted at sharing and exchanging photos or videos, such as YouTube or Flickr.
- SNSs focused on career or professional development through which a user can develop useful professional contacts or find a job. These SNSs involve, for example, LinkedIn or Classroom 2.0.
- SNSs aimed at acquiring information about daily issues such as problems with growing some kind of vegetable or keeping diet. These SNSs include different blogs or forums, which share the same kind of information, for instance, Do-It-Yourself Community SNS.
- SNSs focused on education through which students can consult their study difficulties, work on the joint project, or share their study information. This is, for example, The Student Room SNS.
- SNSs targeted on academic research through which scholars or researchers can cooperate on the joint projects or share their publications. This is, for instance, Academia.edu SNS.

Figure 2 below provides an illustration of these types of SNSs.

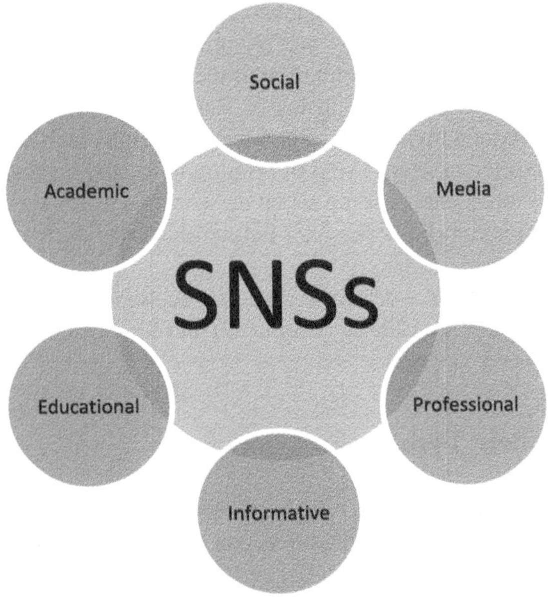

Fig. 2. SNSs and their types

3 Implementation of SNSs in Education

Social network sites are widely used nowadays, not only for entertainment but thanks to their big potential, also in other fields of human activities, including education [8]. However, not much has been written about their implementation and pedagogical principles behind this process so far.

Nadvornik in his study proposes one of the possible approaches to the implementation of a school web presentation the principles of which can serve as a model for the implementation of a social network since there are many similar steps. These steps can be divided into preparatory activities, proposal phase, order of service and its processing and its initial use [9].

The preparatory activities include the following steps:

- mapping school needs and expectations from a social network;
- discovering whether all pupils have access to the Internet;
- decision on the amount of money which is acceptable for the school to invest into the social network; and
- in case there already exists a social network at some other school, discussion on the advantages and disadvantages of this social network.

The proposal phase consists of:

- placing an order to potential companies;

- doing research of a suitable platform which would meet the school requirements [10]; and
- possible buy off of the already existing manual made by other schools.

The order of service and its processing involves:

- selection of the final version and platform from the tender;
- setting up the team which will be in charge of the development of social network site; and
- social network development.

The initial use contains the following steps:

- training of all staff members who will work with the selected social network;
- introduction of the new social network to pupils and training them in its use;
- evaluation of its functioning and its subsequent adjustment to school needs [11]; and
- writing of a manual for all interested subjects which would include the basic strategic information such as learning standards or operational information about the pedagogical methods and approaches which can help meet all the set pedagogical-educational goals (cf. [12, 13]).

Social network does not have to replace the traditional, face-to-face teaching, but it can be a corresponding support for this type of teaching. Primarily, the social network should serve teachers and their pupils, possibly parents. Therefore the basic functions of such a social network should be with respect to the *pupils* as follows: they should have a possibility to have their own account, their own access with the help of login data; they should have a possibility to see learning content, plans, assignments, grading of their school results; they should have access to an overview of important weekly, monthly, quarterly information (e.g., dates of tests or exams); they should have a possibility to communicate with their teachers and other schoolmates and run group discussions; they should be able to see school information about the current events, photos from school trips and events; and they should have some space for uploading their own documents, assignments or projects.

With respect to the *teacher's* needs, the social network should involve the following functions: an account for a teacher who will have more rights and administrative rights than his pupils; a possibility to communicate with pupils individually, in groups and in classes; a possibility to run discussions on a given topic, a chance to add contributions; a possibility to obtain information about the class and other classes; space where a teacher could upload his teaching materials for pupils, worksheets or assignments; space where he could upload pupils' grades, and inform about important dates on a weekly, monthly and quarterly basis; a chance to communicate with children's parents. Teacher should also have a chance to make links to important web pages such as the Ministry of Education, Youth and Sports of the Czech Republic, the Czech School Inspection, the National Institution of Professional Education or the Institute for Information in Education [13].

With respect to the *school management,* the social network could take a role of the present communication interface or the school Intranet which the school management uses in order to communicate with their teachers and other school staff members. In addition, the school management will have a user account for each staff member; space for the selected staff members in which organizational issues could be solved and the selected staff members could access it only on the basis of the set rights. This would, of course, mean that pupils could not access this account. Thus, the school management should pay attention to the fact that any SNS should possess a general yearly plan (e.g., events or important dates); monthly plans and current changes; alternative syllabuses; meeting minutes; current legal changes; current information about finances; school newspapers or journals; extra curricula activities and clubs; competition results; in fact, all that is happening within the school and all other relevant information which is important for smooth functioning of the school (cf. [12]).

With respect to the *parents'* needs, who want to have an overview of their son's or daughter's activities at school, his/her grades or the events the school organizes, it is mainly the special parents' account which is important. In addition, parents want to know what is happening at school; have an overview of the assignments their children have to do, their grades and teaching plans; important events, photos from school events and trips; and a possibility to communicate with their children and their teachers.

As far as the general *public* is concerned, the social network can have a representative function and therefore it could provide some basic information without a necessity of having a user account. This information could include the school contact and school activities; an overview of important dates for public such as the dates of enrolment, entrance exams or Open School Day. In addition, the general public could be informed about the School Educational Programme or job opportunities at a given school.

4 Discussion

At present the Internet is used by the overwhelming majority of school pupils, including teachers since they have easy access to it. Therefore it is not difficult to understand the principle of functioning of a social network. In fact, most of the young generation now uses SNSs in leisure time. They mainly use them for fun, but majority of them also begin to exploit them for their studies at school (cf. [14]). They predominantly use social networks, such as Facebook for their home preparation, access to learning materials, sharing information with their peers, mutual help in solving tasks or a possibility to access it from anywhere and at any time.

The authors also illustrate that there would many benefits for all stakeholders if the school implemented a new educational social network such as easier access to learning materials and their sharing, faster feedback on assignments and tests, current overview of school activities or a complete overview of students' successes and failures for the school management, parents, teachers and pupils themselves. In addition, such an educational social network can be a good public presentation of the school itself.

In addition, present schools are well equipped with technological devices. And although in the present school system the face-to-face form instruction prevails, technologies represent as a suitable support, schools try to implement them in their classes and use new approaches to the teaching with their help. Therefore there seems to be no barrier to using a social network for educational purposes at Czech schools.

Nevertheless, the implementation of any educational social network requires meeting certain pedagogical principles and steps which the authors described above such as an elaboration of preparatory activities, a well-thought-of proposal phase, careful order of service and its processing and its initial use. Moreover, the developers of a new social network for educational purposes could follow universal pedagogical principles, set already by Comenius already in the 17th century [15]. These principles include, for example, to move from simple to more difficult tasks; to understand the essence of the subject, not to learn it by heart, to ease the learning process; or to stimulate pupils to get involved into their studies.

5 Conclusion

Unfortunately, nowadays there is still a lack of research studies which would explore the role of SNSs in education. Nevertheless, those few which already exist show that SNSs can be beneficial in stimulating students in their studies both at school and home. Moreover, some educational social networks already exist, such Piazza [16] or Edmodo [17], which seem to be becoming quite popular among the students (cf. [18]). Therefore next authors' research will concentrate on the evaluation of the existing educational social networks for educational purposes and consequently, on their implementation into real teaching and learning.

References

1. Maslow, A.H.: A theory of human motivation. Psychol. Rev. **50**(4), 370–396 (1943)
2. Hulanova, L.: Internetova Kriminalita Pachana na Detech: Psychologie Internetove Obeti, Pachatele a Kriminality. Triton, Praha (2012)
3. Bezpecny internet. (Safe Internet). http://www.bezpecnyinternet.cz/zacatecnik/socialni-site/co-jsou-socialni-site.aspx
4. Kulhankova, H., Camek, J.: Fenomen Facebook. Jakub Camek, Kladno (2010)
5. Steinfield, C., Ellison, N., Lampe, C., Vitak, J.: Online social network sites and the concept of social capital. In: Lee, F.L., Leung, L., Qiu, J.S., Chu, D. (eds.) Frontiers in New Media Research, pp. 115–131. Routledge, New York (2012)
6. Jain, S.: 40 Most Popular Social Networking Sites of the World. SocialMediaToday.com. http://www.socialmediatoday.com/content/40-most-popular-social-networking-sites-world?page=1
7. White, G.M.: What types of social networks exist? http://socialnetworking.lovetoknow.com/What_Types_of_Social_Networks_Exist
8. Poulova, P., Klimova, B.: Education in computational sciences. In: Proceedings of the International Conference on Computational Science (ICCS) (2015, in press)
9. Nadvornik, V.: Skolni webova stranka a cilove skupiny jejich uzivatelu. In: Ditech 2009: mezinarodni studentska vedecka konference. IKM UHK, Hradec Kralove (2009)
10. Chromy, J., Ryashko, L., Dvorak, D.: Selected Elements of Information Management and Marketing in Higher Education. Extrasystem Praha, Praha (2013)
11. Slavik, J., Novak, J.: Pocitac jako pomocnik ucitele: efektivni prace s informacemi ve skole. Portal, Praha (1997)

12. Zounek, J.: Internet pro pedagogy: [jak hledat a najit]. Ikar, Praha (2001)
13. Cerna, M., Poulova, P.: Social software applications and their role in the process of education from the perspective of university students. In: Proceedings of the 11th European Conference on e-Learning (ECEL 2012), Groningen, pp. 87–96 (2012)
14. Falahah, Rosmala: D. Study of social networking usage in higher education environment. Procedia Soc. Behav. Sci. **67**(1), 156–166 (2012)
15. Comenius, J. A.: The Great Didactic [Didactica Magna]. Translated into English and edited with biographical, historical and critical introductions by M.W. Keatinge. New York: Russell & Russell (1967)
16. Sankar, P.: Our story. https://piazza.com/about/story
17. Bajer, L.: Edmodo. http://wiki.rvp.cz/Kabnet/Online_nástroje/2ZV/U/D/Edmodo
18. Moldrik, K.: Socialni site urcene pro vyuku. http://spomocnik.rvp.cz/clanek/17603/SOCIALNI-SITE-URCENE-PRO-VYUKU.html
19. Marrouat, C.: Social Media–A History: Infographic. http://socialmediaslant.com/social-media-history-infographic-updated/

Virtual Reality Assistant Technology for Learning Primary Geography

Zhihan Lv[1(✉)] and Xiaoming Li[1,2,3]

[1] Shenzhen Institutes of Advanced Technology, Chinese Academy of Science, Chengdu, China
lvzhihan@gmail.com
[2] Shenzhen Research Center of Digital City Engineering, Shenzhen, China
[3] Key Laboratory of Urban Land Resources Monitoring and Simulation, Ministry of Land and Resources, Shenzhen, China

Abstract. A virtual reality based enhanced technology for learning primary geography is proposed, which synthesizes several latest information technologies including virtual reality(VR), 3D geographical information system(GIS), 3D visualization and multimodal human-computer-interaction (HCI). The main functions of the proposed system are introduced, i.e. Buffer analysis, Overlay analysis, Space convex hull calculation, Space convex decomposition, 3D topology analysis and 3D space intersection detection. The multimodal technologies are employed in the system to enhance the immersive perception of the users.

Keywords: VRGIS · Geography learning · Virtual reality · GIS

1 Introduction

With the developments in web, mobile and virtual reality technologies as well as mass adoption of smart and mobile devices by all people in the current society, significant opportunities have emerged for e-learning applications [17]. Location-based mobile phone software has been proved to have the potential in supporting biology, geography and math lessons for students in schools [12]. The latest technologies from video game industry make it becomes easy and efficient to integrate the state-of-the-art graphics/interface and the educational aspect with poor graphics and interaction [1,35]. The technologies of video games [33] have attracted considerable attention to enhance user participation and motivation which should be a key concern in the design of an interactive human-computer-interaction(HCI) interface [5] of the learning enhanced system [10]. Technology enhanced learning brings multidisciplinary, interdisciplinary, and pandisciplinary educational content in different forms [2] oriented to different culture [50]. The dynamic learning environments can deliver educational benefits as educational offerings based upon various characteristics of individual learners [37]. Synthesizing multimedia operations and knowledge sharing aspects has also attracted attention from the research community [16]. The combinations of technology

Z. Gong et al. (Eds.): ICWL 2015 Workshops, LNCS 9584, pp. 31–40, 2016.
DOI: 10.1007/978-3-319-32865-2_4

enhanced learning and other applied information field have been considered as promising practical research topics [46]. It has been argued that integration of concepts from GIS into Information Technology (IT) can provide impressive opportunities for education [48]. The guidelines for the design of 3D virtual learning spaces has been suggested before [36]. The related evaluation process has been proposed in previous research [6,17]. Besides, a lot of other previous related researches have also inspired our research [9,13,38–41,45,49,51,63].

In virtual reality technology trend, geospatial data visualization has never been developing rapidly [44]. With the development of VR (Virtual Reality) technology and widely applications in various areas, the requirements to VR are also increasing rapidly [25]. Virtual Reality Geographical Information System (VRGIS), a combination of geographic information system and virtual reality technology [14] has become a hot topic. Accordingly, '3-D modes' has been proved as a faster decision making tool with fewer errors [43]. Meanwhile, new user interfaces for geo-databases is also expected [3]. With the popularity of network, the VRGIS platform based on the network environment also becomes a trend. The application of VRML, X3D and other online VR technologies have achieved networking of VR systems [21–23,27,29,30,32,47,59,65].

WebVRGIS [25] is preferred in practical applications, especially by the geography and urban planning [20,31], which is based on WebVR [34]. Urban simulation is becoming widely noticed nowadays, and some simulation systems have been developed in this area, e.g. ArcView3D Analyst [24], Imagine Virtual GIS, GeoMedia, etc. WebVRGIS engine supports steadily real time navigation in virtual scenes which are constructed with massive,multi-dimensional data from various sources [18,19,42,52–58,60–62,64,66,67]. 3D urban landscape database with various data sources can be produced to implement spatial analysis and 3D visualization and published in the Internet environment [7,8,11,15]. In this research, we plan to use virtual reality geographic information system technology as an education tool to teach the geography courses.

2 System Overview

3D geometrical analysis education model includes 8 sub-modules: entity set operation, buffer analysis, overlay analysis, space convex hull calculation, space convex decomposition, 3D topology analysis, 3D Minkowski sum calculation, and 3D space intersection detection, as shown in Fig. 1.

3 Functions

Entity set operation includes 4 sub-modules: union, meet, difference, and equilibrium difference. In the space entity, union outputs a new entity including all input entities. Meet outputs the common part of all input entities. Difference outputs spatial features included in the former input entity but excluded from the next space entity.

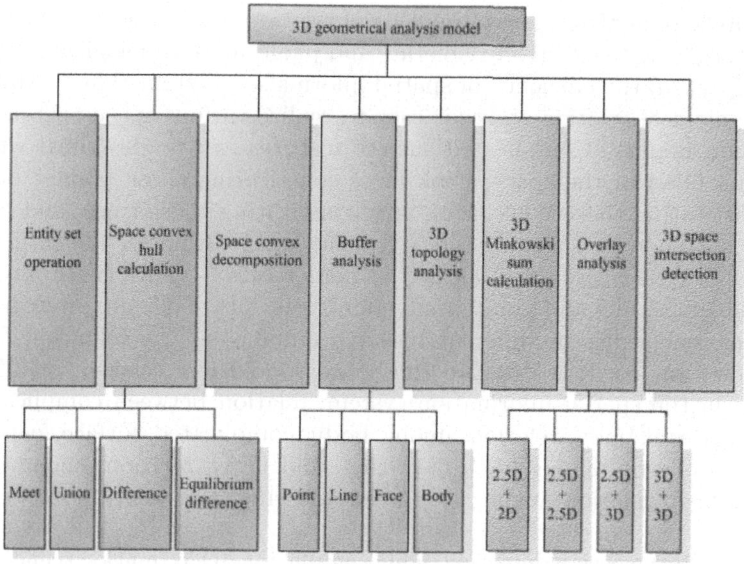

Fig. 1. 3D Geometrical analysis model

Buffer analysis includes point, line, face, and body. Buffer analysis is served as one of spatial analysis tools used to solve proximity-related problems. It is used to realize spatial extension of a spatial entity, determine the scope of influence of this entity in 3D space, and reflect the gradual change law of its influence with distance variation. For instance, the buffer of special sphere with the radius as r (buffer distance R) is a ball with the radius as r+R.

Overlay analysis refers to an analytical method in which two or more geographic element photos in the same region are overlapped under a unified spatial reference system to generate multiple attributive characters of this region. Overlay analysis can be used for new classification of multiple attributes generated after such overlay, so as to establish spatial correspondence among geological objects, and extract quantitative characteristics of some topics within the scope of a certain region.

Space convex hull calculation: in 3D figure application, we often encounter such an issue: determine a convex polyhedron with the minimum volume and including several given points in the space. It is also a form of the minimum coverage problems to calculate the algorithm of convex hull including spatial point sets. It is widely applied in the modeling of buildings.

Space convex decomposition: convex decomposition of a concave polygon is one of basic problems about computation geometry. It is applied in many fields. It realizes the function of decomposing complicated space convex into simple convex polygon. Most existing algorithms are of overall decomposition algorithm. However, fewer researches are made on partial decomposition algorithm. The overall decomposition algorithm is time-consuming. Therefore, it cannot meet application needs of all projects.

3D topology analysis: space topological relation is an important part of spatial analysis. How to effectively generate and judge space topological relation has direct impact on the efficiency of spatial information system. The establishment of 3D topological relation makes it easy to realize various space operations and information inquiry. Complicated surface features can be described with various bodies filled in the space, hook faces constituting those bodies, boundary rings constituting those hook faces, arcs constituting those rings, and nodes on those arcs. Generally speaking, body is basic constitution for the target entity. Any complicated entities are deemed as composed of bodies (natural or artificial). Body, face, line and point are dynamic concepts. They are interconvertible under different scales or different research emphases. The following 6 groups of relations are used to describe the space topological relation of 3D vector structure in the spatial information system: relation between complicated surface feature and body, relation among body, complicated surface feature, and hook face, relation among hook face, ring, and body, relation among ring, arc and hook face, relation among arc, node, and ring, and relation between node and arc.

3D space intersection detection: while simulating 3D animation scenes, numerous collision phenomena will be encountered. Essentially, these collision phenomena are points, lines, faces, and bodies. It is only necessary to judge whether they intersect in 3D space, and work out intersecting points, intersecting lines, intersecting faces, and intersecting bodies.

4 Application Scenarios

The oriented city region simulation WebVRGIS engine is developed based on OpenGL and C++, which integrates VR and GIS seamlessly and supports massive data.

As shown in Fig. 3, the user is watching the virtual geographical scene through the HMD. The HMD is the VR glasses shell by which users could watch the anaglyph 3D scene generated from smartphone screen. The convergence-to-face part of the HMD for light blocking is made by soft holster filling of sponge, so it's not oppressive at all. In addition, it can modify the pupil distance (PD) and depth of field (DOF), so it is suitable for the users with different myopia degree and PD. The input methods include head motion and remote controller. The head motion on VR glasses only supports the rotations around three axis which are controlled by gyroscope sensor of the smartphone. The head rotation actions are synchronous with the rotation of the camera view in the VR scene, which brings the immersive perception to the user in real time. Meanwhile, the remote controller is used to input the displacement of the 3D scene as well as manipulate the menu of the software configuration. The touch-less interaction by swing fingers in the air is also an option [26,28] (Fig. 2).

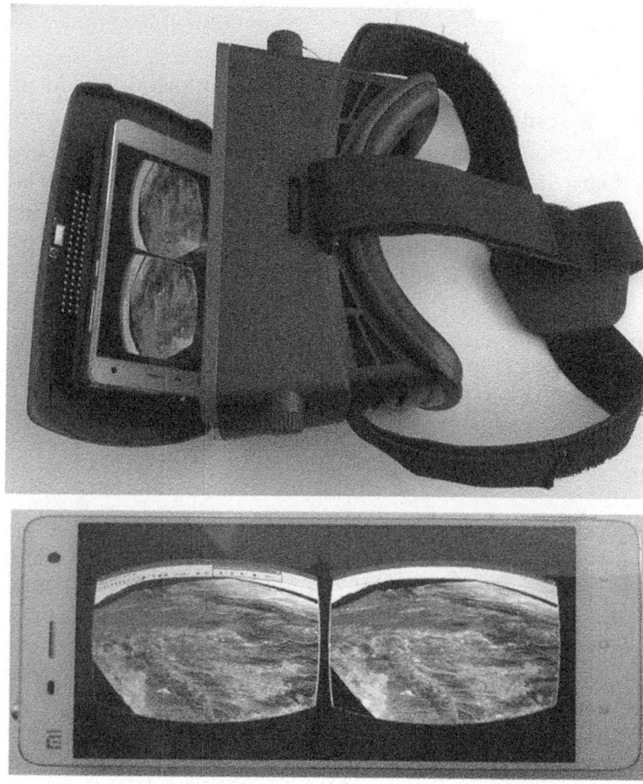

Fig. 2. VRGIS running on virtual reality glassess device

Fig. 3. Left: the user wears the virtual reality Glasses to look at the virtual 3D GIS; Right: the user wears the virtual reality Glasses and use touch-less interaction to manipulate the 3D GIS

5 Conclusion

WebVRGIS is used to show the geographical information intuitively as an enhanced learning tool. Geographical information has several characteristics, i.e. large scale, diverse predictable and real-time, which falls in the range of definition of Big Data defined by Faye Briggs [4]. Virtual reality is a promising and suitable technology to represent geographical bigdata. In future, the new technology will enhance the learning process, for example, multiple users may support the teacher to train a class at the same time.

Acknowledgments. The authors are thankful to the National Natural Science Fund for the Youth of China (41301439), LIESMARS Open Found(11I01) and Electricity 863 project(SS2015AA050201).

References

1. Bellotti, F., Berta, R., Gloria, A.D., Primavera, L.: Enhancing the educational value of video games. Comput. Entertainment (CIE) **7**(2), 23 (2009)
2. Boytchev, P., Kanev, K., Nikolov, R.: Technology enhanced learning with subject field multiplicity support. In: Proceedings of the Joint International Conference on Human-Centered Computer Environments, pp. 39–44. ACM (2012)
3. Breunig, M., Zlatanova, S.: Review: 3d geo-database research: Retrospective and future directions. Comput. Geosci. **37**(7), 791–803 (2011)
4. Briggs, F.: Large data - great opportunities. Presented at IDF, Beijing (2012)
5. Brinkman, W.-P., van der Mast, C., Payne, A., Underwood, J.: Hci for tech-nology enhanced learning. In: Proceedings of the 22nd British HCI Group Annual Conference on People and Computers: Culture, Creativity, Interaction, vol. 2, pp. 185–186. British Computer Society (2008)
6. Carroll, J.M., Rosson, M.B.: A case library for teaching usability engineering: Design rationale, development, and classroom experience. J. Educ. Resour. Comput. (JERIC) **5**(1), 3 (2005)
7. Che, L., Shahidehpour, M., Alabdulwahab, A., Al-Turki, Y.: Hierarchical coordination of a community microgrid with ac, dc microgrids. IEEE Trans. Smart Grid **PP**(99), 1 (2015)
8. Che, L., Zhang, X., Shahidehpour, M., Alabdulwahab, A., Abusorrah, A.: Optimal interconnection planning of community microgrids with renewable energy sources. IEEE Trans. Smart Grid **PP**(99), 1 (2015)
9. Chen, Y.-C.: A study of comparing the use of augmented reality and physical models in chemistry education. In: Proceedings of the ACM International Conference on Virtual Reality Continuum and its Applications, pp. 369–372. ACM (2006)
10. Chen, Z.-H., Chen, S.Y.: A surrogate competition approach to enhancing game-based learning. ACM Trans. Comput. Hum. Interact. (TOCHI) **20**(6), 35 (2013)
11. Dang, S., Ju, J., Matthews, D., Feng, X., Zuo, C.: Efficient solar power heating system based on lenticular condensation. In: International Conference on Information Science, Electronics and Electrical Engineering (ISEEE), vol. 2, pp. 736–739. IEEE (2014)
12. Hansen, F.A., Kortbek, K.J., Grønbæk, K.: Mobile urban drama for multimedia-based out-of-school learning. In: Proceedings of the 9th International Conference on Mobile and Ubiquitous Multimedia, p. 17. ACM (2010)

13. Holzinger, A., Kickmeier-Rust, M.D., Ebner, M.: Interactive technology for enhancing distributed learning: a study on weblogs. In: Proceedings of the 23rd British HCI Group Annual Conference on People and Computers: Celebrating People and Technology, pp. 309–312. British Computer Society (2009)
14. Huang, B., Jiang, B., Li, H.: An integration of gis, virtual reality and the internet for visualization, analysis and exploration of spatial data (2001)
15. Jiang, D., Xu, Z., Lv, Z.: A multicast delivery approach with minimum energy consumption for wireless multi-hop networks. Telecommun. Syst., 1–12 (2015)
16. Klamma, R., Spaniol, M., Jarke, M.: Knowledge multimedia processes in technology enhanced learning. In: Proceedings of the First ACM International Workshop on Multimedia Technologies for Distance Learning, pp. 77–86. ACM (2009)
17. Lahti, J., Siira, J., Törmänen, V.: Development and evaluation of media-enhanced learning application. In: Proceedings of the 11th International Conference on Mobile and Ubiquitous Multimedia, p. 5. ACM (2012)
18. Li, T., Zhou, X., Brandstatter, K., Raicu, I.: Distributed key-value store on hpc and cloud systems. In: 2nd Greater Chicago Area System Research Workshop (GCASR). Citeseer (2013)
19. Li, T., Zhou, X., Brandstatter, K., Zhao, D., Wang, K., Rajendran, A., Zhang, Z., Raicu, I.: Zht: a light-weight reliable persistent dynamic scalable zero-hop distributed hash table. In: IEEE 27th International Symposium on Parallel & Distributed Processing (IPDPS), pp. 775–787. IEEE (2013)
20. Li, X., Lv, Z., Hu, J., Zhang, B., Shi, L., Feng, S.: Xearth: a 3d gis platform for managing massive city information. In: IEEE International Conference on Computational Intelligence and Virtual Environments for Measurement Systems and Applications (CIVEMSA), pp. 1–6. IEEE (2015)
21. Li, X., Lv, Z., Hu, J., Zhang, B., Yin, L., Zhong, C., Wang, W., Feng, S.: Traffic management and forecasting system based on 3d gis. In: 15th IEEE/ACM International Symposium on Cluster, Cloud and Grid Computing (CCGrid). IEEE (2015)
22. Li, X., Lv, Z., Wang, W., Zhang, B., Hu, J., Yin, L., Feng, S.: Webvrgis based traffic analysis and visualization system. Adv. Eng. Softw. **93**, 1–8 (2016)
23. Li, X., Lv, Z., Zhang, B., Wang, W., Feng, S., Hu, J.: Xearth: a 3d gis platform for city bigdata 3d visualization and analysis. In: IEEE International Conference on Computational Intelligence and Virtual Environments for Measurement Systems and Applications (CIVEMSA). IEEE (2015)
24. Li, X., Lv, Z., Zheng, Z., Zhong, C., Hijazi, I.H., Cheng, S.: Assessment of lively street network based on geographic information system and space syntax. In: Multimedia Tools Applications, pp. 1–19 (2015)
25. Lu, Z., Rehman, S.U., Chen, G.: Webvrgis: webgis based interactive online 3d virtual community. In: International Conference on Virtual Reality and Visualization (ICVRV), pp. 94–99. IEEE (2013)
26. Lv, Z.: Wearable smartphone: wearable hybrid framework for hand and foot gesture interaction on smartphone. In: IEEE International Conference on Computer Vision Workshops, pp. 436–443. IEEE (2013)
27. Lv, Z., Chen, G., Zhong, C., Han, Y., Qi, Y.Y.: A framework for multi-dimensional webgis based interactive online virtual community. Adv. Sci. Lett. **7**(1), 215–219 (2012)
28. Lv, Z., Halawani, A., Feng, S., Li, H., Réhman, S.U.: Multimodal hand, foot gesture interaction for handheld devices. ACM Trans. Multimedia Comput. Commun. Appl. (TOMM) **11**(1s), 10 (2014)

29. Lv, Z., Li, X., Zhang, B., Wang, W., Feng, S., Hu, J.: Big city 3d visual analysis. In: 36th Annual Conference of the European Association for Computer Graphics (Eurographics). European Association for Computer Graphics (2015)
30. Lv, Z., Li, X., Zhang, B., Yin, L., Wang, W., Feng, S., Hu, J.: Traffic passenger flow forecasting on virtual reality gis system. In: IEEE International Conference on Computational Intelligence and Virtual Environments for Measurement Systems and Applications (CIVEMSA). IEEE (2015)
31. Lv, Z., Réhman, S.U., Chen, G.: WebVRGIS: a P2P network engine for VR data and GIS analysis. In: Lee, M., Hirose, A., Hou, Z.G., Kil, R.M. (eds.) ICONIP 2013. LNCS, vol. 8226, pp. 503–510. Springer, Heidelberg (2013)
32. Lv, Z., Su, T.: 3d seabed modeling and visualization on ubiquitous context. In: SIGGRAPH Asia Posters, p. 33. ACM (2014)
33. Lv, Z., Tek, A., Da Silva, F., Empereur-Mot, C., Chavent, M., Baaden, M.: Game on, science-how video game technology may help biologists tackle visualization challenges. PloS one **8**(3), 57990 (2013)
34. Lv, Z., Yin, T., Han, Y., Chen, Y., Chen, G.: Webvr-web virtual reality engine based on p2p network. J. Netw. **6**(7), 990–998 (2011)
35. Mayo, M.J.: Games for science and engineering education. Commun. ACM **50**(7), 30–35 (2007)
36. Minocha, S., Hardy, C.L.: Designing navigation and wayfinding in 3d virtual learning spaces. In: Proceedings of the 23rd Australian Computer-Human Interaction Conference, pp. 211–220. ACM (2011)
37. Mulwa, C., Lawless, S., Sharp, M., Arnedillo-Sanchez, I., Wade, V.: Adaptive educational hypermedia systems in technology enhanced learning: a literature review. In: Proceedings of the ACM Conference on Information Technology Education, pp. 73–84. ACM (2010)
38. Mustafa, B.: Visualizing the modern operating system: simulation experiments supporting enhanced learning. In: Proceedings of the Conference on Information Technology Education, pp. 209–214. ACM (2011)
39. Nagel, T., Duval, E., Vande Moere, A.: Interactive exploration of geospatial network visualization. In: CHI 2012 Extended Abstracts on Human Factors in Computing Systems, pp. 557–572. ACM (2012)
40. Ng, K.: Interactive feedbacks with visualisation and sonification for technology-enhanced learning for music performance. In: Proceedings of the 26th Annual ACM International Conference on Design of Communication, pp. 281–282. ACM (2008)
41. Paneva-Marinova, D., Pavlova-Draganova, L., Draganov, L., Georgiev, V.: Ontological presentation of analysis method for technology-enhanced learning. In: Proceedings of the 13th International Conference on Computer Systems and Technologies, pp. 384–390. ACM (2012)
42. Pintus, R., Pal, K., Yang, Y., Weyrich, T., Gobbetti, E., Rushmeier, H.: A survey of geometric analysis in cultural heritage. Computer Graphics Forum (2015)
43. Porathe, T., Prison, J.: Design of human-map system interaction. In: CHI 2008 Extended Abstracts on Human Factors in Computing Systems, CHI EA 2008, pp. 2859–2864. ACM, New York (2008)
44. Rhyne, T.M., MacEachren, A.: Visualizing geospatial data. In: ACM SIGGRAPH Course Notes, p. 31. ACM (2004)
45. Scanlon, E., O'Shea, T., McAndrew, P.: Technology-enhanced learning: evidence-based improvement (2015)

46. Schmees, M.: Organizing technology enhanced learning. In: Proceedings of the 8th International Conference on Electronic commerce: The New e-commerce: Innovations for Conquering Current Barriers, Obstacles and Limitations to Conducting Successful Business on the Internet, pp. 139–150. ACM (2006)
47. Su, T., Lv, Z., Gao, S., Li, X., Lv, H.: 3d seabed: 3d modeling and visualization platform for the seabed. In: IEEE International Conference on Multimedia and Expo Workshops (ICMEW), pp. 1–6. IEEE (2014)
48. Tomaszewski, B., Holden, E.: The geographic information science, technology, information technology bodies of knowledge: an ontological alignment. In: Proceedings of the 13th Annual Conference on Information Technology Education, pp. 195–200. ACM (2012)
49. Underwood, J.: Designing technology enhanced learning contexts. In: Proceedings of the 9th International Conference on Computer Supported Collaborative Learning, vol. 2, pp. 270–272. International Society of the Learning Sciences (2009)
50. Vatrapu, R.: Cultural considerations in learning analytics. In: Proceedings of the 1st International Conference on Learning Analytics and Knowledge, pp. 127–133. ACM (2011)
51. Walczak, K., Wojciechowski, R., Cellary, W.: Dynamic interactive vr network services for education. In: Proceedings of the ACM Symposium on Virtual Reality Software and Technology, pp. 277–286. ACM (2006)
52. Wang, J.J.-Y., Gao, X.: Partially labeled data tuple can optimize multivariate performance measures. In: 24th ACM International Conference on Information and Knowledge Management (CIKM) (2015)
53. Wang, J.J.-Y., Wang, Y., Jing, B.-Y., Gao, X.: Regularized maximum correntropy machine. Neurocomputing **160**, 85–92 (2015)
54. Wang, K., Kulkarni, A., Zhou, X., Lang, M., Raicu, I.: Using simulation to explore distributed key-value stores for exascale system services. In: 2nd Greater Chicago Area System Research Workshop (GCASR) (2013)
55. Wang, K., Liu, N., Sadooghi, I., Yang, X., Zhou, X., Lang, M., Sun, X.-H., Raicu, I.: Overcoming hadoop scaling limitations through distributed task execution
56. Wang, K., Zhou, X., Chen, H., Lang, M., Raicu, I.: Next generation job management systems for extreme-scale ensemble computing. In: Proceedings of the 23rd International Symposium on High-Performance Parallel and Distributed Computing, pp. 111–114. ACM (2014)
57. Wang, K., Zhou, X., Li, T., Zhao, D., Lang, M., Raicu, I.: Optimizing load balancing and data-locality with data-aware scheduling. In: IEEE International Conference on Big Data (Big Data), pp. 119–128. IEEE (2014)
58. Wang, K., Zhou, X., Qiao, K., Lang, M., McClelland, B., Raicu, I.: Towards scalable distributed workload manager with monitoring-based weakly consistent resource stealing. In: Proceedings of the 24rd International Symposium on High-Performance Parallel and Distributed Computing, pp. 219–222. ACM (2015)
59. Wang, W., Lv, Z., Li, X., Xu, W., Zhang, B., Zhang, X.: Virtual reality based GIS analysis platform. In: Arik, S., et al. (eds.) ICONIP 2015. LNCS, vol. 9490, pp. 638–645. Springer, Heidelberg (2015). doi:10.1007/978-3-319-26535-3_73
60. Wang, Y., Bicer, T., Jiang, W., Agrawal, G.: Smart: a mapreduce-like framework for in-situ scientific analytics (2015)
61. Wang, Y., Su, Y., Agrawal, G.: A novel approach for approximate aggregations ver arrays. In: Proceedings of the 27th International Conference on Scientific and Statistical Database Management, p. 4. ACM (2015)
62. Yang, Y., Ivrissimtzis, I.: Mesh discriminative features for 3d steganalysis. ACM Trans. Multimedia Comput. Commun. Appl. **10**(3), 1–27 (2014)

63. Yannier, N., Koedinger, K.R., Hudson, S.E.: Learning from mixed-reality games: Is shaking a tablet as effective as physical observation? In: Proceedings of the 33rd Annual ACM Conference on Human Factors in Computing Systems, pp. 1045–1054. ACM (2015)
64. Zhang, S., Zhang, X., Ou, X.: After we knew it: empirical study and modeling of cost-effectiveness of exploiting prevalent known vulnerabilities across iaas cloud. In: Proceedings of the 9th ACM Symposium on Information, Computer and Communications Security, pp. 317–328. ACM (2014)
65. Zhang, X., Han, Y., Hao, D.S., Lv, Z.: ARPPS: augmented reality pipeline prospect system. In: Arik, S., Huang, T., Lai, W.K., Liu, Q. (eds.) ICONIP 2015. LNCS, vol. 9492, pp. 647–656. Springer, Heidelberg (2015). doi:10.1007/978-3-319-26561-2_76
66. Zhao, D., Zhang, Z., Zhou, X., Li, T., Wang, K., Kimpe, D., Carns, P., Ross, R., Raicu, I.: Fusionfs: toward supporting data-intensive scientific applications on extreme-scale high-performance computing systems. In: IEEE International Conference on Big Data (Big Data), pp. 61–70. IEEE (2014)
67. Zhou, X., Chen, H., Wang, K., Lang, M., Raicu, I.: Exploring distributed resource allocation techniques in the slurm job management system. Illinois Institute of Technology, Department of Computer Science, Technical Report (2013)

Setting up a Virtual Test Environment for User Group Specific Practical Exercises in eHealth eLearning Courses

Alexander Mense[1(✉)], Mathias Forjan[2], Juliane Herzog[1], Philipp Urbauer[1], and Stefan Sauermann[2]

[1] Department of Information Engineering and Security, University of Applied Sciences Technikum Wien, Vienna, Austria
{mense, herzog, urbauer}@technikum-wien.at

[2] Department of Biomedical Engineering, University of Applied Sciences Technikum Wien, Vienna, Austria
{forjan, sauermann}@technikum-wien.at

Abstract. In recent years e-Health – the support for healthcare processes by means of information and communication technology – has become an essential issue for governments, organizations, companies and citizens all over the world. Although at the moment the use of e-Health solutions is expected to bring primarily regional advantages, a series of factors show that the topic has to be considered in an international context and qualified human resources are seen as a key ingredient for success. Therefore the "eLearning4eHealth Network" project at the University of Applied Sciences Technikum Wien aims to develop internationally coordinated eLearning curses for e-Health based on specific knowledge profiles that have been developed in the project. Practical trainings with real world tools (which at best are even in live operation) need to be an important part of the courses. Thus, a set of tools were evaluated and an appropriate suite of them were selected based on knowledge group specific use cases. Currently they are integrated in the eLearning environment and into the courses content.

Keywords: eLearning · eHealth · Practical exercises · Tool environment

1 Introduction

e-Health – support for health care processes by information and communication technology (ICT) – is currently a major topic for governments, organizations, companies and citizens all over the world. As e-Health is expected to have big impact for health care itself as well as to the costs of health care, the interest for specific e-health application is quite high. Highly qualified people and therefore education and qualification are seen as core factors for future successful e-health solutions [1].

The European e-Health Strategy Report states that "Qualified human resources are another key ingredient for success." [1, p. 43] and "The most important part of eHealth investment that needs expanding is the e-Health skills and knowledge of healthcare staff and ICT suppliers' staff. An expanded capability is essential to achieve more success and so help to boost e-Health investment." [1, p. 43].

Z. Gong et al. (Eds.): ICWL 2015 Workshops, LNCS 9584, pp. 41–47, 2016.
DOI: 10.1007/978-3-319-32865-2_5

Even if it seems, that e-Health brings regional advantages, a lot of facts show that it makes sense to consider the topic in a global context (e.g. the requirement for interoperability). Consequently also education in this field has to be seen in a global environment and internationally harmonized educational programs make perfect sense for satisfying current and future e-Health needs.

The "eLearning4eHealth" (eHL) project at the university at Applied Sciences Technikum Wien aims to set up a network of international experts for the development of internationally harmonized academic lectures, training programs and qualification certificates for basic and further education in e-Health. Currently experts from Germany, Canada, Portugal, Czech Republic and Swiss as well as working groups from international organizations in the e-Health domain (e.g. "IHE Education" group, "EU-US Workforce Development Workgroup") are involved.

The developed concepts will be implemented in modern eLearning courses which are offered to students as well as subsequently to companies and organizations as flexible and time-and location-independent learning programs. The courses also enable academic institutions to directly integrate external international experts and their knowledge into their own educational activities. This can be accomplished by using the content as well as directly involving them with communication tools such as communication forums or online conferences. For companies and organizations the courses offer a simple opportunity for further education of their staff.

The technical content of the project is comprised of four main areas:

1. Content: Based on the analysis of existing academic courses and training programs as well as market requirements, learning scenarios and learning content will be developed and implemented as e-learning trainings.
2. Compliance: Conception and definition of processes, frameworks and responsibilities for the issuing of international e-Health qualification certificates
3. Virtual Lab: Selection, specification and implementation of technical simulation tools for integration of practical learning tasks as part of the training programs
4. Transfer: Evaluation of requirements of user groups, organizations, companies and students to develop education profiles. Piloting of the results.

The content developed in area 1 can be combined to target group specific education profiles which are created in the "transfer" section. Contents are implemented in an e-learning environment. As it has been shown that simulations are a valuable part of education and training [2] the courses shall be supported by technical simulation tools developed in the "virtual lab" area.

2 Methods

2.1 Knowledge Profiles

After the evaluation of the state of the art regarding existing learning programs and certifications [3, 4], surveys and interviews done by the network partners were used to get user requirements for the development of knowledge profiles. A knowledge profile is required to perform specific activities in e-Health, individual for each profession.

These profiles are used to structure content to user group specific courses. The finale knowledge profiles are shown in Fig. 1 together with examples of modules (focusing on cross organizational healthcare data exchange) which have to be participated by the different professions.

Thematic content category	Knowledge area	Module	Role		
			Physician	Software designer	Health Information Administrator
Medicine	Fundamentals	Anamnesis, medical specialisations	M	M	M
	Medical terminology – Fundamentals	Wording, definitions, classification principles	M	O	O
	Workflows	Basics & examples of clinical pathways	M	O	M
Engineering	Fundamentals	Data, databases	M	M	M
	Security, Safety and Privacy	IHE Security	O	M	O
	Standards & Interoperability	IHE Basics	O	M	O
		HL7, DICOM, LOINC	O	M	M
		CDA	O	M	M
	Electronic Data Exchange	IHE Profiles, XDS details	O	M	O
	Healthcare Information systems	Examples	M	M	O
Finance Management Law	Fundamentals	Project management, Quality management, process management	M	M	M
		Regulatory & legal issues	M	M	M
	Health Data Management	Methods for collecting and processing health data	M	M	M
	Usability	Usability of EMR (Definitions, principles)	-	M	O

M This module is needed by this role.

- This module is not needed by this role.

O This module is maybe needed by this role

Fig. 1. Knowledge profiles (Source: [5])

The content for the first courses (primarily basic education in e-Health as this is needed by every role) has been already developed and provided as a Moodle course to students.

2.2 Learning Objectives and Use-Case

As a first outcome a general knowledge base regarding cross organizational health data exchange has been defined. Based on the knowledge areas a set of learning objectives and a corresponding practical use case to support the achievement of the objectives were defined. This use case was used as the starting point for the evaluation and selection of tools to offer course participants the possibility to apply their gained theoretical knowledge to a real world environment.

2.3 Tools Evaluation

For the specified use case and the required fields of application a search for tools was done and the tools were evaluated based on the criteria shown in Table 1. Fundamental requirements to be usable as part of the eLearning courses are the online availability and an open source policy. If possible tools available in live operation should be used.

Table 1. Evaluation criteria

Evaluation criteria	Possible answers
Field of application (FA)	Electronic medical record (EMR), interoperability testing, medical practice management, XML/Reference Information Model (RIM) testing, Hospital information system (HIS), Electronic health record (EHR), Providing of code lists, value sets and consistent identification of objects
Experiences gained with the tool (EXP)	yes|no|no information available(n/a)
On-going development (DEV)	yes|no|n/a
Regional versions available (RV)	yes|no|n/a
Availability of a documentation (AD)	yes|no|n/a
Range (complexity) and possibilities of the tool (RP)	high|low|n/a
Access policy (AP)	public|restricted|both|n/a
Possibility of plugins (PLU)	yes|no|n/a
System requirements(SR)	high|low|n/a

3 Results

3.1 Use Case

Based on the learning objectives an appropriate use case was developed. Table 2 shows the learning outcomes (description based on Bloom's Taxonomy [6]) and the corresponding use case. Figure 2 shows the use case diagram based on the knowledge profiles and user roles.

Table 2. Learning outcomes and corresponding use case

Learning objectives	Use case
Describe the structure of CDA documents (content, levels)	Create an implementation guide Create a CDA document
Describe the structure and content of the CDA implementation guidelines	Test a CDA document using a Schematron
Create a CDA for an easy clinical use case, e.g. blood analysis	Test the Schematron using a set of documents
Use the codes from the Austrian terminology server (using the API)	Store and retrieve the document using the XDS environment
Test a CDA using a Schematron	
Describe the general structure of a profile within the IHE	

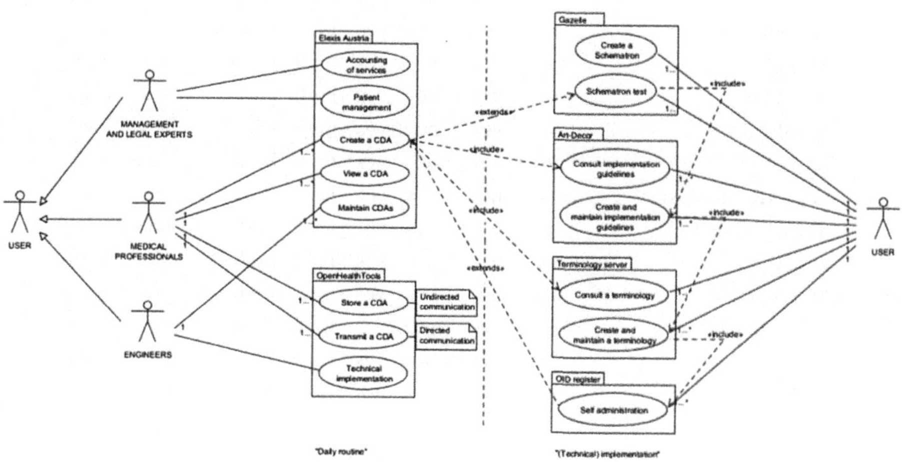

Fig. 2. Use case diagram

3.2 Tool Evaluation and Selection

As a result of the online research 25 tools marked as open source and publicly available were identified and evaluated based on the defined criteria (Table 1). Table 3 shows the results of the evaluation.

The tools installed have been initially tested to be appropriate for the use case. First tests were successful. Based on the evaluation results six tools were selected to implement the defined use case: Art-Decor [7], Elexis Austria [8], Gazelle [9], OpenHealthTools [10], Terminology Server [11], OID register [12].

Three of the tools are online services that can also be used for simulation. The other tools will be packed together to be provided as an "Virtual Lab" environment to course participants.

Table 3. Tool evaluation results

Tool/Criteria	EXP	DEV	RV	AD	RP	AP	PLU	SR
Art-Decor	yes	yes	no	yes	high	public	no	high
Gazelle	yes	yes	no	yes	high	public	no	low
Continua Health Alliance	yes	yes	no	yes	high	both	no	low
OHT	yes	no	no	no	high	restricted	no	high
Term. Server	yes	yes	yes	yes	low	both	no	high
OID register	yes	yes	no	yes	low	public	no	high
Elexis Austria	yes	no	yes	yes	low	restricted	yes	low
AlwaysMed	no	no	no	no	low	public	no	low
CottageMed	no	no	no	yes	high	n/a	no	low
FreeMed	no	yes	no	no	low	public	yes	high
GaiaEHR	no	yes	no	yes	high	public	no	high
GNUmed	no	yes	no	yes	low	both	yes	low
GNU Health	no	yes	no	yes	high	n/a	yes	high
HospitalOS	no	yes	yes	yes	low	restricted	no	high
Mirth	yes	yes	no	yes	high	restricted	yes	high
openEHR	no	yes	no	yes	high	n/a	yes	n/a
openEMR	no	yes	no	yes	high	n/a	yes	low
openMRS	no	yes	no	yes	high	both	yes	high
OSCAR McMaster	no	no	yes	yes	low	n/a	no	low
THIRRA (EHR)	no	no	yes	no	low	both	no	low
VistA	no	yes	no	yes	high	both	yes	high
MedinTux	no	no	yes	yes	low	both	yes	high
OpenDental	no	yes	no	yes	high	public	yes	high
Cypress	no	yes	no	yes	high	n/a	no	high
Laika	no	no	no	no	low	n/a	no	low

4 Discussion

Whilst the content of the courses and lectures as well as the use case have been verified by the international network to be internationally applicable the selection of the tools depend on the specific area and local needs. Therefore the presented selection of tools is unfortunately only partly usable by all international partners and some of the tools have to be replaced by other products.

The next step and challenge in the project will be the needless integration of the Virtual Lab into the learning environment.

Acknowledgements. This project is funded by the City of Vienna Municipal department 23 "Economic Affairs, Labour and Statistics" within the program "Internationalization of Teaching and Science".

References

1. EC: eHealth Action Plan 2012-2020 - Innovative healthcare for the 21st century, Bruessel (2012)
2. Ziv, A., Small, S.D., Wolpe, P.R.: Patient safety and simulation-based medical education. Med. Teach. **22**, 489–495 (2000)
3. Herzog, J., Pohn, B., Forjan, M., Sauermann, S., Urbauer, P.: Education for eHealth - a status analysis. In: eHealth2014 - Health Informatics Meets eHealth, vol. 198, pp. 172–179 (2014)
4. Urbauer, P., Herzog, J., Pohn, B., Forjan, M., Sauermann, S.: Certification programs for eHealth – status quo. In: eHealth2014 – Health Informatics Meets eHealth. Studies in Health Technology and Informatics, vol. 198, p. 164ff (2014). doi:10.3233/978-1-61499-397-1-164
5. Herzog, J., Sauermann, S., Mense, A., Forjan, M., Urbauer, P.: Development of knowledge profiles for international eHealth eLearning courses. In: Medical Informatics Europe 2015 - Digital Healthcare Empowering Europeans, Madrid, Spain, pp. 556–560 (2015)
6. Overbaugh, R.C., Schultz, L.: Bloom's Taxonomy. http://ww2.odu.edu/educ/roverbau/Bloom/blooms_taxonomy.htm
7. The Art-Decor expert group, About art-decor.org/mediawiki/index.php/AboutFreie. Arztsoftware elexis-austria, elexis-austria Standardmodul. http://www.elexis-austria.net/elexis-austria/21-elexis-austria-funktionen/17-elexis-austria-standardmodul.html
8. Freie Arztsoftware elexis-austria, elexis-austria Funktionen. http://www.elexis-austria.net/elexis-austria/21-elexis-austria-funktionen.html
9. IHE International, What's Gazelle. http://gazelle.ihe.net/gazelle-in-few-words
10. Open Health Tools, About OpenExchange. https://projects.openhealthtools.org/sf/projects/openexchange/
11. Bundesministerium für Gesundheit, Medizinische Terminologien und der Terminologieserver. https://www.gesundheit.gv.at/Portal.Node/ghp/public/content/gesundheitssystem-terminologieserver.html
12. Bundesministerium für Gesundheit, OID Portal Österreich. https://www.gesundheit.gv.at/OID_Frontend/

Development of the 'Learning to Learn' Competence Through Wiki Tools in CA-CLIL: Pilot Course

Vladimira Froldova and Ivana Simonova(✉)

University of Hradec Kralove, Rokitanskeho 64, 500 03 Hradec Kralove, Czech Republic
{vladimira.froldova,ivana.simonova}@uhk.cz

Abstract. The paper presents the results of learners' feedback on Social Science lessons at Secondary school for EU administration in Prague, Czech Republic. In the lessons the computer-assisted content and language integrated learning (CA-CLIL), wiki tools and methods of collaborative learning are applied. Such a model aims at developing the 'learning-to-learn' competence as defined by European Union documents. Totally 60 students participated in the pedagogical experiment; its main objective was to prove expected contributions of this approach to the process of instruction. Learners' feedback was collected by the questionnaire and analyzed.

Keywords: Study materials · CLIL · Wiki · Collaborative learning · English · Survey

1 Introduction

Since 2006 the national curriculum for secondary schools in the Czech Republic has been reflecting (among others) the concept of key competences adapted to European Union (EU) legislation [1]. Knowledge and skills to each competence development have been implemented into learning objectives and learning content in each subject. One of the key competences is the 'learning-to-learn' competence; further on the expression 'learning competence' is used. The question is how the competence development is applied in everyday teaching/learning within a selected subject in the Czech education system. Reflecting the popularity and wide spread of latest technologies, new approaches to teaching/learning are currently applied. Moreover, rather strong support is provided to the competence of communication in foreign languages. Putting these two aspects together, the computer-assisted language learning (CALL), or even mobile-assisted language learning (MALL) are relevant 'topics of the day'. The question is what both the teachers' and students' feedback is to such an approach. Therefore, the implementation and application of the learning-to-learn competence from teacher's point of view was briefly monitored within Czech curriculum and (2) evaluation of the learning model exploiting the wiki platform, computer-assisted content and language integrated learning (CA-CLIL) and collaboration in the subject of Social Science was evaluated by students.

Z. Gong et al. (Eds.): ICWL 2015 Workshops, LNCS 9584, pp. 48–56, 2016.
DOI: 10.1007/978-3-319-32865-2_6

2 Theoretical Background

Generally, in the Czech curricular documents and in practice there is a slightly different approach to building the learning-to-learn (or learning) competence compared to educational literature. Lokajíčková [2] (234) states "… learning competences are not always a synonym to the construct of learning to learn, as it is used mainly in English written literature". She suggests them to be considered "dispositions for managing the situations for learning, while learning to learn is regarded as a process which accompanies learning". [2] (234) Lokajíčková also understands the learning-to-learn concept to be super-ordinate to the concept of learning competences. On the other side, taking into account, the exploitation of latest technologies have become standard within the Czech education system, there exist at least two phenomena which might provide substantial didactic support: (1) wiki environment and (2) the content and language integrated learning (CLIL), particularly the computer-assisted CLIL (further on the CLIL abbreviation is used). The CLIL methodology was widely and deeply analyzed and discussed by numerous scientists and authors in last decade, as well as wiki exploitation a few years later (e.g. Dale et al. [3], Dalton-Puffer [4], Mehisto et al. [5] as well as wiki exploitation a few years later (e.g. West and West [6], Ebersbach [7]). To sum up, the computer-assisted activities do not only mean those running on a computer, notebook and other devices but also relating services are included, i.e. those mediated via the Internet. Thus the computer-assisted CLIL can be defined as such an approach to teaching/learning when activities are enhanced by PC/Internet so that the learning content could be acquired in any subject and through a foreign language [8].

The wiki environment (platform) is a website allowing users to create and edit pages easily and collaboratively. It can serve as a tool for synchronous and asynchronous communication and also enables students and teachers to keep track of any changes made into students' learning process. Furthermore, wiki might serve not only as a platform for a teacher's assessment of student's progress or frequency of contributions (adding, deleting), but also it might provide the information about student's interests, motivations and giving space for creativity. The wiki environment provides several properties that make it ideal framework for composing different time and place environment. Wiki applications can support a variety of learning activities ranging from tightly to loosely coupled collaborations. Wiki-based collaborative applications can also support metacognitive tasks, like reflection or self/co-explanation, as Larusson [9] mentions. Moreover, wiki is considered a user-friendly tool. The exploitation of wiki environment brings the collaborative and co-operative learning on the stage. Two approaches to understanding these term may appear. Some authors consider them identical (e.g. MacGregor [10], Cooper and Robinson [11]), the others state collaborative learning takes place any time students work together, e.g. when they help each other with homework whereas co-operative learning means students work together in the same place (on a structured project) in a small group (e.g. Barkely et al. [12]). The type of work may be the distinguisher between the two terms for some authors saying collaboration means to work together on a project, while co-operation puts together work of single team members. Either we prefer the former or the latter approach, positive impact was detected with learners in deeper understanding of the learning content, increased overall achievement, improved self-esteem, higher motivation to learning. Moreover, students become actively and constructively involved in the content, they learn how to solve group conflicts and improve teamwork skills [13]. From the pedagogical point of view, several questions should be answered: 'How can the CLIL approach enrich the collaborative learning, and vice versa, to support the learning competence development?', particularly 'What are students' and teachers' attitudes towards CLIL where wiki tools for collaborative learning are exploited?', 'What is teachers' opinions on promoting the learning competence?', 'What are students' attitudes to collaborative learning?' and many others. Answers to selected questions were collected within the survey described below. In the survey the definition of the learning competence stated in the Czech curriculum was applied, i.e. it represents the capability to apply or use a set of related knowledge, skills, and abilities required to successfully performed tasks in a defined learning objective [14]. In other words, the upper secondary school graduate should:

- have a positive attitude to learning and education,
- know different learning techniques,
- be able to create suitable learning's conditions and learning environment,
- put different ways of working with a text into effect (learning and analytical reading), know effectively how to look up information and process it, be reading literate,
- listen to different oral presentations (explanation, lectures, speeches etc.) with understanding and be able to write down notes from different media sources,
- use different information sources including other people's experience as well as their own,
- follow and evaluate their own learning progress and accomplished tasks and be able to accept other people's assessment of their learning results,
- be aware of future possibilities and opportunities in their education, specifically in the field of their specialisation.

Above mentioned partial learning competences are rather similar to generic skills defined by Petty [15]. He calls them mini key competences; they include synthesis, analysis, evaluation, study skills and affective and social skills. Both learning competences and generic skills reflect skills and abilities which are cross-curricular and enhance desired quality for being competitive on the labour market.

3 Materials and Methods

Before the survey of students' opinions started, teachers in the Secondary School for EU Administration (SSEUA), Prague, Czech Republic, where the CLIL approach is applied, answered two questions to provide ideas about the field researched:

(1) Is the learning competence included in your subject curriculum?
(2) Do you develop the learning competence when teaching your subject?

They expressed their opinions on the learning competence reflection in their work. Out of 34 respondents, 20 of them answered 'yes' to the first question (Is the learning competence included in your subject curriculum?) and 29 respondents answered 'yes' to the second question (Do you develop the learning competence when teaching your subject?). Consequently, those providing the 'yes' answer to the first question were asked to specify three activities they use in this context. The examples revealed that only eight respondents were aware of knowledge, skills and abilities contributing to the learning-to-learn competence development. Twelve respondents gave examples of learning objectives concerning their subjects instead of the learning competence.

Then, the survey was carried out among students of the SSEUA, so that to get their feedback on CLIL, wiki and collaborative learning towards the learning-to-learn competence development. SSEUA has more than 800 students but only 60 students participated in the pilot course. To support meaningful communication in English and enhance English communication skills, in one class of 30 students (aged 16–17) the CLIL approach was applied (experimental group), whereas in the second class of 30 students other (non-CLIL) methods were exploited (control group). Lessons in both classes were supported by the wiki environment. One (45-min) lesson per week was scheduled for the subject of Social Sciences, totally 32 h per school year. All students were divided into ten teams of three students in each class for the whole year. They worked and were assessed both individually and in teams, depending on given tasks. Each student had unlimited access to learning materials, provided by the teacher, which were displayed on the wiki, and to class collaborative web pages. The access to team web pages was provided to the members of each group, student's portfolio pages were open to single students. The teaching/learning processes were designed both to promote maximum communication in English and in mother tongue and to enhance learning competence via collaboration through wiki.

The whole process consisted of three types of activities. *First,* before each face-to-face lesson starts, study materials and links to them are presented to all students on the wiki platform, students read them, analyze and think about the content, they consider the contribution and develop their own opinions. All activities aim at being well-prepared to the topic which will be taught on the face-to-face lesson. This stage refers to neo-behaviourism approach [16] where the teacher is a guarantee of transferring basic information to students, so students are able to gain an insight into the whole issue. *Second,* the face-to-face learning starts. It represents active learning applying the constructivist approach [16]. This stage is structured into two phases. In the school face-to-face phase the students directed by the teacher work in pairs or teams on activities which encourage them to use general classroom communication skills (in English in the CLIL group and in mother tongue in the non-CLIL group), as well as to learn or practise solving higher cognitive tasks. They plan, organise and check outcomes of the texts they read before the lesson, of their projects or take notes from different information sources. Within the home phase, students work in the wiki environment. Each student has their own portfolio page, where they submit their homework, usually based on comparing and discussing information collected from the text to the 'just-learnt' information or giving an opinion on related issues. The students give a short assessment or self-assessment on a current learning issue and their performance during the previous face-to-face lesson. Their essays are collected through the wiki platform. The collection of individual and group-created essays is an efficient tool reflecting students' comprehension of a particular topic, as well as developing their learning competence by learning from others. These activities should help them extend their learning competences and improve in their mother tongue (in the non-CLIL group) and/or professional English in the CLIL group). *Third,* each team creates their own learning space/environment via the team wiki platform consisting of pages of individual students. This process refers to connectivism, where a network of connections helps distribute information. That is the reason why learning gains the power to construct and exceed those networks [17]. Each team member contributes to the team page after each lesson. Students should post there their reflection on a face-to-face lesson as well as add some materials concerning their learning needs and the topic. The team members can see each other portfolio pages, so that they can be inspired while working on their tasks at home. They can discuss and comment team member's contributions and react to their comments and assesses the content of the page from subject-content in both groups and from the foreign-language (in the CLIL group) point of view. They summarise the team's contributions and evaluate their team approach. The whole communication is supervised by the teacher, who posts their own comments and assesses the content of the page from subject-content or foreign language points of view. This supervision should help students stay focused on learning and develop not only academic and general functional language within the CLIL group, but also to learn how to work in teams or look up additional materials on the Internet. Last but not least, students have to manage their learning and accomplish tasks on a wiki to a pre-defined deadline.

This rather complicated process of developing the learning-to-learn competence is displayed in Table 1.

Table 1. Structure of social science lessons.

Group	CLIL	Wiki	School lessons
Experimental	yes	yes	yes
Control	no	yes	yes

At the end of the school year students' feedback was collected on this pilot course embracing the CLIL approach, wiki activities within autonomous home learning. For this purpose the questionnaire was designed consisting of 37 statements evaluated on the six-point Likert scale. The questionnaire was structured into four sub-categories: wiki as a learning environment, evaluating and self-evaluating skills, cooperation, and creativity. The following statements were selected for the purpose of this study:

(1) I really use available wiki materials for my learning.
(2) I consider doing tasks on a wiki platform to be an important part of my learning.
(3) I think that my evaluation and self-evaluation skills improved by working on wiki tasks.
(4) I think that working on a wiki platform supports my creativity development.
(5) I think that working on a wiki platform enables me to use different sources for self-expression.
(6) I think that working on a wiki platform made me to cooperate with others.
(7) I think that team work on a wiki platform supported my learning.

(8) I think that English in non-language subjects was contributory for me.
(9) I think that my English communication skills improved.
(10) I think that I have a better command in English than before the course.
(11) I would appreciate to have more subjects in CLIL.
(12) I consider the wiki-based learning interesting.
(13) I would like to carry on working on a wiki.

This pilot course was conducted in 2013/14 school year; each year consists of two five-month semesters. To keep ethic rules and not to educationally discriminate some students, the experimental (CLIL) group in winter semester worked as the control (non-CLIL) group in the summer semester, and vice versa. Data were collected from both groups after each course and summarized. So as not to be influenced by the other group, students in both groups were not informed about the teaching method exploited in the other group. The survey did not intend to compare students' opinions in CLIL and non-CLIL groups but to get a general reflection on the CLIL exploitation in Social Science subject.

4 Results

Reflecting the above mentioned teacher's subjective feedback, the analyses of team and portfolio pages, plus post-course questionnaires as well as the focus-group discussion show that wiki-based tasks can contribute to development of student's learning-to-learn competences. This conclusion was based on a partial subjective qualitative analysis run by the authors, not published yet, but it served as the background of further steps.

To measure perceived students approaches to wiki-based tasks, the students completed a questionnaire, which consisted of 37 statements divided into four groups (general learning skills, CLIL-language skills, and cooperation/collaboration and wiki environment) scored on a six-point Likert scale from 1 meaning 'I strongly agree with this item' to 6 expressing 'I strongly disagree with this item'. Selected results are displayed in Fig. 1.

The positive feedback on the pilot course is displayed in light colours, the negative opinions are in the black, structured and dark grey colours. From all of the above, it can be seen that the 'worst' score was in statement 7 (S7) saying that team work on the wiki platform supported their learning and improved their evaluation and self-evaluation skills (S3). On the other side, more than 90 % students used the displayed materials on a wiki for their learning (S1). This result is similar to Su and Beaumont [18] results who found about 89 % students perceived that R&D wiki helped to develop their initiative in learning independently. More than 75 % students consider wiki-based tasks important for their learning (S2). More than 70 % students stated that a wiki supported their creativity (S4) and promoted different ways of expressing themselves (S5). Implementing wiki environment into lessons had an impact on about 88 % of students' cooperation (S6), and 80 % of them think that cooperation on a wiki had an impact on their learning. Similarly to Kam and Katerattanakul [19] whose study reveals that synchronicity and group-awareness promote team-based learning.

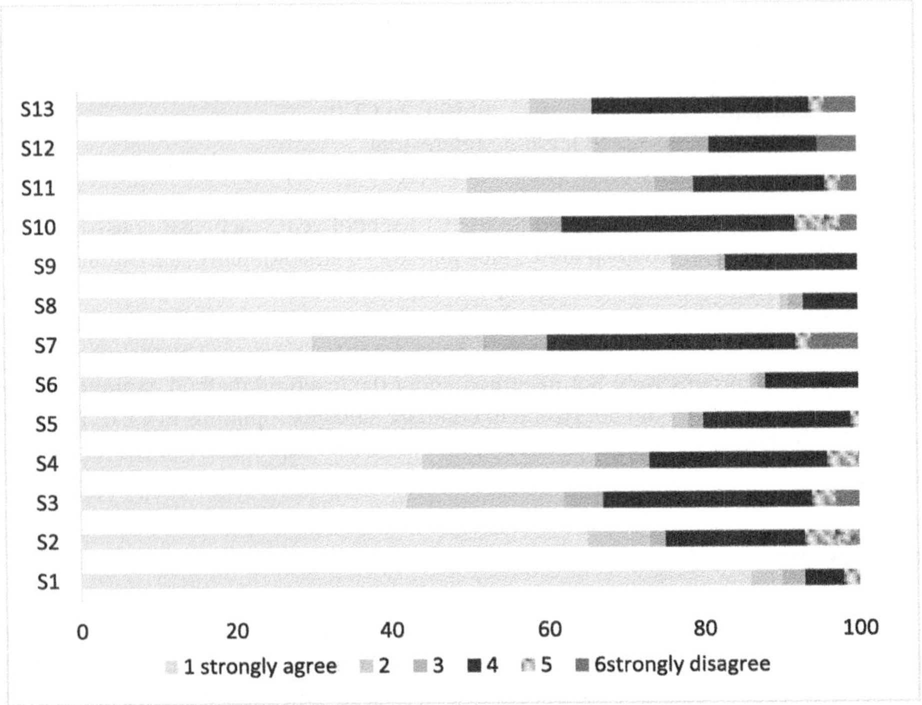

Fig. 1. Students' feedback after the pilot course

To evaluate students' attitudes to CLIL learning, more than 90 % think that using English in non-language subjects was contributory for them (S8). Comparable findings similar to ours were discovered in different parts of world e.g. Furstenberg and Kletzenbauer [20] or Duran and Cruz [21]. Reflecting the focus group discussions on CLIL, students appreciated the fact that they were able to speak/write on different topics in English. The language-advanced students would like to have more English language and materials during the lessons and some of them express their dissatisfaction with their level of English. On the other hand, weak students find CLIL lessons very challenging, the amount of English language and materials were more than enough for them and they would like to be tested only in Czech language. These attitudes represent approximately 20 % of students who are not keen on having more CLIL subjects (S9-11).

More than 80 % students find wiki-based learning interesting (S12). This attitude is supported by focus group discussions, where students expressed their motivation to learn new technology or do new things. Surprisingly, this motivation was gradually wearing off in the non-CLIL group, but not in the CLIL group, although both groups did the same wiki-based tasks. The difference was mainly in working language and extra Internet materials (podcasts, clips, videos, resources etc.) which are in English and rarely in Czech. The next reason for worn off motivation was setting a deadline, which was frustrating for some students. In both groups there were students who do not find not only wiki environment, but also the whole idea of learning anything by means of Internet contributory (see dark grey colour). The findings reflect the difference between 79 % CLIL students who want to have more CLIL subjects to 53 % non-CLIL students (S13).

5 Discussions and Conclusions

In this study the research problem whether/how a wiki environment can support learning competences explored the pedagogical implications arising from the implementation of a wiki tools into an existing curriculum of the subject of Social Science.

First of all, the construct of learning competences was discussed. Reflecting the criteria set on learning competences, which students in Czech higher second education should reach, our focus was on cooperation, evaluation and self-evaluation, and learning skills. We tried to implement a few wiki-based tasks dealing with learning competences into a running experiment on a wiki. Within the applied approach, students most appreciate the fact that they can express themselves in many different ways (graphs, mind maps, pictures, videos etc.), which might reflect their learning styles as outlined in Šimonová and Poulová [22]. The students are in favour of giving feedback not only for the teacher but as well for their peers and team members. According to Schaaf et al. [23] (243) "feedback and reflective thinking are fundamental for learning". As the relevant studies on creativity development supported by a wiki within CLIL are rather rare, we suggest this area for a future research. Most students express their positive attitude to cooperating in teams on a wiki, even though sometimes it wis very challenging. Although there are a few studies, e.g. Kam and Katerattanakul [19], which consider synchrony the most important aspect of collaborative learning, there seems to be enough studies, e.g. Coll et al. [24], which find asynchrony especially in self- and peer-assessment fundamental. Nevertheless, there are a few students who do not like working in teams, and they consider the whole idea of using the wiki neither motivating, nor contributory to their studies.

In conclusion we can state that the idea of implementing a wiki platform into teaching/learning process was approved by this pilot course. Next step will be to make efforts to implement wiki-based tasks, which are predominantly focused on learning competences, into the wiki environment. As mentioned above, the learning competence is an inevitable part of school curriculum, however, it is still not fully integrated into teaching and learning process as it should be in the Czech education system.

Acknowledgment. The paper is supported by the project 'Didactic aspects of Blackboard Mobile Learn implementation into the process of instruction at FIM'.

References

1. Recommendations of the European Parliament and of the Council: on key competences for lifelong learning. 2006/962/ES: Official Journal of the European Union, 394/10 (2006). http://eur-lex.europa.eu/legal-content/CS/TXT/PDF/?uri=CELEX:32006H0962&from=EN

2. Lokajíčková, V.: Kompetence k učení a možnosti jejího rozvíjení a hodnocení: vymezení pojmu a přehled současných přístupů [Learning competence and possibilities of its development and evaluation]. Pedagogická Orientace **23**(3), 318–341 (2013)
3. Dale, L., Van de Es, W., Tanner, R.: CLIL Skills. Expertisecentrum mvt, Leiden (2010)
4. Dalton-Puffer, C., Smit, U.: Empirical Perspectives on CLIL Classroom Discourse. Peter Lang, Frankfurt am Main (2007)
5. Mehisto, P., Marsh, D., Frigols, M.J.: Uncovering CLIL: Content and Language Integrated Learning in Bilingual and Multilingual Education. Macmillan Education, Oxford (2008)
6. West, J., West, M.: Using Wikis for Online Collaboration: The Power of the Read-Write Web. Jossey-Bass, San Francisco (2009)
7. Ebersbach, A.: Wiki: Web Collaboration. Springer, Berlin (2008)
8. Vesela, K.: CA-CLIL: Blending the Unblendable? UKF, Nitra (2011)
9. Larusson, J.A., Alterman, R.: Wikis to support the “collaborative” part of collaborative learning. Int. J. Comput. Support. Collaborative Learn. **4**(4), 371–402 (2009)
10. MacGregor, J.: Collaborative learning: shared inquiry as a process of reform. In: Svinicki, M.D. (ed.) The Changing Face of College Teaching, New Directions for Teaching and Learning, vol. 42 (1990)
11. Cooper, J., Robinson, P.: Small group instruction in science, mathematics, engineering, and technology. J. Coll. Sci. Teach. **27**, 383 (1998)
12. Barkely, E.F., Cross, K.P., Howell Major, C.: Collaborative Learning Techniques: A Handbook for College Faculty. Jossey-Bass, San Francisco (2005)
13. Educational Broadcasting Corporation (2004). http://www.thirteen.org/edonline/concept2class/coopcollab/
14. RVP Veřejnosprávní činnost [Framework programme – Administration and public activity]. In: č. j. 12 698/2007-23. MŠMT (2007). http://zpd.nuov.cz/RVP/ML/RVP%206843M01%20Verejnospravni%20cinnost.pdf
15. Petty, G.: Teaching students’ skills. http://geoffpetty.com/for-teachers/skills/
16. Zounek, J., Sudický, P.: E-learning: učení (se) s online technologiemi: Kniha s online podporou [E-learning: learning/teaching with technologies: Book with online support]. Wolters Kluwer, Praha (2012)
17. Downes, S.: Connectivivism and Connective Knowledge. http://www.downes.ca/post/54540
18. Su, F., Beaumont, C.: Evaluating the use of a wiki for collaborative learning. Innov. Educ. Teach. Int. **47**(4), 417–431 (2010)
19. Kam, H.J., Katerattanakul, P.: Structural model of team-based learning using web 2.0 collaborative software. Comput. Educ. **76**, 1–12 (2014)
20. Furstenberg, U., Kletzenbach, P.: CLIL: from online sources to learnig resources. In: Conference Proceedings, International Conference ICT for Language Learning, 5 edn., Florence, Italy. Libreriauniversitaria.it, 15–16 November 2012
21. Duran, A., Cruz, M.: How to Integrate Stories and ICT in Content-Based Units of Work for English Learning. Porta Linguarum, vol. 19, pp. 219–232 (2013). http://www.ugr.es/~portalin/articulos/PL_numero19/14%20A%20Duran.pdf
22. Šimonová, I., Poulová, P.: Learning Style Reflection within Tertiary e-Education. WAMAK, Hradec Kralove (2012)
23. Van der Schaaf, M., Baartman, L., Prins, F., Oosterbaan, A., Schaap, H.: Feedback dialogues that stimulate students’ reflective thinking. Scand. J. Educ. Res. **57**(3), 227–245 (2013)
24. Coll, C., Rochera, M.J., Gispert, I., Zumbach, J., Hillers, A., Reimann, P.: Supporting online collaborative learning in small groups: teacher feedback on learning content, academic task and social participation. Comput. Educ. **75**, 86–102 (2014)

Learning Styles in the e-Learning Environment: Meta-analysis of Longitudinal Changes

Pavel Doulik[1], Jiri Skoda[1], and Ivana Simonova[2(✉)]

[1] Faculty of Education, Jan Evangelista Purkyne University, Pasteurova 1, 40096 Usti nad Labem, Czech Republic
{Pavel.Doulik,Jiri.Skoda}@ujep.cz

[2] Faculty of Informatics and Management, University of Hradec Kralove, Rokitanskeho 62, 50003 Hradec Kralove, Czech Republic
ivana.simonova@uhk.cz

Abstract. The paper introduces results of meta-analysis focused on the field of learning styles in the e-learning environment held in two periods (2001–2007, 2008–2014) within selected journals in database systems ProQuest Central, Elsevier Science Direct and ERIC. Totally 5,361 relating papers were collected in both periods. The papers were structured according to three criteria. Collected data underwent the chí-squared test for independence and analysis of adjusted residuals on the significance level $\alpha = 0.05$. The results did not prove any statistically significant change. Results were discussed and relating conclusions provided.

Keywords: Learning styles · e-Learning · Meta-analysis

1 Introduction

It is widely accepted that people differ in ways of perceiving situations and circumstances, evaluating them, judging consequences, making decisions etc. In spite of the differences, each person may be right in his/her own manner. Individual strategies applied in the process of learning are called cognitive and/or learning styles [1] and have been defined by numerous authors as e.g. an individual's characteristic and consistent approach to perceiving, remembering, processing, organizing information and problem solving [2]. These individual features differ from abilities. As Sternberg states [3], the ability refers to how *well* someone is able to do something, whereas the style refers to how someone *likes* to do something. Thus the learning style can be understood as a preferred way of using abilities which an individual has. Despite some divergence in the field of learning style stability, reliability and validity of measurements (cf. Coffield [4], Felder [5], Mitchell [6], Gregorc [7], Kolb [8] and others), the research in this field is expected to be of great importance for general and field/subject didactics [9].

Relating to the information and communication technologies (ICT) implemented in education, more than a decade ago Honey was one of those who were asked their opinion on learning styles in e-learning, specifically whether there are *e*-learning styles [10]. In 2000 in the sample group of 242 respondents he ran a research to investigate their

Z. Gong et al. (Eds.): ICWL 2015 Workshops, LNCS 9584, pp. 57–66, 2016.
DOI: 10.1007/978-3-319-32865-2_7

reactions to a long list of potential likes and dislikes about e-learning. Unfortunately, the correlation to the learning preferences did not reveal the significant differences as Honey expected – the likes and dislikes were remarkably similar regardless of learning style preferences [3]. Drilling down into deeper analysis another question appeared, i.e. whether people with different learning style preferences *had the same things in mind* when they signed up for these likes and dislikes. It seemed unlikely to him that e.g. learning 'at my own pace' would be the same for learners with different learning preferences. Honey concluded that despite his initial survey had failed to reveal e-learning styles as such, it discovered some important differences about how people approach online learning. 'One size fits all' has never worked for clothes. 'Why should it for e-learning?' [11].

These findings led us to research the reflection of learning styles in the e-learning environment in periodical publications (journals). As this is a long-time topic of interest for us, the main objective of this paper is to analyze data collected in two periods, compare the results and discover possible changes, particularly those which should be reflected in the process of teaching/learning.

1.1 Position of Learning Styles in the Learning Process

Individual learning styles belong to learner's crucial characteristics [12] – they reflect consistent individual differences in how people organize the processing information and experience [9]. Learning skills, experience, abilities, attitudes, inner motivation as inherited pre-dispositions are added to cognitive styles, thus individualizing learning processes which [13] arise from the inborn basis, have character of the learning meta-strategy, the learner applies them in a certain period of life, they partially depend on the learning content, lead to results of a certain type (e.g. to remembering information, understanding information etc.) and last but not least they are developed by co-impact of outer conditions. As the meta-strategy, learning styles include individual learning strategies, learning tactics and learning operations. They lead the individual to learning results of a certain type but they may limit the process of reaching results of another type, even better ones [14].

Curry [15] introduces a model of individual learning style in the form of onion. The deepest layer is the most stable one as it arises from the inborn basis. The second layer comprising processes of information processing probably arises from the cognitive style but it is partly susceptible through outer impact [16]. The third layer includes social and motivation processes. The fourth, upper layer embraces learner's individual preferences within learning and can be influenced by pedagogical impact of the teacher. All layers penetrate each other, both in the inner - upper and upper - inner directions. Then, the process of learning looks like a whole, a complex of more elements [15].

Currently, the interest in learning style theory and application is slowly decreasing, being replaced by more complex strategies reflecting the latest developments in psycho-didactics and neuro-didactics where more emphasis is paid on self-direction of learning and autonomous learning strategies. These approaches are rather closely connected with the e-learning development. The virtual environment and e-learning directly grew up on principles of autonomous learning and learning strategies. They deal with self-development, self-improvements, self-management, reaching maximum potentialities, keeping the directions, possibly setting adequate correction of mistakes, removing barriers which do not make learning easier and by the level of self-responsibility [17]. Autonomous learning strategies lie in independent planning and prognosticating and in active reaching of objectives and fulfilling tasks, in self-regulation of own independent learning. The main elements of autonomous learning were detected in fields of motivation preferences, volitional approaches, the ability of meta-cognition, awareness of own steps in thinking processes and their impact, to problem solving [18]. Moreover, the autonomous learning also depends on learners' readiness to define their learning objectives, the ability to be pro-active, to appropriately interpret and exploit successes and failures, to be able to define own plans and wishes.

The autonomous learning, which is necessary for efficient process of education conducted in the e-learning environment, requires good knowledge of individual learning styles theory and practice. The presented meta-analysis focuses on papers in periodical publications (journals) dealing with learning styles in the process of education running in the e-learning environment. Both the theoretical and empirical studies focusing on solving concrete research problems were considered.

2 Design and Methodology of Conducting the Meta-analysis

The main research problem of this study is whether any longitudinal changes appeared in learning styles reflection in the e-learning environment in the period of last 14 years. Therefore, two meta-analyses were conducted for 2001–2007 and 2008–2014 periods. This period was framed by the year 2001, when the important document 'National Programme for the Development of Education in the Czech Republic', also called the White Paper, was published by the Czech Ministry of Education, Youth and Sport. The year 2007 is in the centre of the research period as the time, when 'The strategy of Lifelong Learning in the Czech Republic' [19] was published. This document deals with priorities of the education for competitiveness and thus makes impact on framework educational programmes and other curricular documents on all school levels. The year 2007 is in the centre of the research period as the time, when 'The strategy of Lifelong Learning in the Czech Republic' [20] was published. This document deals with educational priorities for competitiveness and thus makes impact on framework educational programmes and other curricular documents on all school levels. Three criteria were applied for both analyses.

1. *Time period for conducting the analysis*. Strong attention has been devoted to questions relating to learning styles in the Euro-Atlantic countries for three decades, which means the field is rather well worked up from the pedagogical and psychological point of view. But, considering the learning styles in the e-learning environment, the time period for conducting the meta-analysis is significantly shorter. The massive development of e-learning began after 2000, when the programme of European Commission "E-learning – new education in digital environment" started, the initiative towards creating electronic Europe (e-Europe) was introduced and

Honey's survey was conducted, as mentioned in the introductory part. From these reasons the first analysis was conducted in the period of 2001–2007. Then, the comparative analysis followed reflecting the 2008–2014 period, when e-learning became standard within the in full-time and part-time process of instruction.
2. *Information sources relevant to the meta-analysis*. Reflecting the topicality of presented data, solely the periodical publications (journals) were considered, as more flexible feedback to latest trends in education was expected in them compared to books. The problem includes several professional fields comprising general pedagogy, pedagogical psychology, andragogy, technology of education, but also geriagogy (senior education), neuroscience, the e-enhanced instruction to some extent etc. As it was not real to analyze the content of each paper in each journal within the period, the search engines of database systems ProQuest Central, Elsevier Science Direct and ERIC were exploited to select appropriate papers.
3. *Relevant key words for conducting the meta-analyses*. Disciplines and fields which are still under the development, as e.g. e-learning (or the ICT in education within the wider context) often suffer from terminological unclearness and disunity. Within the focus of our meta-analysis, the English term of *e-learning* was accepted without changes by other foreign languages. For *learning styles* the situation was more complicated. In the English speaking environment the term of *learning styles* is widely used, been supported by others whose synonymous content is controversial to some extent but they still are exploited as synonyms – *cognitive styles*. Despite this term should rather not be understood in this way (as mentioned in chapter 1.1), in some papers it is. Moreover, the identical situation is with the term of *instructional styles*; the meaning often relates to the *teacher's* style of instruction but in some papers instructional styles evidently mean styles of learning, not teaching or instruction. Considering these reasons, in the ProQuest Central, Elsevier Science Direct and ERIC databases systems following pairs of expressions were searched:
   - learning styles AND e-learning,
   - cognitive styles AND e-learning,
   - instructional styles AND e-learning.

In total, 2,028 papers were detected in periodical publications (i.e. in titles, abstracts, full-texts) for the first period (2001–2007) and 3,333 papers for the second period (2008–2014).

Then, the content analysis was made which included abstracts and full-texts. The purpose was to detect the correlation between the pairs of searched key words and consider whether the paper is relevant to the objective of analysis. Such papers were considered relevant which described diagnostic or other research activities relating to learning styles and the e-learning environment, and papers describing the process of instruction accommodating learning styles (individual learning preferences) in the e-learning environment.

It was found out that the vast majority of pair occurrence of the searched key words was of random type without any correlation. In the first period of 2001–2007, only 38 out of total amount of 2,028 analyzed papers (1.87 %) met the pre-defined parameters and could be considered relevant to the meta-analysis. In the second period of

2008–2014, 256 relevant papers were discovered (7.68 %), significantly most of them in Elsevier Science Direct database.

Sequentially, the comparison of data stratification in two periods (2001–2007, 2008–2014) was made. The statistical significance in differences in occurrence was defined by the chí-squared test for independence and follow-up analysis of adjusted residuals on the significance level $\alpha = 0.05$ was conducted.

3 Results of Meta-analysis

The selected papers were analyzed under three criteria:

1. The field/subject the paper deals with.
2. Level of education the paper focuses on.
3. Diagnostics, i.e. methods applied to detect individual learning styles.

3.1 Results of Analysis Reflecting the Field/Subject

From the point of field and/or subject the paper dealt with, the spectrum was rather wide. Learning styles in the e-learning environment were mostly discussed in fields of computing sciences, social sciences, law, psychology, medicine etc. The papers described educational application of the e-learning environment reflecting individual learning styles within learning contents of various higher education subjects. The stratification of papers under this criterion was made according to the field/subject, not the didactic application. Results are summarized in Table 1.

Table 1. Stratification of papers according to the field/subject

Field	2001/2007		2008/2014	
	n	%	n	%
Computing sciences	18	47.3	81	31.7
Social sciences	9	23.7	77	30.0
Technical sciences	2	5.3	25	9.8
Natural sciences	3	7.9	13	5.1
Medicine	4	10.5	23	9.0
Psychology	2	5.3	27	10.5
Arts	0	0	3	1.2
Non-identified	0	0	7	2.7

The statistical analysis of distribution defined by chí-squared test for independence did not prove any statistically significant change in comparison of both analyses from the view of the field/subject ($\chi^2 = 6.612$; $P = 0.4703$). Papers focusing on computing sciences prevailed, which was not surprising when considering the topic of the meta-analysis. Problems and questions relating to e-learning also appeared in other fields, particularly social sciences, mainly pedagogy, field didactics and andragogy.

The comparison of both periods showed a moderate decrease in computing sciences (from 47.3 % in 2001–2007 period to 31.7 % in 2008–2014 period) and a slow increase in social science (from 23.7 % to 30 %). Rather strong attention was also paid to foreign language education, particularly three papers were detected in art education. On the other hand, the occurrence of papers in natural sciences was rather rare despite they boomed of virtualization in the past [21]. This approach was step-by-step reflected in the science instruction, when modelling of experiments in the virtual environment was emphasized [22].

The low representation of science papers in the meta-analysis may be caused e.g. by the unclear content and scope of the term *e-learning*. Among others, e.g. Heaton-Shrestha et al. [23] introduce several approaches to e-learning, from rather general one (e-learning as the instruction enhanced by technology) to the strict and specific approach (e-learning as process of education exploiting ICT for designing courses, distributing the learning content, for student-student and teacher-student communication, for management of study). In the wide context the e-learning means any support to exploiting ICT (e-support) which includes e.g. computer simulations and visualizations of science topics. In English speaking literature the term of e-learning is frequently replaced by *Computer-Based Training* (CBT), *Internet-Based Training* (IBT) or *Web-Based Training* (WBT). These were not used as key words in the process of search because they (among others) include activities which cannot be involved in the concept of e-learning where active and two-way communication and co-operation within teacher-learner and learner-learner processes are required. But this, in our opinion, crucial characteristic of e-learning is not met by most tools providing e-support. We agree with the definition presented by the information e-learning portal for Europe *Elearningeuropa.info*, where e-learning means application of new multimedia technologies and the Internet into education so that to increase its quality by strengthening the access to sources, services, exchange of information and co-operation. Then, the exploitation of elements of co-operative learning and communication among parties participating in education is expected and required in e-learning.

Low amount of papers relating to natural sciences may be also caused by the fact that the science didactics are focusing mainly on the learning content and ways of mediating it to learners, as concepts of pedagogical content knowledge and didactic re-construction propose [24].

3.2 Results of Analysis Reflecting Levels of Education

Currently, the e-learning environment has been penetrating all levels of education, probably with the partial exception of the pre-primary and primary levels but in wider consequences even on these levels the e-support to learning can be considered. In Table 2 the occurrence of papers is stratified under the level of education.

Statistically significant differences were discovered in comparison of the two periods, 2001–7 and 2008–14 ($\chi^2 = 18.772$; $P = 0.0009$). The analysis of adjusted residuals showed statistically significant differences in relative amounts of papers focused on the upper secondary education level ($e_{Ni} = |3{,}871|$) – in the 2008–14 period the amount is relatively significantly lower (13.2 %; 1.6 %). In relevant papers in both periods the exploitation of learning styles preferences in e-learning environment on the tertiary level dominated (68.3 %; 76.9 %). This state could result from various reasons. One of the most important ones was the fact, that in higher education the self-activity of learners towards the process of learning is increasing. Their learning is becoming an autonomous process which comprises both the cognition and motivation [25]. The process of learning supported by e-learning strongly requires learner's inner motivation. This motivation is primarily given by personal aspirations, effords to increasing qualification and competitiveness on the labor market in the selected field. This level of inner motivation is mostly expected from older learners, which is why the e-learning environment is widely exploited in the tertiary education. Moreover, e-learning is a typical tool supporting the distance education which is predominantly conducted on the tertiary level. And, personal aspirations are also important within this inner motivation [26]. The motivation to e-learning is formed by several factors, e.g. [27] by learners themselves and their ability to learn and exploit efficient auto-didactic strategies, positive self-concept and outer incentives; by the teacher, tutor and his/her personality, including the impact of class climate, even in the e-learning environment; by the family; by the centers providing support to learners; by superiors, co-workers, colleagues who can encourage/make pressure on the learner, define and keep organizational culture etc. Moreover, changes in sensory motoric and memory functions of adult learners should be also considered. On the other hand, they differ from younger learners in rich experience, efforts to independency and self-control [28]. And, the fact should be also considered that individual learning styles can change or modify within the course of life to some extent, which relates to changes in development of cognitive functions and gradual socialization and enculturalization of the individual (including in the working process etc.).

Table 2. Stratification of papers according to the levels of education

Level of education	2001/2007		2008/2014	
	n	%	n	%
Early childhood education	0	0	0	0
Primary education	2	5.3	28	10.9
Lower secondary education	2	5.3	20	7.8
Upper secondary education	5	13.2	4	1.6
Post-secondary education	0	0	0	0
Tertiary education	26	68.3	197	76.9
Lifelong learning	3	7.9	7	2.8

Rather large amount of papers (totally 167) dealt with e-learning within the lifelong learning (LLL) where this environment plays the crucial role as support to individual learning and self-didacting. Nevertheless, only a small amount of papers correlated e-learning to learning styles on the LLL level. Individual learning strategies are important here which relate to learning styles and are determined by them, despite minimum attention was paid to them in the analyzed papers.

3.3 Results of Analysis Reflecting Applied Diagnostic Methods

Under this criterion, direct methods expect to apply direct observation of learners when working, learning, solving tasks, and to make follow-up analyses resulting from the observation. Above all, direct methods are time-consuming and require certain level of experience from the diagnostician. Therefore, indirect methods are much frequently exploited in learning styles detection and some of them are widely used by teachers. They include the analysis of learner's products as concepts, drawings, notes; the analysis of learner's portfolio to monitor learner's development and changes in a certain period; the semi-standardized interview with learner or teacher; the phenomenographic interview, when learners explain their life experience, opinions, concepts of reality, procedures applied in learning; open-type written answers to questions; projective graphic techniques, e.g. the analysis of children drawings; questionnaires and evaluation scales [29]. The stratification of relevant papers reflecting applied diagnostic methods is presented in Table 3.

Table 3. Stratification of papers according to applied diagnostic methods

Diagnostic method	2001/2007		2008/2014	
	n[a]	%	n[a]	%
Questionnaire	12	38.7	54	32.1
Interview	7	22.6	35	20.8
Observation	3	9.7	37	22.0
Experiment	3	9.7	1	0.6
Products analysis	6	19.3	26	15.5
Phenomenography	0	0	6	3.6
Social networks analysis	0	0	9	5.4

[a]*Amount of methods does not correlate to the amount of analyzed papers because in some papers several methods were applied.*

Results of comparative analysis showed large statistically significant differences in occurrence of single diagnostic methods in analyzed papers ($\chi^2 = 21.776$; $P = 0.0013$). The analysis of adjusted residuals detected the largest difference in relative occurrence of the observation method ($e_{Ni} = |3{,}31|$); the increase was significantly higher in the 2008–14 period. The increase was caused mainly by the higher occurence of indirect observations which became much easier with the development of on-line learning. and remote laboratories where the processes of learning were monitored. But, in the analyzed papers the learnings preferences were mostly detected by questionnaires, including those especially designed for individual learning style diagnostics. Rather surprising was the use of experiment and analysis of social networks, which are not commonly applied methods for learning styles diagnosis; but, both methods were used together with the analysis of learner's products. Finally, it should be emphasized the papers dealing with learning styles diagnostics were rather few. The diagnostics was usually marginally mentioned only, focusing on the application of results into the process of efficient management of learner's activities in the e-learning environment.

4 Conclusions

Following conclusions could be deduced from the meta-analysis of the papers dealing with learning styles in the e-learning environment:

Strong attention was paid to the fields of learning styles and of e-learning (considered separately), mainly in diagnostics, research and application. But, joining the two fields together the occurrence was rather rare. One of the reasons could be the fact that the definition of e-learning is wide, vague, sometimes unclear, which makes conducting the content analysis complicated. We understand the active interaction (co-operation, communication) among participants in the process of education to be a fundamental characteristics of e-learning which is enabled by this environment. But this requirement is not met by common e-support which is provided by e.g. multimedia materials, virtual experiments, computer simulations, animations, computer modelling etc.; e-learning is understood much wider. Above all, the problem of learning styles in e-learning is complicated by the fact, that in current pedagogical and psychological concept the individual learning styles are not understood as an isolated entity, but part of more complex approaches to learning processes and acquiring knowledge and particularly processes of interactions with still-existing structures created before. This meta-analysis clearly showed the serious systematic research in this field is still missing. This might be caused by the above mentioned differences in concepts (understanding) the terms of e-learning and learning styles. As a matter of fact, in papers dealing with the research on learning styles application in the e-learning environment, the concepts of e-learning and learning styles (learning strategies) are positioned on a large scale.

Acknowledgments. The paper is supported by the project 'Didactic aspects of Blackboard Mobile Learn implementation into the process of instruction at FIM.'

References

1. Heineman, P.L.: Cognitive styles and learning styles. http://mailer.fsu.edu/~kiw05/metacognition/content/cognitive_styles.pdf
2. Šimonová, I., Bílek, M.: On e-learning adapting to learning styles. Media4u Mag. **1**, 4–11 (2010)
3. Sternberg, R.: Thinking styles. Cambridge University Press, Cambridge (1999)
4. Coffield, F. et al.: Learning styles and pedagogy in post-16 learning. a systematic and critical review. Newcatle University report on learning styles. http://www.Isda.org.uk/files/PDF/1543.pdf
5. Felder, R.M.: Are Learning Styles Invalid? (Hint: No!). http://www4.ncsu.edu/unity/lockers/users/f/felder/public/Papers/LS_Validity(On-course).pdf
6. Mitchell, D.P., et al.: Learning Style: A Critical Analysis of the Concept and Its Assessment. Kogan Page, London (2004)
7. Gregorc, A.F.: Learning/teaching styles: potent forces behind them. Educ. Leadersh. **36**, 234–236 (1981)
8. Kolb, D., David, A.: Kolb's Experiential Learning Theory and the Learning Styles Inventory. http://www.icels-educators-for-learning.ca/index.php?option=com_content&view=article&id=50&Itemid=65

9. Mareš, J.: Styly učení žáků a student. Praha, Portál (1998)
10. Honey, P., Mumford, A.: Using Your Learning Styles. Peter Honey Publications, Maidenhead (2002)
11. Honey, P.: Learning styles – the key to personalised e-learning. www.bbmatters.net/bb_matters.../Learning%20styles_peter%20honey.pdf
12. Entwistle, N.J.: Styles of Teaching and Learning: An Integrated Outline of Educational Psychology for Students, Teachers and Lecturers. Wiley, Chichester (1981)
13. Marton, F., Saljo, R.: On qualitative differences in learning – outcomes and processes. Br. J. Educ. Psychol. **46**, 4–11 (1976)
14. Riding, R.J.: Cognitive styles analysis. Learning and Training Technology, Birmingham (1991)
15. Curry, L.: One critique of the research on learning styles. Educ. Leadersh. **48**, 50–56 (1990)
16. More, A.J.: Learning Styles and the Clasroom. University of British Columbia, Vancouver (1993)
17. de Boer, H., Donker-Bergstra, A.S., Konstons, D.D.N.M.: Effective Strategies for Self-regulated Learning: A Meta-analysis. Gronings Instituut voor Onderzoek van Onderwijs, Rijksuniversiteit Groningen, Groningen (2012)
18. Weinert, F.E.: Lernen lernen und das eigene lernen verstehen. In: Reusser, K., Reusser-Weyeneth, M. (eds.) verstehen. Psychologischer Prozeß und didaktische Aufgabe, pp. 183–205. Huber, Bern (1994)
19. Ministry of Education, Youth and Sport: National Programme for the Development of Education in the Czech Republic – White Paper. Institute for Information on Education (Eds.), Prague (2001). http://info.edu.cz/en/system/files/whitepaper.pdf
20. Ministry of Education, Youth and Sport: The strategy of Lifelong Learning in the Czech Republic. Ministry of Education, Youth and Sports (Eds.), Prague (2007). http://www.msmt.cz/uploads/Zalezitosti_EU/strategie_2007_EN_web_jednostrany.pdf
21. Woodfield, B.F., et al.: The virtual ChemLab project: a realistic and sophisticated simulation of inorganic qualitative analysis. J. Chem. Educ. **81**, 1672–1678 (2004)
22. Lamanauskas, V.: Augmented reality and augmented virtuality in early science/chemistry education. In: Bílek, M., et al. (ed.) Interaction of Real and Virtual Environment in Early Science Education: Tradition and Challenges. Gaudeamus, Hradec Králové, vol. 5, pp. 77–93 (2009)
23. Heaton-Shrestha, C., Gipps, C., Edirisingha, P., Linsey, T.: Learning and e-learning in HE: the relationship between student learning style and VLE use. Res. Papers Educ. **22**, 443–464 (2007)
24. Shulman, L.S.: Those who understand: knowledge growth in teaching. Educ. Res. **15**, 4–31 (1986)
25. Boekaerts, M.: Self-regulated learning: a new concept embraced by researchers, policy makers, educators, teachers, and students. Learn. Instr. **7**, 161–186 (1997)
26. Boekaerts, M.: Motivation to Learn. International bureau of education UNESCO, Geneva (2004)
27. Kwek, G.Y.V., Cheung, W.S.: Investigating the e-learning training need analysis of the faculty members in a business department of a tertiary institution. Int. J. Inf. Educ. Technol. **5**, 368–372 (2015)
28. Becker, K., Newton, C., Sawang, S.: A learner perspective on barriers to e-learning. Aust. J. Adult Learn. **53**, 211–233 (2013)
29. Cassidy, S.: Learning styles: an overview of theories, models, and measures. Educ. Psychol. **24**, 419–444 (2004)

Social Networks Supporting the Higher Education in the Czech Republic

Petra Poulova(✉) and Ivana Simonova

Faculty of Informatics and Management, University of Hradec Kralove, Rokitanskeho 62, 50003 Hradec Kralove, Czech Republic
{petra.poulova, ivana.simonova}@uhk.cz

Abstract. In this paper results of survey focused on social networking, particularly of the exploitation of social networks in the higher education are presented. The research question is what social networks are preferred and who their users are (from the point of gender and study programme). Moreover, the use of mobile devices is also investigated, as they often are the means through which students access to social networks. Data were collected by the method of questionnaire in the research sample of 205 students of the Faculty of Informatics and Management, University of Hradec Kralove, Czech Republic, matriculated in IT and Management study programmes in 2013/14 academic year. Three social networks were detected as the most frequently accessed (Facebook, Google + and LinkedIn) by both male and female users but differences were discovered between the groups of IT students and Management students. The collected data verified didactic recommendations defined by other authors on how the potential of social networks can be used towards independent learning on the higher education level.

Keywords: Higher education · Mobile devices · Social networking

1 Introduction

In last few years numerous Internet applications and services were developed and introduced to users, usually targeted to private use first. Social networks and activities running on them tended to socialize the users for private or professional reasons. Having become step by step widely spread, currently, they have penetrated the field of education as well, with the aim to achieve higher efficiency of the process of instruction by all parties participating in the process of education [1], i.e. by:

- educators exploiting new web software applications for teaching purposes;
- learners undertaking new learning activities and collaborating with other students within after school time;
- educational institutions and everybody interested in using the provided data.

Within the current times of e-society and i-society, social networks have become one of numerous means of socializing. They support joining and building relations/connections among people sharing identical interests and activities. Social networks

Z. Gong et al. (Eds.): ICWL 2015 Workshops, LNCS 9584, pp. 67–76, 2016.
DOI: 10.1007/978-3-319-32865-2_8

enable users to create a profile and share the connections with other people. They have been widely used mainly for entertainment, sharing interests and businesses in various fields, including professional ones. Within the area of education such an approach has been applied in collaborative and cooperative learning [2], in the learning theory of digital age – connectivism [3] and others.

Until recently, in the Czech Republic, traditional non-portable (immobile) devices have been widely implemented into the education. Mobile devices, defined as very small items to accompany users anytime and anywhere, autonomous from the electrical supply, as defined e.g. by [4] or [5], were not available to users to sufficient extent as in other technically developed countries. The situation changed substantially within last few years; now mobile learning can be applied on all levels of education, gradually moving from small-scale, short-term to larger more sustained and blended didactic means.

Reflecting this state, the main objective of this paper is to present results of survey conducted on the higher education level to detect what mobile devices students own and what social networks they use so that the data could be exploited in further instructional strategies.

2 Theoretical Background

Within higher education the mobile learning, which includes social networking via mobile devices, is a way how to extend the face-to-face education and offer students the opportunity to learn in any situation or context they prefer. Social networking services are understood by numerous educators as another (higher) level of learning management systems which brings social and learning tools closer (e.g. [6]). Higher Education institutions understand the possibility to exploit mobile services by students an indicator of better performance and higher quality of education and supported various approaches to wireless devices implementation in the e-learning process (e.g. [6, 7]).

Referring to numerous authors, e.g. Laat [8], Banks [9] etc., the networked learning is understood as the exploitation of internet-based information and communication technologies that provide support to the collaborative and co-operative learning by making connections (learner-learner, tutor-learner, within the whole learning community and its learning resources [9]. The notion of learning in communities [10] has changed the way of teaching/learning – the teacher is no longer in full control and solely source of information but learners actively take responsibility, coordinate and regulate their learning [11].

These, definitely, are the strengths of social networks implemented in the process of instruction. On the other hand, some limits and risks also exist and should be mentioned. Miguel et al. [12] within designing a model for secure learning assessment in on-line web collaborative learning groups also pointed out the information security requirements in online assessment developed in collaborative learning contexts. In addition to many security and privacy issues, virtual world users are exposed to safety issues such as cyberbullying and cyberstalking [13].

3 Methodology

The process of ICT implementation into education started in 1997 at FIM; and it became widely spread after 2000, when the LMS WebCT (since 2008 called Blackboard) started to be used. In this academic year, 250 online courses supporting single subjects have been available to students, either to be used in the part-time and distance forms of education, or to assist the face-to-face teaching/learning process. Traditionally, all online courses are conducted within the LMS. Moreover, they are also available on mobile devices. It means the blended learning model is applied which combines three approaches: (1) the face-to-face instruction, (2) work in online courses and (3) individualized approach to them through mobile devices. This solution satisfies learners' time/place preferences and bridges formal and informal learning [6]. For the work with software not providing free/open access (e.g. MS SQL Server, Enterprise Architect) the 'virtual desktops' have been available to students and teachers since 2012/13 academic year; since 2013/14 the Blackboard Mobile Learn™ version 4.0 for Apple and Android devices has been piloted (Blackboard Mobile Learn™ version 4.0 supports iOS6 +, i.e. iPhone 3GS, iPad 2 +, IPad mini, iPod Touch 4 + and Android OS 2.3 +). Exploiting this application students get mobile access to their study materials, they can create and/or participate in discussion forums, use e-mail service, blogs, follow their progress and/or comment on the learning process.

3.1 Research Questions

Reflecting the above mentioned our research focused on the question *what social networks are preferred by higher education students* so that those frequently accessed ones could be used for educational purposes. Partial questions were as follows:

- What devices do respondents own and use in higher education?
- What social networks do respondents use?
- How often do respondents access the preferred social networks?

3.2 Research Sample

The research was held at the University of Hradec Kralove, Faculty of Informatics and Management (FIM). In the institution students can enroll at three-year bachelor study programmes in Applied Informatics (AI3), Financial Management (FM3), Tourism Management (TM3), Sports Management (SM3), or follow-up two-year master study programmes in Applied Informatics (AI2) and Information Management (IM2), or doctoral study programmes in Knowledge Management (KM) and Applied Informatics (AI). Totally 205 FIM students (male 60 %; female 40 %) matriculated in 2013/14 academic year participated in the research. The research sample was structured as follows:

- Applied Informatics (AI3 + AI2; 83 + 1 students; 41 %),
- Information Management (IM3 + IM2; 44 + 2; 22 %),
- Financial Management (FM, 21; 10 %),
- Tourism Management (TM 54; 27 %).

i.e. totally 128 IT students (63 %) and 75 Management students (37 %) participated in the research. Most of respondents (143) were 20–24 years old, nearly one third of them were older (25 – 29 years old: 27; 30–39 years old: 22), four respondents were younger than 20 years and seven respondents were above 40 years.

3.3 Methods and Tools

The research was held at the Faculty of Informatics and Management, University of Hradec Kralove, Czech Republic, in May 2014.

Data were collected by the online questionnaire within online courses in the LMS Blackboard, in subjects Database Systems 2, Management 2 and English for Specific Purposes 2 and 4. The questionnaire contained 12 items focusing on two main fields of interest – the ownership, use and preferences of (1) mobile and other devices and (2) social networks. Respondents provided answers of the multiple-choice type; four choices could have been made in items 1 and 2, all choices could be marked in items 3–8, one choice was in items 9 – 12. The NCSS2007 statistic software was used for processing the collected data; the method of frequency analysis was exploited and the results were analyzed.

4 Results

The results reflect the above presented research questions and are structured in three parts.

4.1 Question 1: What Devices Do Respondents Own and Use in Higher Education?

The data in Fig. 1 show notebooks were the most frequently possessed mobile device (88 % of respondents have their own notebook), followed by smartphone (86 %) and PC (52 %); 18 % of students still use mobile phones. Moreover, most students own more than one devices, e.g. notebook and smartphone, notebook and mobile phone); and more than a quarter of students have a tablet and/or netbook (10 %), which are other devices to be included in the group of multiple ownership. Above all, TV is a immobile device that widely occurs in parents 'households if students live there (nearly 67 %), followed by mp3 players (49 %), DVD players (39 %), radio (30 %) and HI-FI (27 %).

Another question is *to what extent* students use the immobile and mobile devices. Currently, notebooks were more frequently exploited for education (87 %) than for private matters (45 %), followed by smartphones (83 %) and PCs (42 % of respondents used them for education But, the most frequently used 'device' was personal contact – education-related matters were personally discussed by 92 % of respondents and private topics by 96 % of them.

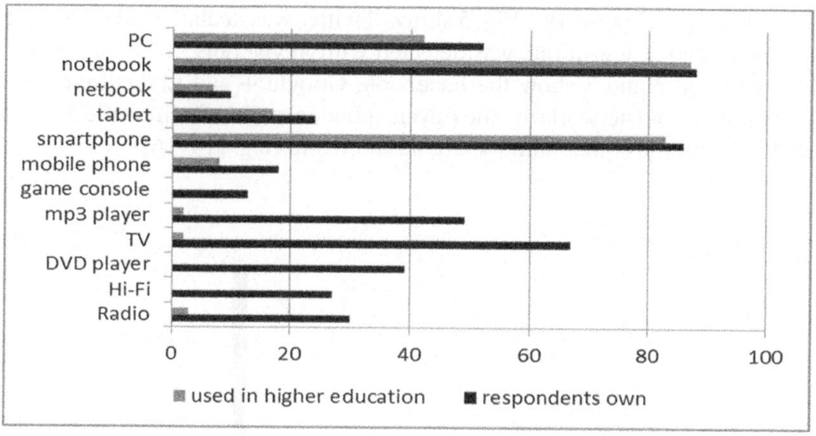

Fig. 1. Devices owned and used in higher education (%)

4.2 Question 2: What Social Networks Do Respondents Use?

The data displayed in Fig. 2 clearly show that there are three social networks which reached significant preference. The first one was Facebook, definitely the most frequently used social network, most users are frequently or all days logged in. The second one was LinkedIn, detected as less frequently used – it was declared as never accessed by more than 60 % of respondents, the others visit it not frequently (20 %), seldom (5 %), not regularly (10 %) and 79 % of respondents have never accessed LinkedIn. And, third was Google +, currently the second-largest social networking site in the world after Facebook. However it was seldom and not regularly accessed by the respondents.

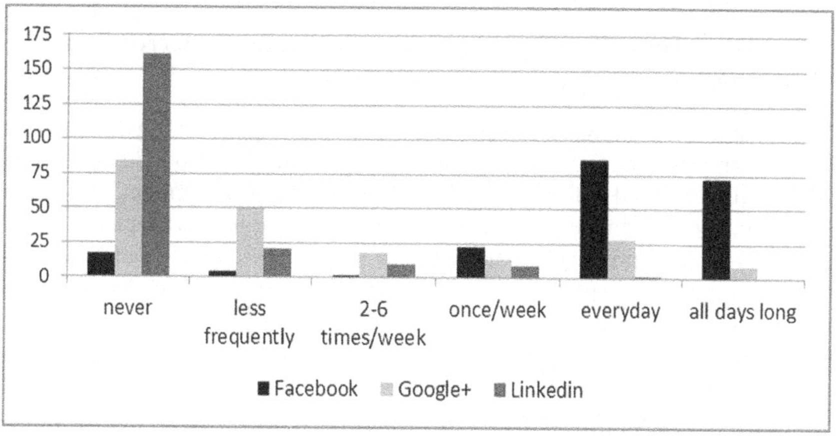

Fig. 2. Selected social networks: respondents' access frequency (n)

As for other social networks, Fig. 5 shows Twitter was declared to be visited by 9 % of respondents and 3 % visit rate was detected with Skype only.

Both the Figs. 2 and 3 show the Facebook, Google + and LinkedIn are the most frequently used social networks by the FIM respondents. This finding reflects the results collected by numerous other authors around the world (e.g. [14–16]).

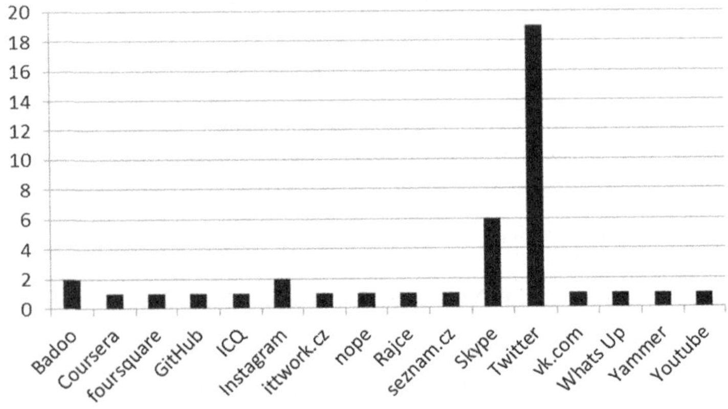

Fig. 3. Other social networks: respondents' access frequency (n)

As analyzed in [17], the social network services work on latest mobile devices (tablets, smartphones, PDAs etc.) which large amount of respondents both own and widely use for private purposes and slightly for education-related communication.

4.3 Question 3: How Often Do Respondents Access the Preferred Social Networks?

Finally, the data were analyzed under two criteria: (1) respondent's gender (M – male, F – female), presented in Fig. 4 and (2) study programme the respondents were administered in (AI – Applied Informatics, IM – Information Management, M – Financial Management, Sports Management), displayed in Fig. 5. The access frequency is detected from 'all days long' expressed by black color to 'never' presented in patterned columns.

As expected, figure displays the strongest preference of Facebook by both male and female respondents, compared to strong rejection of Google + by both genders. The disproportion, from unknown reasons, was detected in LinkedIn, which was 'never' accessed by nearly 80 % of male respondents.

Reflecting the data in figure strong preference of Facebook was detected with respondents in all three study programmes and rejection (hardly any access frequency to LinkedIn network (from 70 to 85 % in all study programmes) and below-average access frequency to Google + (about 40 %).

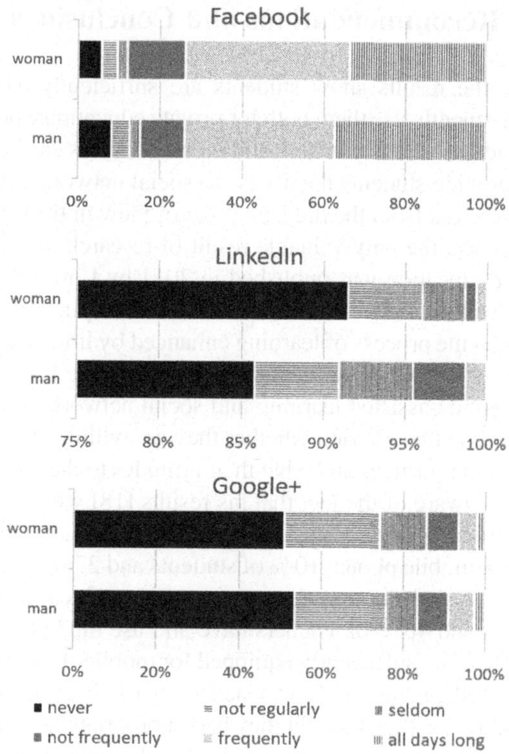

Fig. 4. Access frequency reflecting respondents' gender (%)

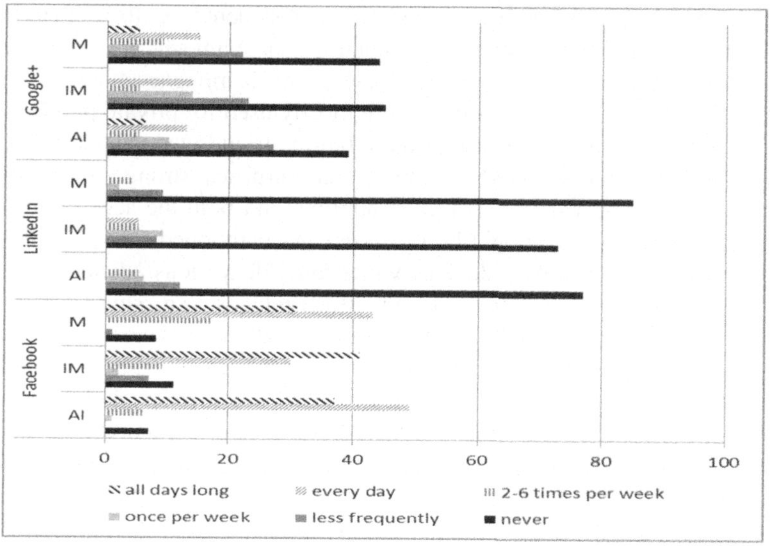

Fig. 5. Access frequency reflecting respondents' study programmes (%)

5 Discussions, Recommendations and Conclusions

As presented above, the results show students are sufficiently equipped with mobile devices, they rather frequently use them both for private educational purposes. This finding means the level of students' literacy is high and mobile devices can be implemented in the higher education to provide students the access to social networks. But, this field has not been adequately worked out from the didactic point of view in the Czech Republic. There are hardly any researches; the only valuable result of research on mobile devices implementation into higher education was published in 2011 by Lorenz [18]. He analyzed the concept of mobile education under the conditions of developing university environment, particularly focusing on the process of learning enhanced by library services. He answered the research question whether both students and teachers have learning/teaching skills to use the potential of mobile-assisted learning and social networking for higher education. Particularly he focused on the criterion whether they are willing and able to bear financial expenses to cover relating services and what their attitudes to the mobile-assisted teaching and learning are. Been aware of the fact that his results [18] were collected in 2010, they can be compared to those collected at FIM in several criteria, e.g. 92 % of students and 85 % of teachers own a mobile phone; 10 % of students and 27 % of teachers have a smartphone (in 2010); 65 % students and the same number of teachers own notebooks or laptops; 61 % students and 46 % of teachers have and use mp3 players. Despite not only students but also teachers are sufficiently equipped for mobile-assisted learning implementation, only 65 % of students and 42 % of teachers proclaimed insufficient readiness for mobile-assisted learning, i.e. they thought they had appropriate learning/teaching skills for efficient use of mobile devices in education. This result contracts to Corbeil and Valdes-Corbeil results where 94 % of students and 60 % of teachers expressed the readiness to exploit mobile devices for educational purposes (from the sample group of 107 students and 30 teachers) [19]. In Lorenz's research totally 57 % of students and 46 % of teachers were willing to pay for education-related services and the same amount of both parties would appreciate/were going to implement mobile devices into learning/teaching.

As widely expected social networks were mostly used for private purposes, particularly for communication and visualization of family, friends and interest-related items. So as this fact could be exploited for educational purposes, strong didactic effort and motivation targeting at learners should be applied, and both the access rate to social networks and their real use should be increased. As mentioned above, in practice the access is made through mobile devices which provide various advantages (e.g. low weight, small size, 7/24/365 access) and disadvantages (e.g. small screen), when presenting the (learning) content. This fact means that study materials, tests, communication and other tools enhancing the process of instruction must be provided in such formats to the social networks' users which are clearly displayed on these small devices. In practice it means e.g. long fulltext materials to be shorten, animations and video-sequences considered from the point of technical, technological and size features, simple presentations with bulleted texts preferred, as well as tests in multiple-choice, true/false, yes/no formats etc. Thus the mobile-assisted learning didactic principles are reflected within social networking. Thus they can be considered an inseparable part of this phenomenon.

The recent technical and technological development being very fast, education should benefit from this fact. Similarly to e-learning two decades ago, the 'mobile-assisted learning didactic principles are necessary to be developed and set in this phase of the process of social networks/mobile devices implementation in the education.

So as to be successful and smooth, following steps should accomplished determining the strategy [20]:

- a learner's needs analysis should be run,
- the feedback collected and communicated,
- adequate infrastructure and technical support ensured,
- professional training to teachers and students should be provided and professional skills towards mobile-assisted learning and social networking literacy should be trained,
- social networking running via mobile devices should be defined for specific educational environments, institutional backgrounds and contexts, including key goals, scope of change, didactic methods distinguishing this strategy from other approaches, standards and educational policies.

So as to optimize time and resources, all these activities, steps and feedback are conducted simultaneously, they do not run linearly.

To sum up, the findings discovered at FIM reflect the research results on mobile-assisted learning and exploitation of social networking for educational purposes. In the Czech Republic

(1) this approach to learning has not become so common and has not been included in official curricular documents and methodologies as e.g. e-learning. Therefore, long-time data still are not available to be published.
(2) Latest (i.e. smart) types of mobile devices reached Czech users later than in economically-strong and developed countries. Currently, in the globalized world, differences are quickly fading in this field and Czech students and teachers are sufficiently equipped with them. However, the scientifically-verified methodology (didactics) on how to implement mobile devices, particularly how to start and apply mobile-assisted learning into the process of instruction, is still missing.

Acknowledgment. The paper is supported by the project 'Didactic aspects of the process of Blackboard Mobile Learn implementation into instruction at FIM'.

References

1. Oberer, B., Erkollar, A.: Cloud eLearning: Transforming education through cloud technology: Preliminaries for generation C. In: Proceedings of the 7th International Conference on eLearning, pp. 363–369. The Chinese University of Hong Kong, Hong Kong (2012)
2. Concept to Classroom, What are cooperative and collaborative learning? http://www.thirteen.org/edonline/concept2class/coopcollab
3. Siemens, G.: Description of Connectivism. Connectivism. http://www.connectivism.ca/about.html

4. Roschelle, J.: Using mobile phones in language learning/teaching. Procedia Soc. Behav. Sci. **15**, 2947–2951 (2011)
5. Liang, L., Liu, T., Wang, H., Chang, B., Deng, Y., Yang, J., Chou, C., Ko, H., Yang, S., Chan, T.: A few design perspectives on one-on-one digital classroom environment. J. Comput. Assist. Learn. **21**(3), 181–189 (2005)
6. Benson, V.: Unlocking the potential of wireless learning. Learn. Teach. Hig. Educ. **2**, 42–56 (2008)
7. Benson, V., Morgan, S.: Student experience and ubiquitous learning in higher education: impact of wireless and cloud applications. Creative Educ. **4**(8A), 1–5 (2013)
8. De Laat, M., Lally, V., Lipponen, L., Simons, R.J.: Online teaching in networked learning communities: A multi-method approach to studying the role of the teacher. Instr. Sci. **35**, 257–286 (2007)
9. Banks, S., Goodyear, P., Hodgson, V., McConnell, D.: Introduction to the special issue on advances in research on networked learning. Instr. Sci. **31**, 1–6 (2003)
10. Lave, J., Wenger, E.: Situated Learning: Legitimate Peripheral Participation. Cambridge University Press, Cambridge (1991)
11. De Laat, M.F., Lally, V.: It's not so easy: Researching the complexity of emergent participant roles and awareness in synchronous networked learning discussions. J. Comput. Assist. Learn. **20**(3), 165–171 (2004)
12. Miguel, J., Caballe, S., Xhafa, F., Prieto, J.: Security in online web learning assessment Providing an effective trustworthiness approach to support e-learning teams. World Wide Web **18**(6), 1655–1676 (2015). Springer, New York
13. Ferencz, S.K., Goldsmith, C.W.: Privacy issues in a virtual learning environment. Cause/Effect, A practitioner's journal about managing and using information resources on college and university campuses **21**, 5–11 (1998)
14. eBizMBA: Top 15 most popular social networking sites. http://www.ebizmba.com/articles/social-networking-websites
15. Gomes, W.: Website metrics within Google analytics (2013). https://www.youtube.com/watch?v=-m7ZPgOB8Y8
16. Skyrms, B., Pemantle, R.: A dynamic model of social network formation. http://arxiv.org/pdf/math.PR/0404101.pdf
17. Poulova, P., Simonova, I.: Mobile technologies within the higher education. In: ICETA Proceedings, to be Published (2014)
18. Lorenz, M.: Kde nechala škola díru: m-learning aneb Vzdělání pro záškoláky [Where school let a hole yawn: m-learning or education for truants]. http://pro.inflow.cz/kde-nechala-skola-diru-m-learning-aneb-vzdelani-pro-zaskolaky
19. Corbeil, J.R., Valdes-Corbeil, M.E.: Are you ready for mobile learning? Educause Q. **30**(2), 51–58 (2007)
20. Pieri, M., Diamantini, D.: From e-learning to mobile learning: New opportunities. In: Mobile Learning: Transforming the Delivery of Education and Training, pp. 183–194. Athabasca University Press, Athabasca (2009)

e-Learning in Practice: Tracking Students' Performance

Ivana Simonova(✉) and Petra Poulova

Faculty of Informatics and Management, University of Hradec Kralove, Rokitanskeho 64, 50003 Hradec Kralove, Czech Republic
{ivana.simonova,petra.poulova}@uhk.cz

Abstract. The hybrid learning exploited as a tool supporting the face-to-face form of instruction started to be implemented in this process two decades ago. Providing a wide rate of tools and strategies to each student, the information and communication technologies make efforts to support efficient learning. As a result students are positively motivated and able to develop their level of knowledge in the shortest time period spending least efforts. To reach such a level in the real process of instruction, the requirement for optimizing the teaching/learning arose, particularly the call for improving the flexibility of the process, mainly by applying the individualized approach.

Keywords: Experiment · e-Learning · Hybrid learning · Learning style · Research · Tracking

1 Introduction

There is no doubt that the hybrid learning, as defined by Bothell [1], has become firmly established methodology, particularly within the higher education [2].

In the Czech Republic, been exploited as a tool supporting the face-to-face form of instruction, it started to be implemented in the process of instruction two decades ago [3]. This process started at the Faculty of Informatics and Management (FIM), University of Hradec Kralove (UHK) in 2001; and more than 250 online courses in the LMS WebCT (renamed Blackboard) have been designed, so as to support the face-to-face instruction in single subjects. Thus it can be stated that up to now both students and teachers have collected rather wide experience in this field. As generally accepted, the information and communication technologies (ICT) provide a wide rate of tools and strategies each student can choose from and learn efficiently. The consequent result is students are positively motivated and able to develop the individual highest level of knowledge in the shortest time period spending least efforts [4].

So as such a level to be reached in the real process of instruction, the requirement for optimizing the teaching/learning appeared, particularly the call for improving the flexibility of the process, mainly by applying the individualized approach [5]. Considering this requirement, following questions should be answered:

(1) Do students learn more, if the hybrid process of instruction is tailored to their learning preferences?
(2) How does the process run?

Z. Gong et al. (Eds.): ICWL 2015 Workshops, LNCS 9584, pp. 77–86, 2016.
DOI: 10.1007/978-3-319-32865-2_9

(3) What can help students show what they know?

2 Theoretical Background

When considering the research results in learning styles published by Felder [6], Gregorc [7], Mitchell [8], Coffield [9], Mares [10, 11] and many others, methodology on how to implement learners' preferences into instruction was deeply worked out. Honey was the first one who asked the question about learning styles in e-learning, i.e. in the ICT-enhanced process where technologies are implemented to some extent [12]. The likes and dislikes about e-learning having been monitored in the group of 242 respondents, he concluded their opinions did not differ as he had expected, despite various types of learners definitely had different features in mind, when speaking e.g. about learning at my own pace.

The Ross and Schulz's approach (in [10]) and Gregorc's concept [7] were applied in hybrid learning reflecting learning styles preferences in the Czech education environment. This field was researched mainly by Mares who proposed to adjust the World Wide Web to various learning styles, i.e. to sensory, social and cognitive preferences, and design [11]:

- the visual Web providing static texts, images, graphs, animations, video-recordings etc.,
- the auditive Web with recordings of lectures, music, discussions,
- the kinesthetic Web providing hands-on activities and practical examples,
- the Web adapted to social preferences reflected in independent, pair or team work.

Student's awareness of individual preferences to be the pre-requisite of efficient learning was determined by Gregorc, as well as the teacher's ability to apply a sufficiently wide range of teaching methods, activities, assignments and types of feedback and communication corresponding to students' individual preferences. Therefore, he designed the concrete/sequencing, abstract/sequencing, concrete/random and abstract/random Webs. It can be seen from the presented results that it is important for a student to be aware of their learning style preferences, to know what their strengths and weaknesses are and to be provided a variety of instructional methods to choose the most suitable ones [10].

The research on the flexibility of hybrid learning conducted at FIM arose from the theory by Johnston [13]. She partly agrees with theories of Piaget, Jung, Skinner, cognitive psychologists etc., who work with the tripartite theory of the mind, i.e. feelings, thoughts and behaviour, which are expressed in cognition, conation and affectation. Johnston describes the whole process of learning as a combination lock where the cognition (processing), conation (performing) and affectation (developing) are the interlocking tumblers; if they are aligned, they unlock individual's understanding of his/her learning combination. The will is situated in the center of the model, and interaction is the key. She compares human learning behaviour to a patterned fabric, where the cognition, conation and affectation are the threads of various colours and quality. Then, it depends on the individual weaver (learner) how s/he combines them and what the final pattern is [13].

Johnston designed the Learning Combination Inventory (LCI) which focuses on not the product of learning, but the process of learning, on how to unlock and what unlocks the learner's motivation and ability to learn. Respondents' answers create the schema (pattern) consisting from four categories of learners [13]:

- sequential processors, defined as the seekers of clear directions, practiced planners, thoroughly neat workers;
- precise processors, identified as the information specialists, into-details researches, answer specialists and report writers;
- technical processors, specified as the hands-on builders, independent private thinkers and reality seekers;
- confluent processors, described as those who march to a different drummer, who are creative imaginers and unique presenters.

To sum up the most frequent responses to LCI [14], students of all types of processors do not like to be disturbed from work, to be lack of time, they like to have entertaining environment at schools and select such ways of assessment which do not stress but motivate them to further study. These approaches should be applied in both the face-to-face and hybrid learning process of instruction individually according to the student's learning style pattern as we did in version 1 of the online course (see below). Gregorc proved that only students with very strong preferences did not study efficiently if another style was required [7]. On the other side, Felder said that partial mismatching supported the development of new learning strategies [6].

3 Research I on Students' Individual Learning Preferences Within Hybrid Learning at FIM

In this paper two related researches are described: *Research I* focused on individual learning preferences within hybrid learning and the follow-up *Research II* dealt with tracking learners' performance in hybrid learning. The complete pedagogical experiment is described in detail in [15]. The individualized hybrid learning concept was verified by the pedagogical experiment [15, pp. 56–57]. The main objective of this research was to answer the above mentioned question, i.e. whether students learn more if the hybrid process of instruction is tailored to their learning preferences, how the process runs and what can help students show what they know.

3.1 Methodology I

The pedagogical experiment following the pretest – hybrid instruction – posttest structure was applied. The hybrid process covered the face-to-face instruction in the subject Library services – Information competence in education. This subject was taught 90 min per week and supported by autonomous study in the online course to fix and practise the learning content, develop new knowledge and be able to apply it in practice.

The sample group consisted of nearly 400 students of University of Hradec Kralove at the beginning of the research. However, only 324 respondents finished the complete process of research, from various reasons. The research sample can be described as follows:

- totally 62 % of male and 38 % of female students participated in the research;
- respondents were from 20–50 years old, 80 % in the 20–24 year-old group;
- 65 % of them graduated from secondary professional schools, 33 % from grammar schools and others (2 %);
- 63 % of respondents declared no experience in studying the distance online courses before the research started, approximately 20 % of them had studied one course and 5 % were experienced online learners passing four or more distance courses.

All students were randomly divided in three groups, each of them studying one of three versions of the same online course:

- In version 1, students in the experimental group 1 (group LCI) worked in the flexible online course which was tailored to their learning preferences. The flexibility (individualization) was made by the electronic application (plug-in) which automatically generated individualized course content which reflected student's preferences detected by the LCI. For the individualization the database of study materials, exercises, assignments, ways of communication and other supportive activities was prepared where each material was designed in six versions to be selected from. Thus a course was created which suited individual learning preferences of each student.
- In version 2, students in experimental group 2 (group CG – content general) had access to all types of materials, exercises, assignments etc. and the process of selection was the matter of their individual decision.
- In version 3, students in the control group (group K) used the common course according to teacher's directions, i.e. they were made to accept the teacher's style of instruction.

3.2 Results I

Unfortunately, no statistically significant differences were discovered in learners' performance [15, pp. 58–84]. The mean test scores in LCI, CG and K groups in pretests (monitoring the entrance level of students' knowledge) and posttests (showing the final level of knowledge after the face-to face instruction and autonomous work in one of three versions of the supportive online course) are displayed in Fig. 1.

The differences in test scores in LCI/K group and CG/K group are displayed in Fig. 2.

In previous researches dealing with hybrid learning which had been conducted at FIM the statistically significant differences were discovered in favor of hybrid learning, e.g. [16]. Therefore, the findings of this research were surprising and rather disappointing for the research team. We expected, considering the research results of above mentioned authors ([6, 9, 13] and others), that if not significant, at least some statistical differences would be detected in the LCI group where the face-to-face learning was supported by the online course individually tailored to students' learning preferences by the e-application.

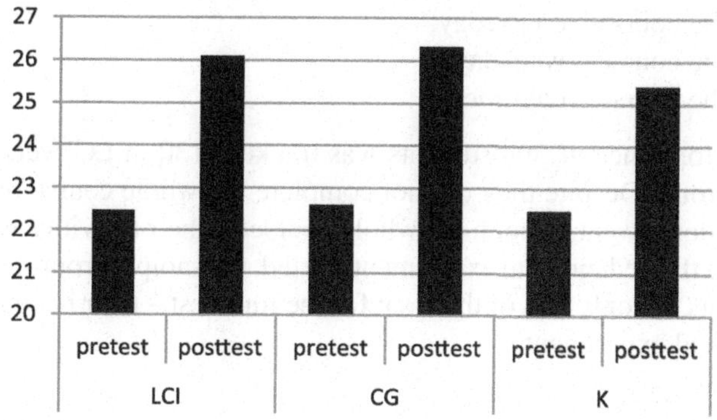

Fig. 1. Mean test scores in pretests and posttests in LCI, CG and K groups

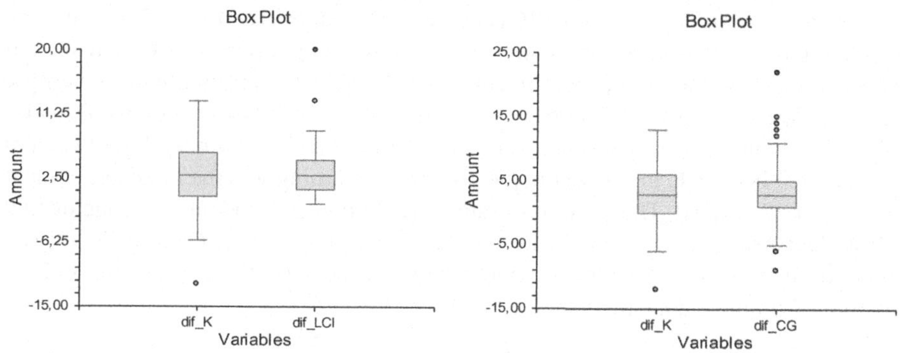

Fig. 2. Pretest and posttest scores: differences in K/LCI (left) and K/CG groups (right)

4 Follow-up Research II in Tracking Learners' Performance in Hybrid Learning

As the learning content in any course was identical for all students irrespective to their learning style preferences, the causes of non-significant differences in students' knowledge in single versions of the online course were expected to be discovered in their independent work in the courses. That was the reason why we focused on answering the question how the process of hybrid learning was running. The process of instruction in all groups (courses) was tracked by the LMS.

4.1 Methodology II

The data collected from tracking were analyzed so as to discover whether there exist some differences which could explain the disappointing results. The data were collected within the LMS Blackboard and analyzed under following five criteria:

(1) visit rate to the online course;
(2) exploitation of single tools (i.e. hits detected in each version of the online course);

(3) access to the course – courseday;
(4) access to the course – weekday;
(5) access to the course – daytime.

Totally, performance of 394 students was tracked: 130 in LCI version, 131 in CG and 134 in K group. Despite they did not complete the whole course by sitting for the exam, these students went through the whole course so their activities were included in tracking. Before the pedagogical experiment started, the sample group consisted of more than 400 students but only 324 of them sat for the final test – their results were included in the pedagogical experiment.

4.2 Results II

Criterion 1 monitored within the tracking was the visit rate to the online course, i.e. these data show students who really accessed the course. Totally 12,556 visits were detected in three versions of the online course; and strong differences were discovered between single courses. Whereas students visited the LCI course tailored to their preferences 5,501 times, the visit rate was half in the K course where they were made to follow directions reflecting teacher's style of instruction (2,784 times). In-between rate was detected in the CG group where the process of learning was the matter of student's decision (4,271 times). The mean visit rate was 32 times per student. We concluded the LCI students preferred working in the course whereas those in the K group downloaded e.g. study materials to their local computer or did the activities (exercises) offline (if possible). Complete data are displayed in Table 1.

Table 1. Visit rate to online courses

	CG	LCI	K
Students (n)	131	130	133
Visits (n)	4,271	5,501	2,784
Visit per student (n)	32.60	42.32	20.93

Criterion 2 reflected the visit rate to single tools in the course. Under this criterion, the visit rate is expressed in amount of hits in each version of the online course. The data show the Content was the most frequently exploited tool, which was not surprising, as Study material were available there. Nearly all students were monitored as they had used this tool (total mean 92.7 %); those missing there hardly could have succeeded in the subject. However, all materials in the Content were available in the university library but to use those from the course might have been more convenient than borrowing them. Discussion was the second frequently used tool, but amount of hits was much lower – about 5 % of students participated in discussions. The reason might have been that current discussions were held on social networks (mostly on Facebook, Google+ and LinkedIn, as detected with FIM students [17]. Nevertheless, each student participated in discussion within the course twice. Other tools were exploited exceptionally only. The highest amount of hits by one student was 235 times per the whole course. Data are displayed in Table 2. The amount of hits was similar in all three versions of the course

as well as the exploitation of the Content tool. In the LCI group this fact means students preferred the work online.

Table 2. Visit rate to single tools

Hits	All courses (n = 394)		LCI (n = 130)		K (n = 133)		CG (n = 131)	
	n	%	n	%	n	%	n	%
Announcements	223	1.78	42	0.76	100	3.59	81	1.90
Calendar	16	0.13	3	0.05	6	0.22	7	0.16
Content	11,584	92.27	5,301	96.36	2,491	89.48	3,79 2	88.78
Discussion	653	5.20	131	2.38	150	5.39	372	8.71
My grades	78	0.62	22	0.44	37	1.33	19	0.44
Total	12,554		5,501		2,784		4,271	

Criterion 3 reflected the students' access frequency (expressed in amount of hits) to the course within 20-day period, when the course was available to students. The total mean frequency was 739.8 hits per day, reaching from 254 to 1,774 hits per day. As expected, the increased amount of hits was detected in the last third of the study period, when students intensified their study activities.

From the view of single courses several differences were detected, e.g. low amount of hits in the CG course on 16 March (47), 17 March (72) and 18 March (78) and high amount on 31 March, the last-but-one day of the course availability (714 in CG, 719 in LCI).

As single courses differ in absolute amount of hits, a more exact results are received if hits per courseday are rated to the total amount to each course. When considering three periods within the 20-day time (starting period: days 1–7, middle period: days 8–13, final period: days 14–20), hardly any differences in courses were detected in the middle period, whereas increased amount of hits was detected in starting and final ones. The data in all three courses show.

- 19 – 29 % of hits in the starting period,
- slight decrease in the LCI and K courses and increase in the CG course in the middle period,
- sharp increase in all three courses in the final period; in the CG course the amount of hits reached no fewer than 60 % of all hits detected in this course during 20 days.

As the amount of hits was different in each course, amount of hits per day was rated to the total amount of students. Under this criterion the amount of detected hits was from 0.36 in the CG course to 5.64 hits per day in the LCI course.

Criterion 4 considered the access frequency to the course from the point of weekday. Amounts of hits do not differ much in single days of week in each course, except Wednesday in the LCI course. The reason was not discovered as students from different study programmes were working in this course, so the result could not be influenced by e.g. their schedule. Totally, the highest amount of hits was detected on Wednesdays (2,707 hits) compared to lowest amount on Sundays (1,697 hits).

Criterion 5 monitored the access frequency to the course from the point of daytime. Generally, people differ in the preferred work time, and so do the students. If the work time is the matter of individual choice, the individual preference is expected to be expressed even more strongly. Totally, the highest amount of hits was detected between 8 pm–9 pm (1,533 hits) and slowly decreased towards midnight. The second top period was between 10 am–1 pm (10 am: 1,320 hits; 11 am: 1,244; 12 am: 1,185; 1 pm: 1,032). As expected, students were not active in early morning hours (from 2 am to 6 am: max 35 hits). Differences were detected in single courses. Whereas in the CG course two top periods appeared (10 am–11 am and 8 pm–9 pm), in the LCI and K courses three top periods were discovered (10 am–11 am, 8 pm–9 pm; and 1 pm–2 pm in the LCI and 12 am–1 pm in the K course).

5 Conclusions

As clearly seen from the above presented data, tracking the learners' performance in online courses which were part of hybrid learning at FIM did not provide sufficient explanation why no statistically significant differences were detected in the instruction reflecting students' individual learning preferences and thus tailoring the process to their needs. Several differences in learner's performance were discovered in the LCI course which was the one reflecting preferences, e.g.

- more than 96 % of students exploited the Content tool compared to 89 % in the K and 88 % in CG courses;
- amount of hits in the final period was much higher (719 hits) compared to the K course (341 hits), but not to CG course (714 hits);
- neither maximum, nor minimum top was detected in the LCI course, the maximum top was in the CG group;
- highly preferred day for study was Wednesday compared to other courses where no preferences were detected.

Having considered these findings, we cannot state that any or all of them could have been the cause of such a result. So, how can we answer the last question on what can help students show what they know, what measures should be taken for the future?

For future didactic improvements in hybrid learning we propose to apply the Bloom's *digital* taxonomy of educational objectives [18]. This tool/database provides numerous activities so that learners of all learning style patterns can select those which will suit their learning preferences, as well as they can easily avoid those which they do not prefer. Despite Prensky described current learners to be digital natives compared to digital immigrants, i.e. their parents and teachers, results of both our research and tracking might let us express the opinion the time changed – the border between digital natives and immigrants has not been so sharp nowadays, when new generation has appeared, some digital natives have become teachers and naturally understand needs and preferences of their learners. Other teachers, former digital immigrants, have become highly ICT literate, experienced in exploiting modern technologies in lessons and thus applying the hybrid learning in a wide extent [19]. As a result of these and other factors students have become so flexible that no significant differences can be discovered in their performance and knowledge, whichever teaching strategies and methods are used in lessons.

To sum up, reflecting both the results of pedagogical experiment and tracking, and activities provided by the digital taxonomy, this state might indicate a shift in approach to learning styles and the requirement to reflect them in the process of instruction. Our research findings in hybrid learning environment give us opportunity to support those studies mentioned by Coffield which do not support the positive contribution of learning styles theories [9], no matter how much we would like to prefer them. And, the Churches' approach can be a way how to develop the didactics (pedagogy) of current hybrid learning, when mobile devices and social networks are widely exploited for education purposes. We believe the time came to adjust the hybrid learning to these new conditions, i.e. to let digital native teachers implement latest technologies to flexible learners.

Acknowledgments. The paper is supported by the project 'Didactic aspects of Blackboard Mobile Learn implementation into the process of instruction at FIM.'

References

1. Hybrid Learning, University of Washington – Bothell (2015). http://www.uwb.edu/learningtech/elearning/hybrid-and-online-learning/hybrid-learning/about-hybrid-learning/definition-hybrid-learning
2. Porter, W.W., Graham, C.R., Spring, K.A., Welch, K.R.: Blended learning in higher education: institutional adoption and implementation. Comput. Edu. **75**(6), 185–193 (2013)
3. Frydrychova Klimova, B., Poulova, P.: Forms of instruction and students' preferences - a comparative study. In: Cheung, S.K., Fong, J., Zhang, J., Kwan, R., Kwok, L.F. (eds.) ICHL 2014. LNCS, vol. 8595, pp. 220–231. Springer, Heidelberg (2014)
4. Poulova, P., Simonova, I.: Borderless education: InterUniversity study – successful students' feedback. In: Cheung, S.K., Fong, J., Zhang, J., Kwan, R., Kwok, L.F. (eds.) ICHL 2014. LNCS, vol. 8595, pp. 232–242. Springer, Heidelberg (2014)
5. Poulova, P., Simonova, I.: Flexible e-learning: online courses tailored to student's needs. In: Proceedings of the 9th International Scientific Conference on Distance Learning in Applied Informatics (DIVAI 2012), Nitra, UKF, pp. 251–260 (2012)
6. Felder, R.M.: Are learning styles invalid? (Hint: No!) (2010). http://www4.ncsu.edu/unity/lockers/users/f/felder/public/Papers/LS_Validity(On-Course).pdf
7. Gregorc, A.: Gregorc's mind styles (2004). http://www.colorfulleadership.info/papers/concrete.htm
8. Mitchell, D.P.: Learning Style: A Critical Analysis of the Concept and Its Assessment. Kogan Page, London (1994)
9. Coffield, F., et al.: Learning styles and pedagogy in post-16 learning. A systematic and critical review. Newcatle University report on learning styles (2004). http://www.Isda.org.uk/files/PDF/1543.pdf
10. Mareš, J.: Styly učení žáků a student (Learning Styles of Pupils and Students). Portál, Praha (1998)
11. Mareš, J. e-Learning a individuální styly učení. Československá psychologie [e-Learning and Individual Learning Styles], vol. 48, no. 3 (2004)

12. Honey, P. Learning styles – the key to personalised e-learning? (2010). http://www.bbmatters.net/bbmatters.../Learning%20stylespeter%20honey.pdf
13. Johnston, C.A.: Unlocking the will to Learn. Corwin Press, Inc., Thousand Oaks (1996)
14. Poulová, P., Šimonová, I.: Didactic Reflection of Learning Preferences in IT and Managerial Fields of Study, Information Technology Based Higher Education and Training (ITHET 2013). IEEE, Piscataway (2013)
15. Šimonová, I., Poulová, P.: Learning Style Reflection within Tertiary e-Education. Hradec Kralove, Wamak (2012)
16. Šimonová, I., Poulová, P., Sokolová, M.: Klíčové kompetence a jejich reflexe v terciárním e-vzdělávání [Key Competences and Their Reflection in Tertiary e-Education]. M&V Publishers, Hradec Kralove (2011)
17. Šimonová, I., Poulová, P.: Cloud computing in higher education exploiting social networks and mobile devices (published)
18. Churches, A.: Bloom's digital taxonomy. http://edorigami.wikispaces.com/Bloom%27s+Digital+Taxonomy
19. Prensky, M. Digital Natives, Digital Immigrants, On the Horizon, vol. 9, no. 5. MCB University Press (2001)

Investigating the Determinants of Information Sharing Intentions of Learners in Collaborative Learning

Yong Wee Sek[1,2(✉)], Hepu Deng[1], Elspeth McKay[1], and Wei Xu[3]

[1] School of Business IT and Logistics, RMIT University, Melbourne, VIC, Australia
{yongwee.sek,hepu.deng,elspeth.mckay}@rmit.edu.au
[2] Faculty of Information and Communication Technology, Universiti Teknikal Malaysia Melaka, Melaka, Malaysia
ywsek@utem.edu.my
[3] School of Information, Smart City Research Center, Renmin University of China, Beijing, China
weixu@ruc.edu.cn

Abstract. This study investigates the determinants of learners' information sharing intentions in collaborative learning through the adoption of open learner models. Statistical analyses are performed on the data collected from 235 undergraduate students in Malaysian universities through survey to test the relationship between perceived usefulness, perceived ease of use, trust and the information sharing intention of learners. The result reveals that all three factors have a significant impact on learners' information sharing behaviors in collaborative learning through the adoption of open learner models. Such findings are useful for educational institutions in their adoption of open learner models for information sharing in technology-based collaborative learning.

Keywords: Open learner models · Information sharing · Collaborative learning

1 Introduction

With the rapid development of information and communication technologies, technology-based collaborative learning (TBCL) is becoming important for improving the performance of teaching and learning in universities [1]. The popularity of TBCL is due to the benefits that collaboration technologies have providing learners with effective learning environments. The utilization of collaboration technologies can improve learners' participation in collaborative learning. It can facilitate the sharing of learning information. To fully realize the benefits of collaboration technologies, many universities have integrated open learner models (OLMs) in their teaching and learning processes as a collaborative learning tool for promoting the engagement of learners in TBCL.

An OLM is a learning data visualization and collaboration tool. It can be used to visualize learners' knowledge status and their misconceptions in a specific subject area [2]. The adoption of OLMs in TBCL allows learners to share their learning information and compare with each other's progresses. It provides learners with an effective learning environment so that learners have an opportunity to develop their self-reflection and self-assessment skills. Furthermore, the use of an OLM in web-based educational

Z. Gong et al. (Eds.): ICWL 2015 Workshops, LNCS 9584, pp. 87–97, 2016.
DOI: 10.1007/978-3-319-32865-2_10

settings has the potential to enhance the sharing and dissemination of learning information by facilitating inter-personal interaction and collaboration.

Despite the benefits of OLMs for facilitating the sharing of learning information in TBCL, the utilization of this technology is not encouraging [3]. Existing studies try to address this issue mainly through introducing new methods of interactions between OLMs and learners and suggesting different knowledge representation formats [2]. Few studies have empirically investigated the determinants of learners' information sharing intentions in collaborative learning.

This study aims to investigate the determinants of learners' information sharing intentions through the adoption of OLM. Scenario-based and web mediated prototyping is adopted for the introduction of OLM. Statistical analyses are performed on the data collected through an online survey. The result reveals that there is a significant positive relationship between perceived usefulness, perceived ease of use, trust, and the information sharing intention of learners in the adoption of OLM for improving the performance of collaborative learning. The findings can assist educational institutions to develop appropriate strategies and policies in their development of collaborative teaching and learning in TBCL.

2 Literature Review and Motivation

TBCL is a social interaction that involves the acquisition and sharing of experience and knowledge in a community of learners and instructors through the support of collaboration technologies [6]. It is becoming popular for improving learners' cognitive performance and stimulating learners' engagement in their knowledge construction [1]. In TBCL, the utilization of collaboration tools facilitates the sharing of learning information and encourages learners' participations in learning. The successful implementation of TBCL depends on the willingness of learners to share learning information through the adoption of collaboration technologies [7].

Information sharing refers to the provision and acquisition of information between individuals [7]. Learners' active involvements in generating and transferring information and making collaboration an essential and highly valued process are the prerequisite for the successful information sharing in TBCL [7]. Recognizing the importance of the collaboration tool in facilitating the sharing of learning information in TBCL, collaboration tool such as OLM have been introduced.

OLM is an effective collaboration tool for facilitating the sharing of learning information in TBCL [2]. It is used to visualize learners' learning information such as learning progresses, knowledge status, competency, misconception, and concepts [2]. The benefit of adopting this tool is its ability to allow a direct engagement of learners with their own pedagogical models. This openness of the tool allows learners to directly contribute to the development and maintenance of their own content models. It facilitates the sharing of learning information by allowing stakeholders to have an opportunity to get involved in this pedagogical practice. Such a learning information exchange provides learners with opportunities to compare their own learner models with their stakeholders as well as enables learners to collaborate critical reflection [2].

Despite various benefits associated with the sharing of learning information through the utilization of OLM, there are many factors impeding the information sharing between learners. Often learning information is not shared effectively in OLM-based collaborative learning due to the low engagement rate on the utilization of OLM as a collaboration tool for sharing learning information in learning processes.

To address this issue, many initiatives have been proposed. Chen et al. [3], for example, represent OLM as animal companions to encourage learners' engagement in collaborative learning. Kerly et al. [8] adopt a conversation agent in their adoption of OLM to facilitate collaboration between learners. These studies are conducted for improving learners' motivation to utilize OLM to share their learning information with a focus on the technical issues of OLM such as the interaction method and the knowledge representation format [9]. There is a dearth of empirical studies from the perspective of learners. Little research has been done in investigating the determinants of learners' information sharing intentions through the adoption of OLM.

Many studies have been conducted in identifying the determinants of learners' information sharing intentions through the adoption of various collaboration tools. Hung and Cheng [4] investigate learners' information sharing intentions through adopting social networks in virtual learning communities. Hwang [10] explores the factors that affect learners' willingness to exchange learning information in the Backboard learning management system. Liu et al. [11] examine the determinants of learners' readiness in sharing their learning information in the creative commons sharing platform. Table 1 presents a summary of the literature discussed above.

Table 1. Summary of the determinants that affect learners' information sharing intentions

References	Context	Methodology	Factors
Hung and Cheng [4]	Virtual communities in social networks	Quantitative approach with web-based survey and experience virtual community users	Perceived usefulness, perceived ease of use, technology readiness index, and the factor of compatibility
Hwang [10]	Blackboard	Quantitative approach with questionnaire on learners have experience in using Blackboard	Self-identity, social identity, affective commitment, and perceived enjoyment
Liu et al. [11]	Creative Commons	Quantitative and qualitative approaches with questionnaire and interview on learners have experience in using creative commons	Trust, knowledge sharing self-efficacy, and outcome expectation

The studies above in exploring the determinants of learners' information sharing intentions focus on the adoption of different collaboration tools in TBCL. These studies show that learners' willingness in sharing learning information is influenced by the features of the technology and the characteristics of learners [12, 13]. Different collaborative technologies have their own characteristics. As a result, the information sharing intention of learners in different collaboration technologies would be different [12, 13]. There is little research in the investigation of the determinants of learners' information sharing intentions in OLM-based collaborative learning.

3 A Conceptual Framework

In OLM-based collaborative learning, learners are able to utilize the collaboration tool to perform various activities such as (a) sharing learning information, (b) accessing learning information, (c) comparing learning progress with peers, and (d) obtaining constructive feedback and assistance from peers and instructors [2]. To facilitate these activities, a well-design interface with simple and easy-to-use features as well as easy-to-understand learning information representation is essential [9].

With the comprehensive review of the related literature on the factors affecting the adoption of collaboration tools for information sharing, a conceptual framework consisting of trust, perceived ease of use, and perceived usefulness is developed for facilitating the investigation of the determinants of learners' information sharing intentions through the adoption of OLM, given as in Fig. 1.

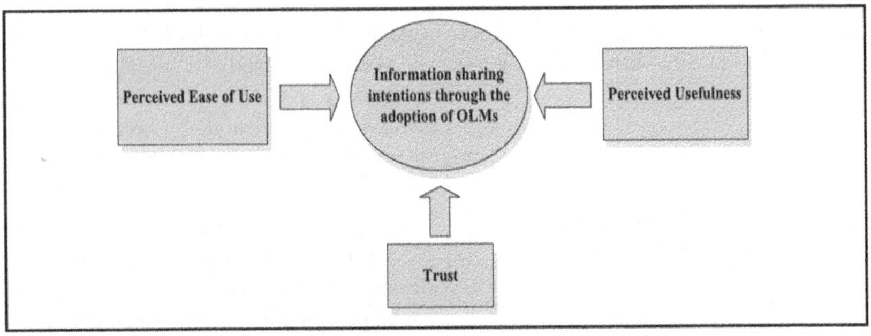

Fig. 1. A conceptual framework for the information sharing intentions

Trust is about an individual learners' willingness in dealing with the risks which come from actions conducted by other learners in TBCL [11]. It is an influential factor that affects the willingness of learners in exchanging and disseminating their learning information [14]. Trust not only plays a critical role in promoting the dissemination and sharing of learning information and knowledge among learners. It also influences learners' intentions for actively sharing learning information [11].

Trust can help to create and facilitate the formation of interpersonal relationships in the teaching and learning process, leading to effective knowledge creation and sharing [11]. It encourages the engagement of learners in TBCL. Trust allows learners to exchange learning information more effectively and efficiently. Existing research shows that the successful implementation of collaboration tools in facilitating the sharing of learning information is built on trust [14]. Tamjidyamcholo et al. [15], for example, reveal that trust is essential for creating a successful knowledge sharing atmosphere in virtual communities. Liu et al. [11] point out that trust has a significant effect on learners' willingness to share their learning information for supporting the acquisition of knowledge and learning information. In OLM-based collaborative learning, learners' willingness to share learning information would increase if a trust relationship can be built. The above argument leads to the following hypothesis:

H1. There is a positive and significant relationship between trust and the information sharing intention of learners in OLM-based collaborative learning.

The technology acceptance model is widely used for explaining the acceptance of collaboration tools for information sharing [4, 16]. In this situation, the perceived usefulness refers to an individual learner's belief of the likelihood with which information sharing behaviors can help improve his/her learning performance through the adoption of collaboration tools [1]. Learners' intention to share their learning information through the adoption of collaboration tools would further increase if they are able to improve their academic performance [1]. Cheung and Vogel [16] show that learners' willingness to actively engage in TBCL is affected by the usefulness of the collaboration tool. In OLM-based collaborative learning, learners' willingness to share their learning information will increase if they are able to improve their academic performance through the adoption of OLM. If learners believe that the adoption of OLM for sharing their learning information can enhance their academic performance, their willingness to share learning information would be improved. Based on this discussion, the following hypothesis is proposed.

H2. There is a positive and significant relationship between perceived usefulness and the information sharing intention of learners in OLM-based collaborative learning.

The perceived ease of use is about the degree to which a learner believes that using collaboration tools for information sharing is free of efforts [16]. If learners are able to adopt a collaboration tool for information sharing without difficulties, the intention to share their learning information would be higher [17]. Cheung and Vogel [16] indicate that the perceived ease of use has a significant positive impact on the willingness of learners to adopt a collaboration tool in transferring learning information. In OLM-based collaborative learning, learners' willingness to share their learning information through OLM would be encouraged if learners can utilize this collaboration tool without difficulties. Thus, the following hypothesis is presented.

H3. There is a positive and significant relationship between perceived ease of use and the information sharing intention of learners in OLM-based collaborative learning.

4 Research Design and Methodology

This study aims to investigate the determinants of information sharing intentions of learners in collaborative learning through the adoption of OLM. To achieve this objective, the research question is formulated as follows: *What are the determinants of learners' information sharing intentions through the adoption of OLM?*

To adequately answer this question, a quantitative research design with a scenario-based and web-mediated prototyping tool is employed. Such a design is frequently used in human-computer interaction research for describing the design specifications and the functionality of a prototype [18, 19]. This technique is practical in the initial development of an information system where the feedback from learners would put into consideration [18, 19]. Scenario-based and web mediated prototyping is appropriate for the introduction of new information systems to specific users [18]. In this study, the description of the pedagogical features of OLM such as the functionalities and interaction tools for facilitating the sharing of learner information are made available for each respondent. This transparency affords the respondent to become aware of the adaptable features available in OLM for information sharing.

Surveys are commonly utilized for gathering information directly from respondents on their views, attitudes and behaviors about the adoption of specific technologies [21]. They are suitable for this study because direct questioning is used to investigate respondents' acceptance on their adoption of OLM for information sharing.

The measurement items for measuring the perceived usefulness and the perceived ease of use are adopted from [22]. The construction of the trust measurement item is adopted from [23]. A seven-point Likert scale is employed for each statement ranging from one describing strongly disagree to seven to indicate strongly agree. Before administering the pilot study, the survey is reviewed by four experts to ensure the semantics correspondence between measurement items in the item pool and the underlying variables intended to be measured. The questionnaire consists of three parts. Part-1 involves the participant's profile. Part-2 is about individual learning styles. Part-3 is related to OLM scenarios presented to each participant. The focus of these scenarios is to explore an individual learner's acceptance of OLM for sharing learning information. A pilot study is conducted to test and validate the reliability of the questionnaire. Several of the original items are revised based on the test results. The improved version of the survey instrument is used for the actual study.

Convenience sampling [21] is adopted in this study because the selection of respondents is based on voluntary and availability [24]. The participants are undergraduate students with experience in engaging learning management systems in their studies in Malaysian universities. Obtaining the learning experience from these participants provides reliable data regarding their OLM acceptance for information sharing. This study employs a web-mediated survey to collect data from the participants. Before assessing learners' acceptance of OLM for information sharing, participants are introduced to OLM through a scenario-based OLM prototype by using Adobe Captivate 7 [25]. The online survey is distributed to 270 undergraduate students in universities in Malaysia. A total of 235 participants have responded.

A correlation analysis is used for evaluating the strength and direction of the relationship between perceived usefulness, perceived ease of use, trust, and information sharing intentions [26]. The use of correlation analysis is due its ability to show how strong these relationships are in OLM-based collaborative learning.

A multiple regression analysis is adopted for predicting the information sharing intention of learners in OLM-based collaboration learning [26]. The applicability of the correlation analysis in this study is due to its ability to investigate how well the perceived usefulness, perceived ease of use, and trust are able to predict the information sharing intention of learners.

5 Data Analysis and Results

A correlation matrix for showing the strength and the direction of the relationship between perceived usefulness, perceived ease of use, trust, and information sharing intentions of learners is presented in Table 2. The correlation coefficient (r) is used as the indicator for representing the strength and direction of the relationship. In the correlation analysis, the r value between 0.5 and +1.0 indicates a strong positive linear relationship [26]. The r value in Table 2 for all the factors ranging from 0.694 to 0.760 is more than +0.5. This shows that there is a strong positive linear relationship between perceived usefulness, perceived ease of use, trust, and information sharing intentions of learners. In particular, the highest r value of 0.76 between the perceived usefulness and the information sharing intention of learners indicates a strong positive relationship. This shows that learners' perceived usefulness positively affects the information sharing intention of learners in OLM-based collaborative learning.

Table 2. The correlation coefficient of the factors that affect information sharing intentions

	Perceived usefulness	Perceived ease of use	Trust	Information sharing intentions
Perceived usefulness	1	0.728[a]	0.739[a]	0.760[a]
Perceived ease of use	0.728[a]	1	0.674[a]	0.671[a]
Trust	0.739[a]	0.674[a]	1	0.694[a]
Information sharing intentions	0.760[a]	0.671[a]	0.694[a]	1

[a] Correlation is significant at the 0.01 level.

The results of the multiple regression analysis for predicting learners' information sharing intentions in OLM-based collaborative learning is presented in Table 3. The value of the variance inflation factor (VIF) for all the factors is less than 10 indicating that no factors are highly correlated between each other. This shows that the identified factors distinctly predict the information sharing intention of learners in OLM-based collaborative learning. The F-test is used to test the fitness of the regression model. A significant F-test value ($F = 131.66$, Sig. $F < 0.01$) implies that the research model is not much difference from the perfect base model.

Table 3. The statistical results of the multiple regression analysis

Independent variables	Beta value	t	Significant level	Results	Tolerance	VIF
Perceived usefulness	0.446	6.767	0.000	Accepted	0.357	2.801
Perceived ease of use	0.163	2.970	0.003	Accepted	0.429	2.332
Trust	0.220	3.833	0.000	Accepted	0.415	2.409

Overall model $F = 131.66$, $p < 0.01$, coefficient of determination = 0.631, Durbin-Watson = 1.727

Table 3 shows that the coefficient of determination R^2 is 63.1 %. This indicates that the proposed factors in this study are able to predict 63.1 % of the information sharing intention of learners in OLM-based collaborative learning. The multiple regression analysis is applied to test the research hypotheses empirically through examine whether the beta values of perceived usefulness, perceived ease of use, and trust are non-zero [26]. Significant and positive beta values imply strong support for the hypothesis. The higher the beta value is, the more influential the corresponding variable is on the information sharing intention of learners in OLM-based collaborative learning. Based on the information in Table 3, the corresponding beta values for perceived usefulness, perceived ease of use, and trust are 0.446, 0.163, and 0.022 respectively. As a result, hypotheses H1, H2 and H3 are all supported.

6 Discussion

This study aims to investigate the determinants of learners' information sharing intentions through the adoption of OLM in TBCL. The findings show that the perceived usefulness, perceived ease of use, and trust are critical for the information sharing intention of individual learners in OLM-based collaborative learning.

The perceived usefulness is critical in determining the willingness of learners to share their learning information through the use of OLM. This result is consistent with the finding in [27], suggesting that learners' intention to share information would increase if they are able to improve their work by utilizing the collaboration tool in sharing learning information. The adoption of OLM in facilitating the sharing of learning information in TBCL are able to attract learners' attentions because it helps promote learners' self-reflection and improve their academic performance. This result suggests that educational institutions need to have experienced and properly trained OLM educators to promote the advantages of using OLM in fostering the sharing of learning information. Furthermore, explaining the benefit to learners about integrating OLM into TBCL would further enhance the adoption of OLM in TBCL.

The significant impact of the perceived ease of use on the information sharing intention of learners in OLM-based collaborative learning identified in this study is in line with previous findings in the information sharing literature [4]. The perceived ease of use plays an important role in determining the successful implementation of collaboration technologies in facilitating the sharing of learning information in TBCL. Learners are willing to adopt a technology for information sharing if they are able to use that technology without any difficulties [4]. The positive relationship between the perceived ease of use and the information sharing intention of learners suggests that OLM is considered as an easy-to-use collaboration tool for facilitating the sharing of learning information in TBCL. This means that OLM instructional designers need to design simple and easy-to-use OLM interfaces in order to encourage the active engagement of learners in sharing their learning information in TBCL.

Trust shows a significant relationship with the information sharing intention of learners in OLM-based collaborative learning. This finding is consistent with the previous studies including Chai and Kim's [28] and Ye et al.'s [29]. Trust is critical for effective knowledge and information exchange [28–30]. In this study, the positive relationship between trust and information sharing intentions of learners reveals that the adoption of OLM can establish a learning environment in which learners can obtain reliable and trustworthy learning resources shared by each other learners.

The contributions of this study are twofold. Firstly, the study provides a better understanding of the determinants of learners' information sharing intentions in OLM-based collaborative learning. Secondly, this study provides insight towards the adoption of OLM for information sharing from the perspective of learners. This can assist practitioners to apply appropriate instructional strategies for effective integration of OLM in TBCL. The research findings in this study have practical implications for educational institutions in the development of efficient and effective strategies and policies that promote the adoption of OLM for facilitating the sharing of learning information in collaborative learning.

7 Conclusions, Limitations and Future Research

This study examines the determinants of learners' information sharing intentions in OLM-based collaborative learning. It shows that perceived usefulness, perceived ease of use, and trust affect learners' information sharing intentions in OLM-based collaborative learning. Such findings provide educational instructors with insights on the acceptance of OLM for information sharing in TBCL.

There are some limitations in this study. Firstly, the sample of this study is only from universities in Malaysia. To generalize the findings, the sample should be extended. Secondly, scenario-based and web-mediated prototyping is used in this study. Further study can be conducted in a real environment in which learners can reflect on their real experience in engaging with OLM tools for information sharing.

Acknowledgement. This research is supported by the Ministry of Education of Malaysia and University Teknikal Malaysia Melaka and the Humanities and Social Sciences Foundation of the Ministry of Education (No. 14YJA630075), China, the Beijing Nova Program (No. Z131101000413058), the Fundamental Research Fund for the Central Universities, and the Research Fund of Renmin University of China (No. 15XNLQ08).

References

1. Huang, Y.M.: Exploring the factors that affect the intention to use collaborative technologies: the differing perspectives of Sequential/Global learners. Australas. J. Educ. Technol. **31**, 278–292 (2015)
2. Bull, S., Kay, J.: Open learner models. In: Nkambou, R., Bordeau, J., Miziguchi, R. (eds.) Advances in Intelligent Tutoring Systems, pp. 318–338. Springer, Heidelberg (2010)
3. Chen, Z.H., Chou, C.Y., Deng, Y.C., Chan, T.W.: Active open learner models as animal companions: motivating children to learn through interacting with my-pet and our-pet. Int. J. Artif. Intell. Educ. **17**(2), 145–167 (2007)
4. Hung, S.W., Cheng, M.J.: Are you ready for knowledge sharing? An empirical study of virtual communities. Comput. Educ. **62**, 8–17 (2013)
5. Liou, D.K., Chih, W.H., Hsu, L.C., Huang, C.Y.: Investigating information sharing behavior: the mediating roles of the desire to share information in virtual communities. Inform. Syst. E-Business Manage. **14**(2), 1–30 (2015)
6. Stahl, G., Koschmann, T., Suthers, D.: Computer-supported collaborative learning: an historical perspective. In: Cambridge Handbook of the Learning Sciences, pp. 409–426 (2006)
7. Pai, F.Y., Yeh, T.M.: The effects of information sharing and interactivity on the intention to use social networking websites. Qual. Quant. **48**(4), 2191–2207 (2014)
8. Kerly, A., Ellis, R., Bull, S.: CALMsystem: a conversational agent for learner modelling. Knowl.-Based Syst. **21**(3), 238–246 (2008)
9. Sek, Y.W., Deng, H., McKay, E.: A multi-dimensional measurement model for assessing the pre-adoption of open learner models in technology-mediated teaching and learning: a pilot study. In: Proceedings of the 19th Pacific Asia Conference on Information Systems, July 5 – 9, Singapore (2015)
10. Hwang, Y.: A preliminary examination of the factors for knowledge sharing in technology mediated learning. J. Inf. Syst. Educ. **19**(4), 419–429 (2008)
11. Liu, C.C., Lin, C.C., Deng, K.Y., Wu, Y.T., Tsai, C.C.: Online knowledge sharing experience with creative commons. Online Inform. Rev. **38**(5), 680–696 (2014)
12. Sun, Y., Jeyaraj, A.: Information technology adoption and continuance: a longitudinal study of individuals' behavioral intentions. Inform. Manag. **50**(7), 457–465 (2013)
13. Brown, S.A., Dennis, A.R., Venkatesh, V.: Predicting collaboration technology use: integrating technology adoption and collaboration research. J. Manag. Inform. Syst. **27**(2), 9–54 (2010)
14. Liou, D.K., Chih, W.H., Hsu, L.C., Huang, C.Y.: Investigating information sharing behavior: the mediating roles of the desire to share information in virtual communities. In: Information Systems and E-Business Management, pp. 1–30 (2015)
15. Tamjidyamcholo, A., Baba, M.S.B., Tamjid, H., Gholipour, R.: Information security-professional perceptions of knowledge-sharing intention under self-efficacy, trust, reciprocity, and shared-language. Comput. Educ. **68**, 223–232 (2013)
16. Cheung, R., Vogel, D.: Predicting user acceptance of collaborative technologies: an extension of the technology acceptance model for e-learning. Comput. Educ. **63**, 160–175 (2013)
17. Su, A.Y., Yang, S.J., Hwang, W.Y., Zhang, J.: A web 2.0-based collaborative annotation system for enhancing knowledge sharing in collaborative learning environments. Comput. Educ. **55**(2), 752–766 (2010)
18. Carroll, J.M.: Five reasons for scenario-based design. Interact. Comput. **13**, 43–60 (2000)

19. Sek, Y.W., Deng, H., McKay, E.: Investigating learner preferences in an open learner model program: a malaysian case study. In: Proceedings of the 25th Australasian Conference of Information Systems (2014)
20. Sek, Y.W., McKay, E., Deng, H.: A conceptual framework for enhancing the motivation in an open learner model learning environment. In: 2014 IEEE Conference on e-Learning, e-Management and e-Services, pp. 105–110 (2014)
21. Creswell, J.W.: Research Design: Qualitative, Quantitative and Mixed Methods Approaches, 2nd edn. Sage Publications, California, CA (2003)
22. Davis, F.D.: Perceived usefulness, perceived ease of use and user acceptance of information technology. MIS Quart. **13**(3), 319–340 (1989)
23. Zhou, T.: An empirical examination of initial trust in mobile banking. Internet Res. **21**(5), 527–540 (2011)
24. Battaglia, M.: Convenience sampling. In: Lavrakas, P.J. (ed.) Encyclopedia of Survey Research Methods, pp. 149–150. Sage Publications, Thousand Oaks, CA (2008)
25. De Voge, J.M., Bass, E.J., Atia, M., Bond, M., Waggoner-Fountain, L.A., Borowitz, S.M.: The development of a web-based resident sign-out training program. In: Systems, Man and Cybernetics IEEE International Conference, pp. 2509–2514 (2009)
26. Hair Jr., J.F., Black, W.C., Babin, B.J., Anderson, R.E.: Multivariate Data Analysis: A Global Perspective, 7th edn. Pearson Prentice Hall, Upper Saddle River, NJ (2010)
27. Papadopoulos, T., Stamati, T., Nopparuch, P.: Exploring the determinants of knowledge sharing via employee weblogs. Int. J. Inform. Manag. **33**(1), 133–146 (2013)
28. Chai, S., Kim, M.: What makes bloggers share knowledge? An investigation on the role of trust. Int. J. Inform. Manag. **30**(5), 408–415 (2010)
29. Ye, S., Chen, H., Jin, X.-L.: An empirical study of what drives users to share knowledge in virtual communities. In: Lang, J., Lin, F., Wang, J. (eds.) KSEM 2006. LNCS (LNAI), vol. 4092, pp. 563–575. Springer, Heidelberg (2006)
30. Sridharan, B., Deng, H., Corbitt, B.: Critical success factors in e-learning ecosystems: a qualitative study. J. Syst. Inform. Technol. **12**(4), 263–288 (2010)

Towards an Architecture for e-Learning Infrastructures on a National Level: A Case Study of AfgREN

Salim Saay[1(✉)], Alex Norta[2], and Mart Laanpere[3]

[1] Computer Science Faculty, Kabul University, Kabul, Afghanistan
saay@tlu.ee
[2] Department of Informatics, Tallinn University of Technology, Akadeemia tee 15A, 12816 Tallinn, Estonia
alex.norta.phd@ieee.org
[3] Institute of Informatics, Tallinn University, Narva Road 25, 10120 Tallinn, Estonia
mart.laanpere@tlu.ee

Abstract. National Research and Education Networks (NRENs) are for sharing resources between member organizations. NRENs play an important role in e-learning activities as they provide necessary communication. Heterogeneous infrastructures used for e-learning are a challenge for system design, integrity and interoperability. This paper proposed a NREN e-learning reference model and affiliated NREN e-learning architectural patterns that considered communication, reliable access, cooperation between e-learning infrastructures and interoperability. Research exists about different architecture including services oriented Cloud computing, For example, the E-School Systems and other institutional e-learning systems use traditional client server architectures. However, no research has been carried out on NREN e-learning architectures. For deeper insight, we investigate and compare in this paper the Estonian Education and Research Network (EENet) as an NREN example of a developed country, the Pakistan Education and the Research Network (PERN) as an example of a developing country and the Afghanistan Research and Education Network (AfgREN).

Keywords: e-Learning · Reference model · Architecture pattern · NREN e-learning

1 Introduction

E-learning is one of the new learning platforms for gaining knowledge at universities and other educational institutions. The main purpose of e-learning systems is to utilize knowledge and skills of educators in such a way that education services can be provided anywhere and anytime without limitation of time and space [1].

The quality of e-learning depends on the content and infrastructure that is available, such as infrastructures for course- and content delivery, effectiveness of delivery, interactivity, and personalization of e-learning courses [2]. The e-learning platform is

Z. Gong et al. (Eds.): ICWL 2015 Workshops, LNCS 9584, pp. 98–107, 2016.
DOI: 10.1007/978-3-319-32865-2_11

also very important for the delivery of content to learners and for successful collaboration interaction. There are different e-learning platforms including the Learning Activity Management System (LAMS) [3], the blackboard e-learning environment [4], WiKi and blogs environment for the collaboration of knowledge development and content writing by learners that offer the chance to them to write their personal views informally [5] and many other systems for e-learning.

Using different platforms for e-learning systems that operate via the Internet poses a challenge for integrity and interoperability. Ricardo Queiros, Lino Oliveira et al. [6] studied the interoperability of e-learning in a school project called PEACE. The PEACE project is for the interoperability strategy of e-Learning environments. However, the project only considers the application layer and does not take into account architectural interoperability. For this reason, IEEE developed the Learning Technology Service Architecture (LTSA) for the standardization, modeling, knowledge sharing and content exchange of e-learning systems [4]. Current e-learning platforms mostly focus on theoretical content and the evaluation of students based on their theoretical knowledge, Antonio Robles-Gómez [7] proposes a client server e-learning architecture to provide more prcatical knowledge for learners. Client-server based platforms composed of a Web server, storage server and learning management systems (LMS) offer e-learning services via the Internet. In this case, the communication- and network layer of such e-learning architectures are very important.

The E-School System architecture [1] provides a flexible, scalable, and modular platform for wide-ranging domain knowledge. It is generating space for all new content types by using interactive media assets and access control for users of the e-learning system. The E-learning School System Architecture is composed of a presentation tier, common services tier, e-schools service tier, and resource tier. However, a communication tier is not considered in the mentioned e-learning systems.

In this paper, we address this gap by answering the research question of how to systematically create an architecture for a NREN e-learning infrastructure. The specific focus is on the communication layer and related e-learning patterns. To achieve a reduction of complexity, we create a separation of concerns by deducing the following sub-research questions. What development methodology is suitable for the NREN e-learning architecture? What are the identified steps of creating a standard- and a concrete architecture? What are the differentiating aspects of our NREN e-learning architecture versus other e-learning platforms. This paper presents our NREN e-learning architectural pattern to provide guidance for the implementation of e-learning systems in NRENs. Patterns are part of concrete architectures that allow for a best-practice development and analysis of differences of existing systems.

The paper is organized as follows, Sect. 2 gives background material pertaining to e-learning infrastructures and the roles of NRENs. In Sect. 3 we discuss the development methodology and Sect. 4 proposes the specific design approach for a tentative NREN e-learning standard architecture. Section 5 explores applicable NREN e-learning architectural patterns for specifying a concrete architecture for Afghanistan. Section 6 concludes the paper and gives future work.

2 e-Learning Infrastructure and NREN Roles : Common Practices

Different terminologies and methods are used for e-learning systems [8]. Using appropriate applications, and networks in e-learning is important, because it affects directly the quality and accessibility of an e-learning system. In computer based learning cases, communication and networking for the delivery of services is a challenge in e-learning systems [9]. The reason for that challenge is the lack of agreed upon communication protocols and network infrastructures. Consequently, certain traditional infrastructures and Cloud computing infrastructures [10] are used in e-learning systems. Cloud computing is a computer based infrastructure which provide computation and storage resource as a services [11], alongside with traditional e-learning systems. Using Cloud computing infrastructures is one of the efficient ways of e-learning implementations in countries that have reliable, inexpensive, and sustainable Internet [12].

Cloud computing has a distributed data center with a large number of resources that guarantees quality of services. Cloud computing supports flexible application offers, rapid troubleshooting and real-time configuration. Cloud computing infrastructures are composed of an infrastructure layer, a content layer, and an application layer [11]. Cloud computing has four models including, private Cloud for a single organization that utilizes multiple services. Public Clouds offer resources to the public as service providers while community Clouds are for sharing resources between specific communities that are concerned with specific security- and community policies. Finally, hybrid Clouds are compositions of more than one Cloud model [13].

The National Research and Education Networks (NRENs) are extensible to Cloud computing. NRENs interconnect multiple education- and research organizations for sharing research resources [14] and are the key driver of educational organizations that want to collaborate with each other and they drive the growth of e-learning at academic- and educational organizations. Additionally, NRENs provide video conferencing, voice over Internet-protocol services, application management, and single sign-on user authentication services [15]. The latter is missing for the E-learning systems in the Estonian Education and Research Network (EENet), the Pakistan Education and Research Network (PERN) and the Afghanistan Research and Education Network (AfgREN). Consequently, we study and compare these platforms are as cases in this paper.

2.1 NRENs as e-Learning Infrastructure

The National Research and Education Networks (NRENs) are a good infrastructure for e-learning systems and are positioned between traditional e-learning methods and Cloud-computing methods. A.E. Oldehoeft [16] reveals that NRENs provide a high performance of computing and communication infrastructure that is extended to scientific, technical and educational communities. A linking together of educational centers, libraries, laboratories and industry are the main targets of NRENs, which the natural interconnectivity of the Internet enables.

Table 1. NRENs e-learning infrastructure adapter from [17].

Layers		PERN	EENet	AfgREN
Application layer		AAA for access to HEMIS, LMS, CMS	AAA for access to resources (LMS, OIS, HITSA and city services), it provides confidentiality	Authentication for accessing to HEMIS, and digital library
Service layer	common services	Social communication solution (Video, IP telephone, Email), monitoring, security	Social communication (Email, Internet, Video), monitoring, security	Social communication (Email, Video) monitoring
	e-learning services	CMS, HEMIS, LMS, Telemedicine	Eduroam, Moodle, OIS, digital library	HEMIS, LMS
Database layer		Student database, library database, HR database, course content database	LMS database, HITSA database, student database, HR database	Student database, HR database, Library database

NRENs are a good headstock and infrastructure for e-learning systems, because NRENs provide high speed domestic connection and inexpensive Internet for educational and academic organizations. In many cases, NRENs provide storage facilities in NREN data centers. Most of NRENs are using fiber optic cable, dense wavelength division multiplexing (DWDM) and high capacity border routers for backbone network infrastructures that provide high national- and international bandwidth. The E-learning services of three NRENs we compare in the Table 1 are based on three layers including an application layer, services layer, and database layer.

3 Methodology

The design-science research method [18] is practiced to design artifacts in a relevant and rigorous way. For the domain of e-learning systems we consider design science not to be a good method for creating complex e-learning architectures. The reason is that design science is more suitable as a research method for the development of a rather formal and technology focused system architectures, while this research deals to a much greater degree with sociotechnical system issues, i.e., people work individually or as groups, or even as parts of organizations together collaboratively while they try to solve complex problems with the help of very diverse sets of technologies.

Action-design science [19] is applicable as an experimental method, but as it is too related to running live system development that organizations develop in an evolutionary way. Thus, since we don't have ongoing NREN e-learning system development projects available, we consider action-design science also an unsuitable research method for this paper.

The case study research method [20] we choose for this research to answer the selected research questions. Case study is a method of research that can be used in a broad area, including architecture, implementation of IT system, social concepts, organizational concepts and so on. The case study method has several research strategy including exploratory, descriptive, explanatory, and improving. Exploratory case study research has the strategy of understanding a specific situation, seeking new insight, generate new ideas and hypotheses, Thus, we selected exploratory strategy for this research, more specifically, inductive empirical research.

4 Proposed Approach

This section proposes an architecture of NREN e-learning system, for which we first give short definitions. An architecture is a description of components, functions and connections among functional components that comprise an overall system [21]. A pattern provides a solution on an architectural level and it serves as a guideline for developing a high-quality specification of new e-learning systems [22]. There are two types of patterns, including design patterns and architectural patterns. Architectural patterns present the best practice for specifying an architecture infrastructure of systems, whereas design patterns focus on the functionality of systems [23]. Thus, a standard architecture for a domain such as e-learning NRENs result from analyzing used reference models that must be incorporated, and also from related architectural patterns in order to provide a concrete architecture [24]. For example, a concrete very context-specific architecture would be AfgREN. We design the architecture-development process in Fig. 1 for more clarification and to show a method for architecture development. Figure 1 depicts a flow for concrete architecture design, however domain knowledge, patterns and a standard architecture are the prerequisite for establishing a high quality concrete architecture that is very context-specific.

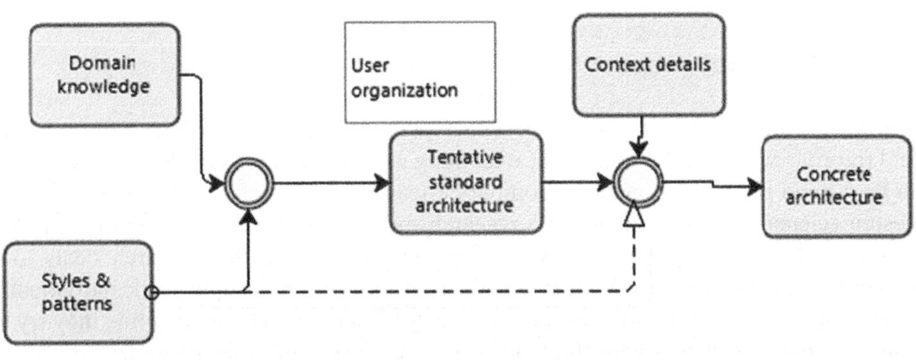

Fig. 1. Steps of architecture types development adapted from [21].

In Fig. 2, we depict the four important layers of an NREN e-learning architecture, namely the top layer that checks credential for access on the Application layer, and additionally layers for services, databases and network elements. We design an NREN e-learning architecture that results from knowledge gained from the qualitative interviews. Currently, the university information technology infrastructure of Afghanistan is hard-wired via Kabul University central server that a cable connects with the University of Vienna. This way it is not feasible to develop an extensible, modifiable and

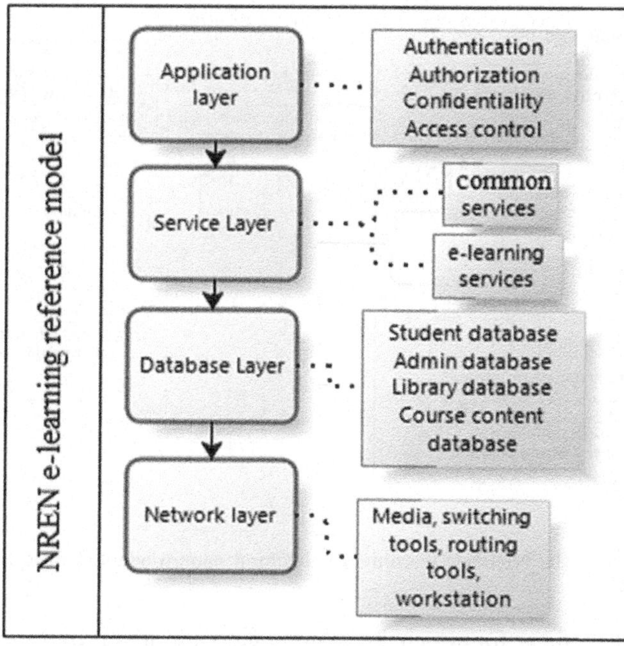

Fig. 2. NREN e-learning reference model.

inter-operable service-layer on top that establishes an NREN for a cross-border e-learning system integration. On the other hand, reference models for easy service-layer development such as a private Cloud model, public Cloud model, community Cloud model and hybrid Cloud model, do not consider a suitably developed network layer. However, the latter must necessarily allow for an integration on top of the pre-existing information technology infrastructure.

5 The NREN Architecture and Affiliated Patterns

In this section we give the resulting NREN standard architecture or e-learning that is depicted in Fig. 3. The latter is adapted from the so-called eSourcing Reference Architecture eSRA [24] and shows a three-layer style that comprises an external-, conceptual, and internal layer. On the external layer, an eLearning_Exchange component is replicated into each respective e-learning concrete architecture, i.e., in Fig. 3 we assume AfgREN, PERN and EENet engage in a cross-national e-learning NREN with their own respective concrete architectures. The eLearning_Exchange component is present in all concrete architectures and they synchronize each other during setup and enactment time of an e-learning exchange. Inside of the eLearning_Exchange component there reside a facade component to shield a respective national e-learning platform from cybersecurity threats that may arise from other national e-learning platforms. Furthermore, there is a component to facilitate the cross-national setup of

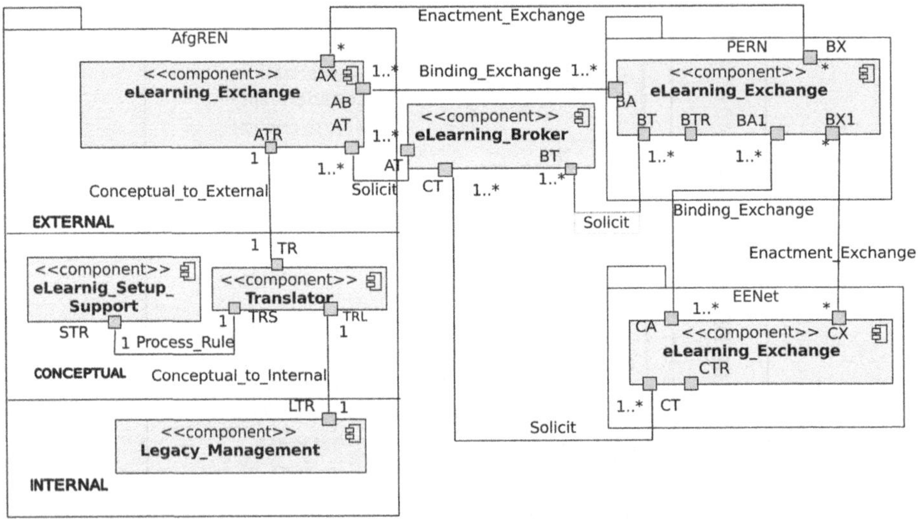

Fig. 3. The NREN e-learning architectural pattern adapted from [24].

collaboration agreement for which we assume they are driven by process-aware services. Thus, the eLearning_Exchange component also contains a component for distributed e-learning process enactment. Finally, the eLearning_Exchange component includes a rules engine that supports the distributed e-learning process enactment engine in, e.g., for deciding rules attached to OR-branches of an e-learning process. To enable the setup phase of an e-learning collaboration, a trusted third party exists in the middle in the form of an eLearning_Broker component. The latter facilitates the rapid matching of e-learning needs with requests. Such a matching is possible using advanced algorithms and recommendation systems.

The concrete architectures in Fig. 3 with the labels AfgREN, PERN and EENet all share the same three-layer style, while PERN and EENet only show the external layer component due to space limitation. Focusing on the fully depicted layers in AfgREN, the conceptual layer comprises an eLearning_Setup_Support component in which e-learning services are composed collaboratively in a crowd-sourcing way. These e-learning services are process aware have rules attached and link to rich multi-media content. Additionally, the Translator component converts heterogeneous data-formats between the external- and internal layer. The latter contains a Legacy_Management component in which local process enactment engines orchestrate information technology infrastructure that is wrapped as a Web-service. Additionally, there exist also local rules engines and local database systems.

The NREN e-learning architecture with embedded concrete national e-learning architectures are easily projectable to a Cloud environment. For that the internal layer corresponds to the so-called Infrastructure-as-a-Service (IaaS) layer in a Cloud, the conceptual layer corresponds to the Platform-as-a-Service (PaaS) layer and the external layer of Fig. 3 corresponds to the Software-as-a-Service (SaaS) layer. The NREN as such could be maintained as a totally public Cloud into which respective national e-learning platforms may join as a national community Cloud, which yields in its composition a hybrid Cloud.

5.1 Affiliated Styles and Patterns

For the NREN e-learning architecture in Fig. 3, we adopt the set of styles and patterns that are also part of eSRA [24]. Thus, a layering style for the domains of respective national e-learning system structures components into groups at a particular level of abstraction. These abstraction layers are the external collaboration layer, the conceptual layer, and the internal layer to manage and orchestrate legacy systems. The layers assure that there is only communication with each adjacent layer.

The eLearning_Broker component uses a publish/subscribe style in which publishers submit new e-learning services and all subscribers receive a notification automatically. The notifier forms the central component of a star topology where the publishers and subscribers are the leaves. The advantage of this style in a multi-party collaboration environment with large numbers of potential e-learning service consumers and providers is enhanced system performance because of a reduced communication overhead and an enhancement of flexibility and integrability of additional national e-learning platforms.

For the remaining way of data management, the NREN employs an abstract-data-repository style. This style keeps the e-learning service consumers and providers of shared data from having knowledge of each other's existence if they wish so, and the details of their respective internal implementations. In addition, using a layering style and by interposing an intermediary protocol between the producer and consumers of shared e-learning services also realizes the abstract data repository style. The abstract data repository style requires an abstract interface to the data repository that further reduces the coupling between the data producers and consumers.

A whole-part pattern aggregates the parts of an e-learning collaboration. Dedicated components exist on the external- and internal layer in the form of the global and local process-enactment- and rules engine.

The broker pattern in NREN is the eLearning_Broker component between the domains of collaborating parties. A broker is a separate component that interacts with the remainder of the architecture. Its purpose is the redirection and bundling of communicating with many collaborating parties. Hence, since the broker pattern stops parties from having to find, contact and investigate every potential collaborating party separately, it affects performance positively.

The eLearning_Exchange component comprises a façade pattern that is a unified interface and offers to a collaborating counterpart access to a set of interfaces of a subsystem, namely the replicated components of the external layer. Hence, this supports the interoperability between e-learning parties and enhances the security in a collaboration as it shields the legacy systems behind the façade of the external layer.

On the conceptual layer of NREN, a pipes-and-filters pattern facilitates establishing communication channels between the external- and internal layer via the conceptual layer. This pattern provides a structure for processing streams of heterogeneous data while filter components encapsulate each processing step. Hence, data passes through pipes between adjacent filters from the external layer to the internal layer and vice versa.

6 Conclusion

In this paper we recognize the need for NREN systems that allow the cross-national exchange of rich e-learning services. The paper explores suitable research methods for NREN development and a discussion of the state of the art shows the existing gap for NREN e-learning systems. With qualitative interviews the commonalities and disparities between existing national e-learning systems are revealed. Furthermore, we suggest a development approach of the architecture and give a tentative reference model that indicates elements an NREN should comprise. Finally, we give an NREN e-learning standard architecture in which national e-learning architectures become part of concrete architectures. Affiliated architecture styles and patterns assure the NREN has high utility.

We show that an exploratory case study-based research method approach is most suitable since NRENs are very much sociotechnical systems where the human factor is very important. Thus, other more formal and technical results oriented research methods such as design science or action-design research do not allow for taking the human factor into account to the same degree. The proposed NREN-development approach should be rigorous in a second step and should aim for methodically developing a standard architecture for NRENs that allows national e-learning systems to become part as standard architectures. Finally, we give a concrete NREN architecture that is deduced from the so-called eSourcing Reference Architecture eSRA. The affiliated relevant architectural styles are layering, publish/subscribe, and abstract data repository. The affiliated architecture patterns are whole-part, broker, and façade.

For future work, we aim to further investigate how the proposed architecture can be refined so that it becomes evident how national e-learning systems can fit in. Additionally, a technical feasibility study must be conducted to estimate the feasibility of establishing an NREN with a service- and communication layer on top of the existing cross-national information-technology infrastructure.

References

1. Pandit, S., Acharya, H., Sanvedi, A., Nahar, P., Soni, S.K., Saxena, P., Ramani, A.K.: An architecture solution for e-learning system – ESSA. In: 2010 International Conference on Technology for Education, T4E 2010, pp. 56–62 (2010)
2. Blundo, D., Martino, M.: E-learning methodologies. Caracalla, 00153 Rome, Italy, FAO (2011)
3. Yan, L., Yang, J., Yang, Z.-K., Liu, S., Huang, L.: Research and application of learning activity management system in college and university e-learning. In: Pan, Z., Zhang, X., El Rhalibi, A., Woo, W., Li, Y. (eds.) Edutainment 2008. LNCS, vol. 5093, pp. 171–179. Springer, Heidelberg (2008)
4. Zenker, F., Gottschall, C., Newen, A., van Riel, R., Vosgerau, G.: Designing an introductory course to elementary symbolic logic within the blackboard e-learning environment. In: Blackburn, P., van Ditmarsch, H., Manzano, M., Soler-Toscano, F. (eds.) Tools for Teaching Logic. LNCS, vol. 6680, pp. 249–255. Springer, Heidelberg (2011)
5. Yau, J., Lam, J., Cheung, K.S.: A review of e-learning platforms in the age of e-learning 2.0. In: Wang, F.L., Fong, J., Zhang, L., Lee, V.S. (eds.) ICHL 2009. LNCS, vol. 5685, pp. 208–217. Springer, Heidelberg (2009)

6. Queirós, R., et al.: Interoperability on e-Learning 2.0: the PEACE case study. In: Cruz-Cunha, M.M., Varajão, J., Powell, P., Martinho, R. (eds.) ENTERprise Information Systems. CCIS, vol. 220, pp. 276–285. Springer, Heidelberg (2011)
7. Robles-Gómez, A., Tobarra, L., Ros, S., Hernández, R., Caminero, A.C., Pastor, R.: A new e-learning architecture for the automatic assessment of network services. In: Proceedings of the 2011 11th IEEE International Conference on Advanced Learning Technologies, ICALT 2011, pp. 56–57 (2011)
8. Moore, J.L., Dickson-Deane, C., Galyen, K.: E-Learning, online learning, and distance learning environments: are they the same? Internet High. Educ. **14**(2), 129–135 (2011)
9. Adami, D., Callegari, C., Giordano, S., Mustacchio, F., Secchi, R.: Teaching experiences with e-learning network infrastructures. In: Teaching Experiences with E-Learning Network Infrastructures, vol. 2005, pp. 510–515 (2005)
10. Masud, M.A.H., Huang, X.: An e-learning system architecture based on cloud computing. World Acad. Sci. Eng. Technol. **62**, 74–78 (2012). Albury, Australia
11. Caminero, A.C., Ros, S., Hernández, R., Robles-Gómez, A., Pastor, R.: Cloud-based e-learning infrastructures with load forecasting mechanism based on exponential smoothing: a use case. In: Proceedings - Frontiers in Education Conference, FIE 2011, pp. 11–16 (2011)
12. Dong, B., Zheng, Q., Yang, J., Li, H., Qiao, M.: An e-learning ecosystem based on cloud computing infrastructure. In: Proceedings of the - 2009 9th IEEE International Conference on Advanced Learning Technology, ICALT 2009, pp. 125–127 (2009)
13. Bora, U.J., Ahmed, M.: E-Learning using cloud computing. Int. J. Sci. Mod. Eng. **1**(2), 9–13 (2013)
14. Savory, B.: Build vs. Buy : The NREN Network Connectivity Dilemma : About Building Research & Education Fibre Networks. UbuntuNet Alliance, Malawi (2012)
15. Patel, A.: New models for NREN's and universities in era of broadband and Web 2.0 applications and innovations. In: Proceedings and Report of the 3rd UbuntuNet Alliance Annual Conference, 2010, pp. 15–24, September 2010
16. Oldehoeft, A.E.: Foundations of a Security Policy for Use of the National Research and Educational Network, February, U.S Department of commmerce, pp. 1–64 (1992)
17. Palanivel, K., Kuppuswami, S.: Service oriented reference architecture for personalized E-learning systems 'SORAPES'. Int. J. Comput. Appl. **24**(5), 35–45 (2011)
18. Vaishnavi, V.K., Kuechler, B.: Design research in information systems. MIS Q. **28**(1), 75–105 (2010)
19. Rossi, M., Lindgren, R., Sein, M.K., Henfridsson, O., Purao, S.: Design research in information systems. MIS Q. **35**(2), 37–56 (2011)
20. Runeson, P., Host, M., Rainer, A., Regnell, B.: Case Study Research in Software Engineering. Wiley, Hoboken (2012)
21. Castelán, E., Brigos, M.A., Fernández, J.: A software reference architecture for the design and development of mobile workflow learning applications. In: International Technology, Education and Development Conference Valencia - 10th–12th March 2014 (2014)
22. Norta, A., Mahunnah, M., Tenso, T., Taveter, K.: An agent-oriented method for designing large socio-technical service-ecosystems. In: IEEE World Congress on Services, pp. 242–249 (2014)
23. Martnez-Fernndez, S., Ayala, C., Franch, X., Marques, H.M., Ameller, D.: A framework for software reference architecture analysis and review. In: CIbSE 2013 16th Ibero-American Conference on Software Engineering - Memorias del 10th Workshop Latinoamericano de Ingeniería en Software Experimental, ESELAW 2013, pp. 89–102 (2013)
24. Norta, A., Grefen, P., Narendra, N.C.: A Reference Architecture for Managing Dynamic Inter-organizational Business Processes, vol. 91, pp. 1–39. Elsevier, Amsterdam (2014)

User Modeling for Web-Based Learning

Predicting Pre-knowledge on Vocabulary from e-Learning Assignments for Language Learners

Di Zou[1], Haoran Xie[2], Tak-Lam Wong[2], Yanghui Rao[3(✉)], Fu Lee Wang[4], and Qingyuan Wu[5]

[1] English Language Centre, The Hong Kong Polytechnic University, Hong Kong, China
dizoudaisy@gmail.com
[2] Department of Mathematics and Information Technology, The Education University of Hong Kong, Hong Kong, China
hrxie2@gmail.com, tlwong@eduhk.hk
[3] School of Data and Computer Science, Sun Yat-sen University, Guangzhou, China
raoyangh@mail.sysu.edu.cn
[4] Caritas Institute of Higher Education, Hong Kong, China
pwang@cihe.edu.hk
[5] School of Management, Beijing Normal University, Zhuhai, China
wuqingyuan@bnuz.edu.cn

Abstract. In the current big data era, we have witnessed the prosperity of emerging massive open online courses, user-generated data and ubiquitous techniques. These evolving technologies and applications have significantly changed the ways for people to learn new knowledge and access information. To find users' desired data in an effective and efficient way, it is critical to understand/model users in applications involving in such a large volume of learning resources. For instance, word learning systems can be promoted significantly in terms of learning effectiveness if the pre-knowledge on vocabulary of learners can be predicted accurately. In this research, we focus on the issue of how to model a specific group of users, i.e., language learners, in the context of e-learning systems. Specifically, we try to predict the pre-knowledge on vocabulary of learners from their previous learning documents such as writing assignments and reading essays. The experimental study on real participants shows that the proposed predicting model is very effective and can be exploited for various applications in the future.

Keywords: Learner profile · Word learning · Vocabulary pre-knowledge

1 Introduction

In the current big data era, we have witnessed the prosperity of emerging massive open online courses, user-generated data and ubiquitous techniques.

Z. Gong et al. (Eds.): ICWL 2015 Workshops, LNCS 9584, pp. 111–117, 2016.
DOI: 10.1007/978-3-319-32865-2_12

These evolving technologies and applications have not only offered a plenty of learning resources on the web but also changed the ways significantly for people to learn new knowledge and access information. To find users' desired data in an effective and efficient way, it is critical to understand/model users in applications involving in such a large volume of learning resources. For instance, word learning systems can be promoted significantly in terms of learning effectiveness if the pre-knowledge on vocabulary of learners can be predicted accurately [2,13]. Another example is that the personalized search or recommendation can be facilitated by user models (i.e., user profiles constructed by social tags) on the domain of social media [11,12].

Therefore, in this research, we focus on the issue of how to model a specific group of users, i.e., language learners, in the context of e-learning systems. As the fast development and popularity of e-learning systems [7], a collection of user learning documents such as writing assignments, reading essays and accessed lecture notes are available in log database of such systems. In the context of language learning, we try to predict the pre-knowledge on vocabulary of learners from their previous learning documents (i.e., writing assignments and reading essays), as these writing assignments and reading essays can reflect both receptive and productive knowledge of words [10]. The contribution of this paper are listed as follows.

- We propose a rating function based on a 5-rating vocabulary knowledge scale (VKS) for extracting pre-knowledge levels;
- We present the framework using the rating function for two kinds of learning documents (i.e., writing assignments and reading essays);
- We compare accuracy of the proposed framework with two baselines by inviting real participants.

The remaining sections of this paper are organized as follows. The proposed framework for learner model construction is introduced in Sect. 2. In Sect. 3, we report the experimental processes and results. Section 4 reviews the related work to our research. Section 5 summarizes this research and discusses some potential future directions.

2 Framework for Learner Modeling

The framework for learner model construction is consisted of three sub-processes. Firstly, the learning documents including writing assignments and reading essays are collected from an e-learning system. Secondly, we identify the set of vocabulary and the degree of pre-knowledge on the vocabulary by employing adapted vocabulary knowledge scale. Finally, we build learner profiles based on the pre-knowledge on vocabulary.

As mentioned above, we mainly exploit two kinds of learning documents (i.e., writing assignments and reading essays) from e-learning systems. However, the proposed framework can be easily extended for incorporating other kinds of documents. For learning documents, we assume that they can be represented by

Table 1. The vocabulary knowledge scale

Scales	Descriptions
1	The learner has never seen this word
2	The learner has seen this word before, but he/she don't know what it means
3	The learner has seen this word before, and he/she know the meaning of this word
4	The learner knows the meaning of this word, and he/she can use the word in a sentence with non-intrusive errors
5	The learner knows the meaning of this word, and he/she can use the word in a sentence correctly

a bag-of-words. However, the conventional term-weight paradigms (e.g., Term Frequency (TF) or Term Frequency Inverse Document Frequency (TF-IDF)) in information retrieval (IR) may be inadequate for modeling the degree of pre-knowledge. These paradigms generally assume that higher frequency reflects higher relevance. However, we should take more issues into consideration for the domain of word learning. For example, grammatical knowledge on a word is obviously neglected according to the assumption if a student knows the semantics of a word but uses an incorrect form of the word in a sentence. To address this problem, we employ and adapt a 5-rating vocabulary knowledge scales (VKS) proposed by Paribakht and Wesche [9] as shown in Table 1. Formally, we convert the above VKS as a piecewise function for ratings as follows.

$$s_i(w_a) = \begin{cases} 0, & \text{if } w_a \notin D_i^{'} \cup D_i^* \\ 0.2 + \alpha f(w_a), & \text{if } w_a \in D_i^{'}, w_a \notin D_i^*, f(w_a) < \eta \\ 0.4 + \alpha(f(w_a) - \eta), & \text{if } w_a \in D_i^{'}, w_a \notin D_i^*, f(w_a) \geq \eta \\ 0.6 + \beta g(w_a), & \text{if } w_a \in D_i^*, g(w_a) < \theta \\ 0.8 + \beta(g(w_a) - \theta), & \text{if } w_a \in D_i^*, g(w_a) \geq \theta \end{cases} \quad (1)$$

where w_a is a word in the corpus, $s_i(w_a)$ denotes the degree of pre-knowledge in the range of [0,1] $D_i^{'}$ is the reading essays and D_i^* is the writing assignments of learner i respectively, α and β are two bonus parameters, η and θ are two thresholds, $f(w_a)$ is the frequency of w_a in $D_i^{'}$, and $g(w_a)$ is the frequency of the correct sentences reduced by the frequency with non-intrusive errors in writing assignments D_i^*.

By employing this function, we can obtain the degree of pre-knowledge of each learner on each word as

$$L_i =< w_1 : s_i(w_1); w_2 : s_i(w_2); ...w_n : s_i(w_n) > \quad (2)$$

where L_i is the learner profile/model for learner i, w_n is a word in the corpus, and $s_i(w_n)$ denotes the degree of pre-knowledge on the word as defined in Eq. (1). The larger value of $s_i(w_n)$ indicates more pre-knowledge of learner i on the word.

3 Experiments

3.1 Subjects and Comparative Methods

To verify the effectiveness of the proposed framework, we invite 25 real participants who are fresh undergraduates from a local university to join the experiment. All participant enrolled an English course lasting for a semester. We have collected 61 read essays and 42 from the online learning system for the course. For the purpose of comparison, we adopt two baselines which use only writing assignments (notated as WA) or reading essays (notated as RE) to calculate the degree of pre-knowledge on words[1].

3.2 Experimental Results

To evaluate the effectiveness of the proposed framework, we adopt the mean square error (MSE) to measure the accuracy of all methods for comparison. The ground truth is from standard English word knowledge tests on subjects. The experimental results are illustrated in Fig. 1. We can observe that our proposed framework has the least mean square errors (0.1763) which reflects the higher accuracy than other two baselines exploiting only one kind of learning documents via the student t-test ($p < 0.05$).

An explanation for the result is that the proposed framework using the vocabulary knowledge scales is more accurate to interpret the levels of pre-knowledge on words from learning documents than baselines. Essentially speaking, both RE and WA baselines can be considered as a simplified vocabulary knowledge scale of Eq. (1). Take the RE baseline as an example, the degree of pre-knowledge of a word is calculated based on the frequency of the word in the reading essays (i.e., $s_i(w_a) \propto f(w_a)$ if $w_a \in D_i^{'}$), which is a simplified presentation of first three parts of Eq. (1). Similarly, the WA baseline is also a simplified representation of remaining two parts (the fourth and fifth lines in Eq. (1)). The experimental results support our assumption and effectiveness of using the 5-rating vocabulary knowledge scales (VKS).

4 Related Work

The research on modeling language learners has been extensively studied in the research communities. To facilitate effective language learning, Chen et al. [1] presented a personalized intelligent mobile learning system which can appropriately recommend English news articles to learners based on the learners' reading abilities evaluated by the proposed fuzzy item response theory. Jung & Graf [5] developed a word association game to facilitate the personalized vocabulary learning by identifying the individual learning needs. Ogata et al. [8] developed a novel ubiquitous learning log system named SCROLL, which builds the student profiles based on their learning activities in the daily life. Huang et al. [4]

[1] We re-scale the degree of the value to [0,1] for the two baselines.

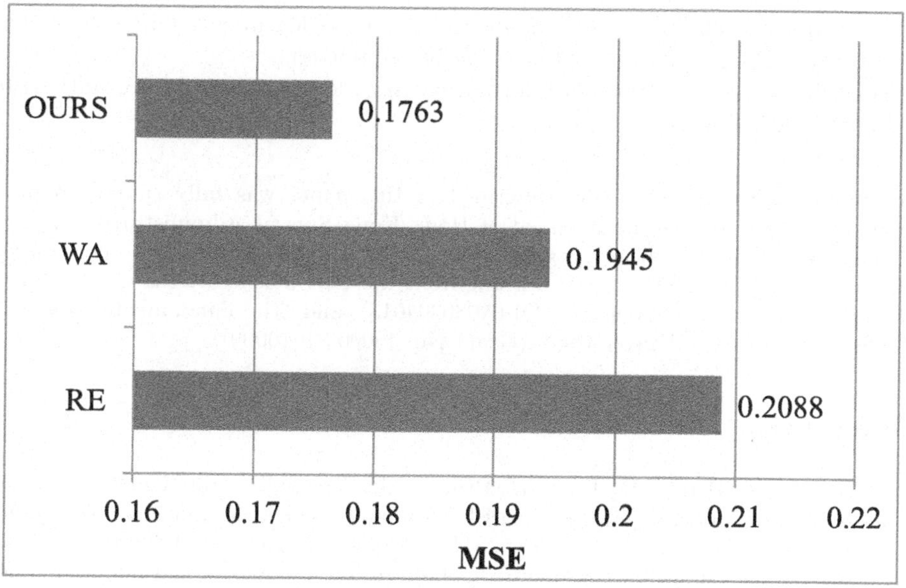

Fig. 1. The performance by using three methods

employed the learning preferences and test results to model learners and assist students in experiencing a systematic vocabulary learning process.

Furthermore, Hsu et al. [3] developed a mobile learning system to recommend reading material for guiding EFL (English as Foreign Language) students to read articles that match their preferences and knowledge levels, a prominent feature of which is that they can allow students to take notes of English vocabulary translations for the reading content in individual or shared annotation mode. Recently, Zou et al. [13] applied the involvement load hypothesis [6] for constructing load-based learner profiles so that incidental word learning tasks can be recommended. The effectiveness of a hybrid use of paper-based and electronic dictionaries has been investigated in [14].

5 Conclusion

In this paper, we present a novel framework based on an adapted vocabulary knowledge scale to predict degree of pre-knowledge of learners on vocabulary. Furthermore, we demonstrate the effectiveness of the proposed framework through the experiments on real learners. In the future, we plan to continue our research in the following directions

- We will investigate the accuracy of various vocabulary knowledge scales and try to find an optimal VKS for typical learning documents from e-learning systems;

- We will adapt the proposed framework to various learning documents so that various vocabulary learning tasks can be supported;
- We will integrate contextual information (e.g., location-based information) to improve learning effectiveness.

Acknowledgement. The work described in this paper was fully supported by a grant from Research Grants Council of Hong Kong Special Administrative Region, China (UGC/FDS11/E06/14), a grant from the National Natural Science Foundation of China (Grant No. 61502545), a grant from the Soft Science Research Project of Guangdong Province (Grant No. 2014A030304013), and "the Fundamental Research Funds for the Central Universities" (Grant No. 46000-31610009).

References

1. Chen, C.-M., Hsu, S.-H., Li, Y.-L., Peng, C.-J.: Personalized intelligent m-learning system for supporting effective english learning. In: IEEE International Conference on Systems, Man and Cybernetics, SMC 2006, vol. 6, pp. 4898–4903. IEEE (2006)
2. Chen, C.-M., Li, Y.-L.: Personalised context-aware ubiquitous learning system for supporting effective english vocabulary learning. Interact. Learn. Environ. **18**(4), 341–364 (2010)
3. Ching-Kun, H., Gwo-Jen, H., Chih-Kai, C.: A personalized recommendation-based mobile learning approach to improving the reading performance of efl students. Comput. Educ. **63**, 327–336 (2013)
4. Yueh-Min, H., Yong-Ming, H., Shu-Hsien, H., Yen-Ting, L.: A ubiquitous english vocabulary learning system. Comput. Educ. **58**(1), 273–282 (2012)
5. Jung, J., Graf, S.: An approach for personalized web-based vocabulary learning through word association games. In: International Symposium on Applications and the Internet, SAINT, pp. 325–328. IEEE (2008)
6. Laufer, B., Hulstijn, J.H.: Incidental vocabulary acquisition in a second language: The construct of task-induced involvement. Appl. Linguist. **22**(1), 1–26 (2001)
7. Li, Q., Lau, R.W.H., Wah, B.W., Ashman, H., Leung, E.W.C., Li, F., Lee, V.: Guest editors' introduction: emerging internet technologies for e-learning. IEEE Internet Comput. **13**(4), 11–17 (2009)
8. Ogata, H., Li, M., Hou, B., Uosaki, N., El-Bishouty, M.M., Yano, Y.: Scroll: supporting to share and reuse ubiquitous learning log in thecontext of language learning. Res. Pract. Technol. Enhanced Learn. **6**(2), 69–82 (2011)
9. Paribakht, T.S., Wesche, M.B.: Reading comprehension second language development in a comprehension-based esl program. TESL Can. J. **11**(1), 09–29 (1993)
10. Webb, S.: Receptive and productive vocabulary learning. Stud. Second Lang. Acquisit. **27**(1), 33–52 (2005)
11. Xie, H., Li, Q., Mao, X.: Context-aware personalized search based on user and resource profiles in folksonomies. In: Sheng, Q.Z., Wang, G., Jensen, C.S., Xu, G. (eds.) APWeb 2012. LNCS, vol. 7235, pp. 97–108. Springer, Heidelberg (2012)
12. Xie, H., Li, Q., Mao, X., Li, X., Cai, Y., Rao, Y.: Community-aware user profile enrichment in folksonomy. Neural Netw. **58**, 111–121 (2014)

13. Zou, D., Xie, H., Li, Q., Wang, F.L., Chen, W.: The load-based learner profile for incidental word learning task generation. In: Popescu, E., Lau, R.W.H., Pata, K., Leung, H., Laanpere, M. (eds.) ICWL 2014. LNCS, vol. 8613, pp. 190–200. Springer, Heidelberg (2014)
14. Zou, D., Xie, H., Wang, F.L., Wong, T.-L., Wu, Q.: Investigating the effectiveness of the uses of electronic and paper-based dictionaries in promoting incidental word learning. In: Cheung, S.K.S., Kwok, L.-F., Yang, H., Fong, J., Kwan, R. (eds.) ICHL 2015. LNCS, vol. 9167, pp. 59–69. Springer, Heidelberg (2015)

A Density-Based Clustering Algorithm with Educational Applications

Zitong Wang[1], Peng Kang[1], Zewei Wu[1], Yanghui Rao[1(✉)], and Fu Lee Wang[2]

[1] School of Data and Computer Science, Sun Yat-sen University, Guangzhou, China
{wangzt3,kangp3,wuzw3}@mail2.sysu.edu.cn, raoyangh@mail.sysu.edu.cn
[2] Caritas Institute of Higher Education, Tseung Kwan O, Hong Kong
pwang@cihe.edu.hk

Abstract. With the rapid development of Web 2.0 and interactive technologies, learning resources are proliferating online. Confronting such large volume of educational data, users require effective and efficient methodologies to organize and manage them, which reveals the importance of clustering. In this paper, we first propose a method to estimate the data density, and then apply it to merge learning resources. The proposed algorithm estimates the confidence of any two learning resources to be a pair of neighbors, and conducts clustering by combining the above confidence with the similarities among resources. Experiments are designed to evaluate the performance of our algorithm using the standard clustering datasets. We also demonstrate how to employ the proposed algorithm in educational applications, including e-learner grouping, resource recommendation and usage patterns discovery.

Keywords: Clustering analysis · Data density · E-learning · User modeling

1 Introduction

With the rapid development of interactive technologies, such as Web 2.0, social media and mobile internet, more and more people tend to obtain learning resources and knowledge online [1]. Most online learning environments are based on Web 2.0 applications that allow learners to collaborate in generating resources, giving rise to social networks that profoundly influence the learning process [2]. Thus, it is quite valuable to conduct clustering and remove redundant information, in addition to employ it in user and resource modeling for Web-based learning, such as e-learner grouping, resource recommendation and

Y. Rao—The research work described in this article has been substantially supported by the Fundamental Research Funds for the Central Universities (Project Number: 46000-31610009).

Z. Gong et al. (Eds.): ICWL 2015 Workshops, LNCS 9584, pp. 118–127, 2016.
DOI: 10.1007/978-3-319-32865-2_13

usage patterns discovery. We here aim to propose an effective clustering algorithm which could be used to discover users' learning patterns and group their learning resources and logs.

The goal of clustering is to discover the natural grouping(s) of a set of unlabeled objects such as learning resources. An operational definition of clustering can be stated as follows: Given a set of N objects, find K groups that satisfy the objects within the same group are similar, while the objects in different groups are dissimilar with each other.

Clusters differ in terms of shape and density. An ideal cluster can be defined as a set of objects that is compact and isolated [3]. In this paper, a clustering algorithm based on the density of learning resources is proposed. For each resource in the e-learning dataset, a circle with a specific radius is drawn to define the neighbors of this resource. The circle defines that any two resources within it are near enough to be a pair of neighbors. For any two resources in the dataset, the frequency they co-occur at the same circle indicates the possibility that they are actually a pair of neighbors, or in a same cluster.

The remainder of this paper is organized as follows. Some related works are discussed in Sect. 2. The proposed algorithm is described in Sect. 3. To evaluate the performance of our method, some experiments are designed in Sect. 4. In Sect. 5, we discuss the possible educational applications for the proposed algorithm. We present our conclusions and future work in Sects. 6 and 7, respectively.

2 Related Work

Clustering algorithms can be mainly divided into two groups: hierarchical and partitional.

Hierarchical clustering algorithms recursively find nested clusters either in the agglomerative mode (i.e., first assign each object to its own cluster, and then merge the most similar pair of clusters to form a cluster hierarchy) or the divisive (top-down) mode (i.e., first assign all objects to one cluster, and then divide the cluster into smaller clusters recursively). The most well-known hierarchical algorithms are single-link and complete-link [4,5].

Partitional clustering algorithms find all clusters simultaneously as a partition of the data and do not impose a hierarchical structure. One of the most popular partitional algorithm is K-means, which has a rich and diverse history as it was independently discovered in different scientific fields by Steinhaus [6], Lloyd [7], Ball and Hall [8] and MacQueen [9]. Even though K-means was first proposed about 60 years ago, it is still one of the most widely used algorithms for clustering.

Furthermore, many methods are proposed to find an appropriate measurement for distance and similarity, such as Cosine similarity, Minkowski distance [10], Mahalanobis distance [11], Pearson correlation [12], and so forth.

In the area of education, there are a large number of case studies employing clustering algorithms. For example, Perera et al. [13] used clustering and sequential pattern mining to identify problems in the collaborative learning groups automatically. They further provided the positive advice to such a kind of learning group in real-time. Huberty et al. [14] focused on the clustering of learning groups and the improvement of learning efficiencies. They suggested the following steps of clustering analysis in higher educational researches: select analysis units (e.g., students); select the set of response variables; the measurement of response variables; determine the variable score metric; select the similarity index; select the clustering method; determine the initial cluster typology; provide evidence of cluster validity; interpret the final cluster typology.

3 Methodology

E-learning occupies an increasing prominent place in education [2]. The clustering algorithm is necessary to identify groups of online resources with similar topics, in addition to distill valuable information from redundant data. For convenience of describing the proposed clustering algorithm, we use the following scenario as an example. During the break time, students are gathering to talk with each other. Then, you walk into this classroom with a camera and take photos randomly. Next, you will find the more two students appears in one photo, the higher the possibility they are friends. The idea of our algorithm derives from it.

This algorithm consists of four steps as follows:

1. For each learning resource in the dataset, draw a circle with radius r (a predefined value) around this resource. For each two resources p_i and p_j, the relevance of them can be estimated by

$$relevance[i][j] = \frac{1}{Distance(i,j)},$$

   where $Distance(i,j)$ is the norm-2 distance of p_i and p_j.
2. If the relevance of two resources p_i and p_j is larger than a predefined value $threshold1$, assign them to one cluster.
3. Remove those clusters with a small number of learning resources, set these resources as unclassified to prune the noisy data.
4. To process the rest of learning resources, we use the following two strategies:
   - **Extend:** it means for two resources p_i and p_j, if $relevance[i][j]$ is larger than a predefined value $threshold2$, which is much smaller than $threshold1$, and only one of the two resources is unclassified, assign the unclassified resource to the cluster where the classified resource belongs to.
   - **New cluster:** it means for two resources p_i and p_j, if $relevance[i][j]$ is larger than a predefined value $threshold2$, and both p_i and p_j is unclassified, assign the two resources to a new cluster.

   The above procedure is described in Algorithm 1.

If there are other learning resources unclassified after the above four steps, repeat Step 3 and Step 4 with a lower threshold.

Algorithm 1. Merging learning resources based on the relevance.

for Any two resources p_i and p_j satisfy $relevance[i][j] > threshold2$ **do**
  if both p_i and p_j are unclassified **then**
    Assign the two resources to a new cluster
  else if only p_i is unclassified **then**
    Assign p_i to the cluster where p_j belongs to
  else if only p_j is unclassified **then**
    Assign p_j to the cluster where p_i belongs to
  else
    Merge the two clusters where p_i and p_j belong to
  end if
end for

This algorithm can gather online learning resources with high similarity into one cluster and prune noisy data efficiently. Thus, it is useful for smart educational systems dealing with massive resources. The typical applications include e-learner grouping, resource recommendation and usage patterns discovery. We will introduce it in detail in Sect. 5.

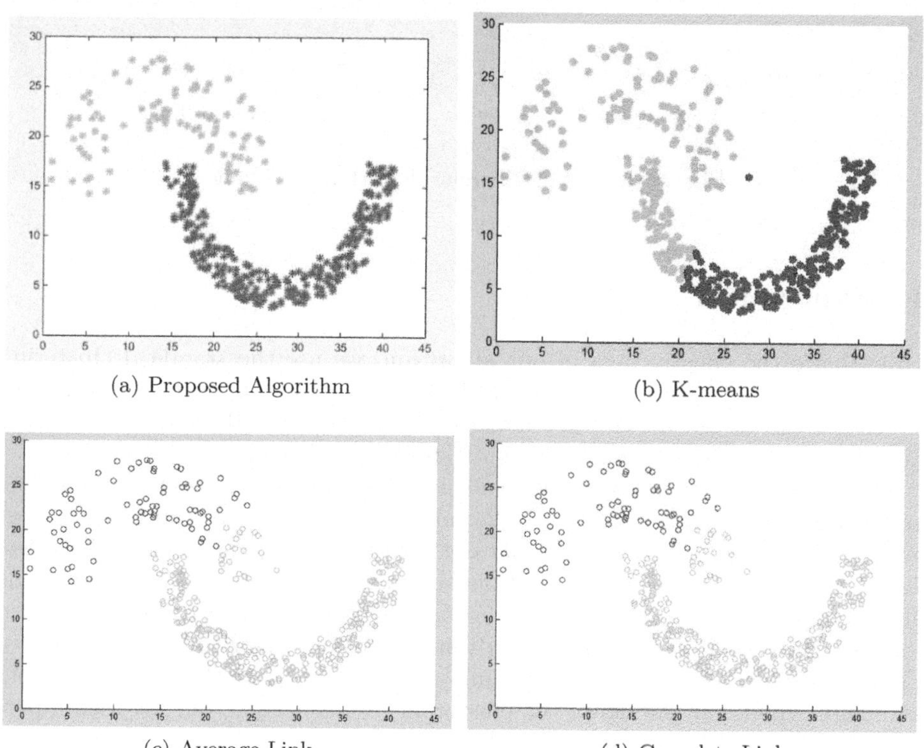

(a) Proposed Algorithm (b) K-means

(c) Average Link (d) Complete Link

Fig. 1. Results of different algorithms on Jain

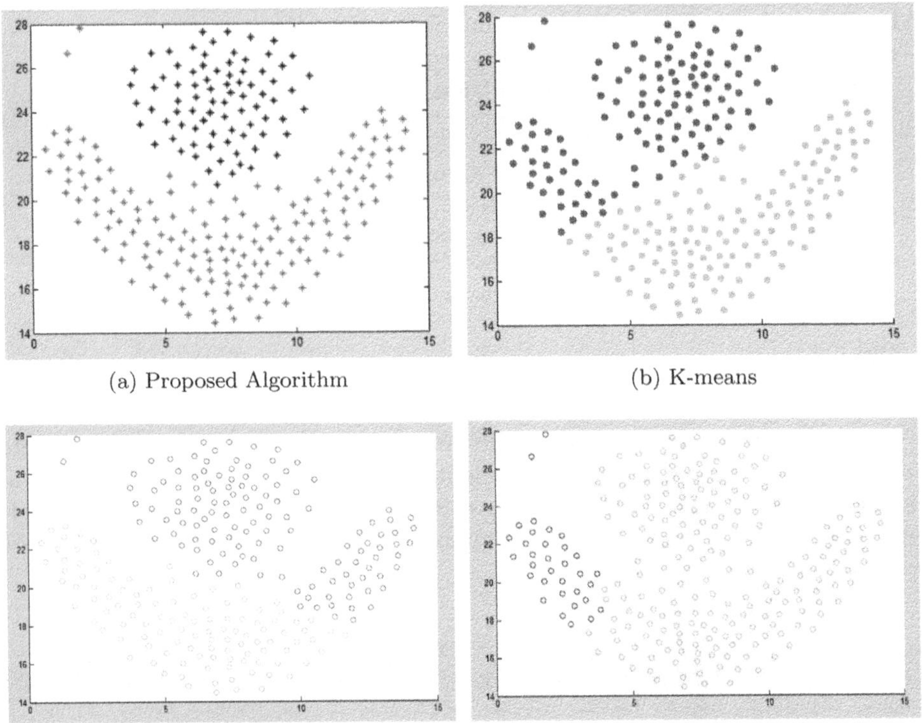

(a) Proposed Algorithm

(b) K-means

(c) Average Link

(d) Complete Link

Fig. 2. Results of different algorithms on Flame

4 Experiment

To evaluate the effectiveness of our algorithm, we use the standard clustering datasets provided by the University of Eastern Finland [15]. Some quantitative metrics, such as the normalized mutual information (NMI) and classification rate (CR) [16] are employed as the indicator of performance.

The clustering results of different algorithms on three datasets, Jain, Flame and Smileface are shown in Figs. 1, 2 and 3, respectively. We can observe that our algorithm performed well on datasets with different shapes and densities. Table 1 presents the performance of our algorithm and three baselines in terms of NMI and CR, where the value of 1 means a perfect clustering result. Compared to other clustering algorithms, the advantages of our algorithm are as follows: First, we do not need to set the number of clusters and the initial centroid manually, which may influence the clustering result. Second, our algorithm performed better on the datasets with different densities than other density-based algorithms.

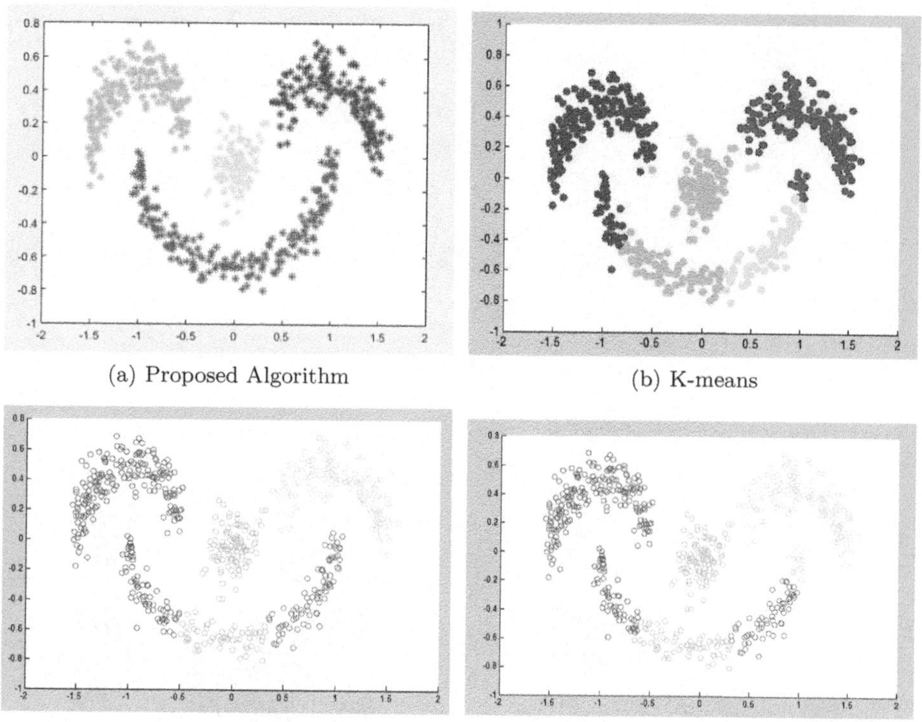

(a) Proposed Algorithm

(b) K-means

(c) Average Link

(d) Complete Link

Fig. 3. Results of different algorithms on Smileface

Table 1. Performance of different algorithms

Datasets	Proposed algorithm		K-means		Average link		Complete link	
	NMI	CR	NMI	CR	NMI	CR	NMI	CR
Jain	**0.9700**	**1**	0.3343	0.7828	0.3887	0.9464	0.3887	0.9464
Flame	**0.9100**	0.9300	0.3881	0.8375	0.6413	**1**	0.3031	0.8250
Smileface	**0.9850**	**0.9960**	0.6471	0.7888	0.5383	0.6863	0.5412	0.6863

To further test the robustness of our algorithm over clusters with different densities, we also employed other three datasets [17], Path-based1, Path-based2 and Aggregation. The clustering results and the truth result of Aggregation are shown in Fig. 4, from which we can observe that our algorithm can discover clusters with different densities effectively.

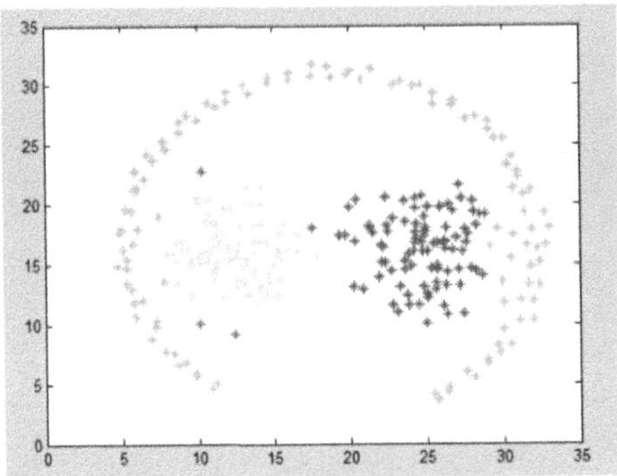

(a) Path-based1

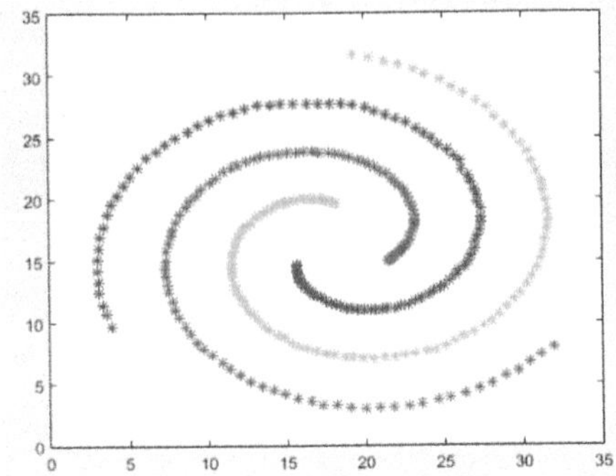

(b) Path-based2

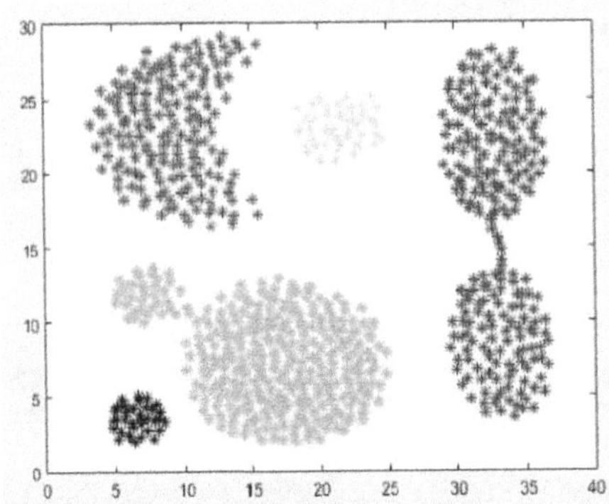

(c) Aggregation

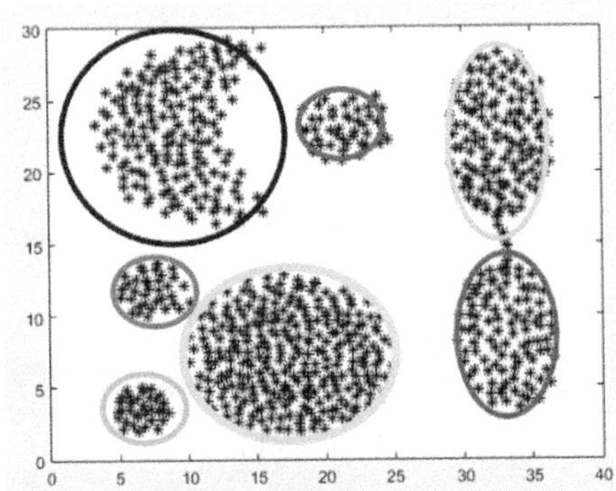

(d) Truth result of Aggregation

Fig. 4. Results of our algorithm on Path-based1, Path-based2 and Aggregation

5 Educational Applications

In this section, we briefly discuss how to apply the proposed algorithm in educational applications, as follows:

- **E-learner grouping.** E-learner grouping is critical to build both personalized e-learning systems and adaptive cooperative learning environment, especially when more than thousands of learners enrolling in a single course in popular MOOCs platforms [18], e.g., Coursera (www.coursera.com) and EdX (www.edx.org). The objective of our study is to develop an automatic algorithm that will discover the natural groupings in the unlabeled data, in which the learning effectiveness can be improved by identifying common features in each learner group.
- **Resource recommendation.** With the rapid development of educational platforms online, learners need an efficient way to achieve suitable learning resources. It is thus valuable to cluster similar objects and recommend personalized data to learners [19]. However, because of the diversity of learning

resources and noise objects, it is difficult for learners to get the right resources. The proposed algorithm was conducted based on the density of data, which can be applied to recommend a set of objects that is compact and isolated to users.

- **Usage patterns discovery.** An important research area in education and technology is how learners use e-learning systems. By exploring the learners' usage patterns, we can get an insight into learners' behaviors for adaptive e-learning. A key process in discovering the learners' usage patterns is to construct personal user profiles to help understand learners' behavior [20]. To achieve this goal, we can employ our algorithm to refine the discovery of usage patterns by distinguishing learners with different ages, interests, and other features.

6 Conclusions

In this paper, we proposed a density-based algorithm to cluster datasets with different shapes and densities. It can be applied to the user modeling for e-learning [21], event detection [22], and community discovery [23,24], which are based on clustering primarily. Furthermore, due to the fact that representative objects are important to social emotion detection [25] and many other classification-based models, the proposed clustering algorithm can be served as a preliminary step for those studies.

7 Future Work

Although our algorithm performed well on many datasets, we plan to improve the methodology and conduct more experiments to make it better in real-world educational applications.

First, our algorithm need to set a predefined value of radius r, and two threshold values which may affect the clustering results. We plan to alleviate the influence of those parameters by multi-clustering, i.e., conduct some tests by a series of values of r and thresholds, and this will produce a matrix of objects representing how many times each pair of objects can be clustered into the same cluster. We also plan to employ some methods introduced in [26]. As our algorithm with a range of values tends to obtain good results as shown in Sect. 4, we consider that with some novel multi-clustering and related methods, our algorithm will obtain more satisfied results for educational applications.

Second, the L2-norm was used as the distance measurement in our algorithm, which may be difficult for selecting the optimal thresholds for datasets with different scales. Thus, we plan to improve the distance measurement of the proposed clustering algorithm.

Acknowledgements. The research described in this paper has been supported by a grant from the Research Grants Council of the Hong Kong Special Administrative Region, China (UGC/FDS11/E06/14).

References

1. Li, Q., Lau, R.W.H., Wah, B., Ashman, H., Leung, E., Li, F., Lee, V.: Guest editors' introduction: emerging Internet technologies for e-learning. IEEE Internet Comput. **13**(4), 11–17 (2009)
2. Cela, K.L., Sicilia, M.Á., Sánchez, S.: Social network analysis in e-learning environments: a preliminary systematic review. Educ. Psychol. Rev. **27**(1), 219–246 (2015)
3. Jain, A.K.: Data clustering: 50 years beyond k-means. Pattern Recogn. Lett. **31**(8), 651–666 (2010)
4. Everitt, B.S., Landau, S., Leese, M., Stahl, D.: Cluster Analysis. Wiley, Chichester (2011)
5. Kaufman, L., Rousseeuw, P.J.: Finding Groups in Data: An Introduction to Cluster Analysis. Wiley, Hoboken (1990)
6. Steinhaus, H.: Sur la division des corp materiels en parties. Bull. Acad. Polon. Sci. **IV**(C1. III), 801–804 (1956)
7. Lloyd, S.: Least squares quantization in PCM. IEEE Trans. Inf. Theor. **28**(2), 129–137 (1982)
8. Ball, G., Hall, D.: Isodata, a novel method of data anlysis and pattern classification. In: Stanford Research Institute, Stanford, CA., Technical report (1965)
9. MacQueen, J.: Some methods for classification and analysis of multivariate observations. In: Fifth Berkeley Symposium on Mathematics, Statistics and Probability, pp. 281–297 (1967)
10. Hathaway, R., Bezdek, J., Hu, Y.: Generalized fuzzy -means clustering strategies using l_p norm distances. IEEE Trans. Fuzzy Syst. **8**(5), 576–582 (2000)
11. Mao, J., Jain, A.: A self-organizing network for hyperellipsoidal clustering (hec). IEEE Trans. Neural Netw. **7**(1), 16–29 (1996)
12. Eisen, M., Spellman, P., Brown, P., Botstein, D.: Cluster analysis and display of genome-wide expression patterns. Proc. Nat. Acad. Sci. **95**(14), 863–868 (1998)
13. Perera, D., Kay, J., Koprinska, I., Yacef, K., Zaiane, O.: Clustering and sequential pattern mining of online collaborative learning data. IEEE Trans. Knowl. Data Eng. **21**(6), 759–772 (2009)
14. Huberty, C.J., Jordan, E.M., Brandt, W.C.: Cluster analysis in higher education research. In: Smart, J.C. (ed.) Higher Education: Handbook of Theory and Research, vol. 20, pp. 437–457. Springer, Amsterdam (2005)
15. http://cs.joensuu.fi/sipu/datasets/
16. Strehl, A., Ghosh, J.: Cluster ensembles - a knowledge reuse framework for combining multiple partitions. J. Mach. Learn. Res. **3**, 583–617 (2002)
17. Chang, H., Yeung, D.-Y.: Robust path-based spectral clustering. Pattern Recogn. **41**(1), 191–203 (2008)
18. Perna, L.W., Ruby, A., Boruch, R.F., Wang, N., Scull, J., Ahmad, S., Evans, C.: Moving through MOOCs: understanding the progression of users in massive open online courses. Educ. Researcher **43**, 421–432 (2014)
19. Manouselis, N., Vuorikari, R., Assche, F.V.: Collaborative recommendation of e-learning resources: an experimental investigation. J. Comput. Assist. Learn. **26**(4), 227–242 (2010)
20. Leung, E.W.C., Li, Q.: A dynamic conceptual network mechanism for personalized study plan generation. In: Zhou, W., Nicholson, P., Corbitt, B., Fong, J. (eds.) ICWL 2003. LNCS, vol. 2783, pp. 69–80. Springer, Heidelberg (2003)

21. Zou, D., Xie, H.R., Li, Q., Wang, F.L., Chen, W.: The load-based learner profile for incidental word learning task generation. In: Popescu, E., Lau, R.W.H., Pata, K., Leung, H., Laanpere, M. (eds.) ICWL 2014. LNCS, vol. 8613, pp. 190–200. Springer, Heidelberg (2014)
22. Rao, Y.H., Li, Q.: Term weighting schemes for emerging event detection. In: IEEE/WIC/ACM International Conference on Web Intelligence and Intelligent Agent Technology (WI-IAT), pp. 105–112 (2012)
23. Xie, H.R., Li, Q., Cai, Y.: Community-aware resource profiling for personalized search in folksonomy. J. Comput. Sci. Technol. **27**(3), 599–610 (2012)
24. Xie, H.R., Li, Q., Mao, X.D., Li, X.D., Cai, Y., Rao, Y.H.: Community-aware user profile enrichment in folksonomy. Neural Netw. **58**, 111–121 (2014)
25. Rao, Y.H., Li, Q., Wenyin, L., Wu, Q.Y., Quan, X.J.: Affective topic model for social emotion detection. Neural Netw. **58**, 29–37 (2014)
26. Mimaroglu, S., Erdil, E.: Combining multiple clusterings using similarity graph. Pattern Recogn. **44**(3), 694–703 (2011)

Personalized Resource Recommendation for Staff Training in Complaint Management Systems

Li Guangjie[1], Ling Junmin[1], Shengguang Meng[2], and Liao Yumin[2(✉)]

[1] China Mobile Group Guangxi Company Limited, Nanning, China
{liguangjie,lingjunmin}@gx.chinamobile.com
[2] Zhuhai Faster Software Technology Co. Ltd., Zhuhai, China
{mengsg,liaoym}@fastersoft.com.cn

Abstract. In this paper, a personalized resource recommendation method is proposed for staff training in complaint management systems. Historical processing logs are extracted to form a complaint space. Complaint processing skills of staff members are assessed in terms of quantity, efficiency and quality on various topics. Similar staff members are clustered according to their behavioral characteristics. A resource recommendation algorithm is proposed to recommend complaint processing records from highly skilled colleagues in the cluster for the staff member to learn. Preliminary experiment results show good performance of the proposed method.

Keywords: User modeling · Staff training · User clustering · Complaint management system

1 Introduction

As the development of major modern companies, the scales of their customers grow fast and the businesses become much complex. Complaint management has become one of the most important tasks in order to ensure quality service [1]. Partially due to the frequent flow of personnel, the skills of staff members for processing customer complaints can be varied. Personalized and targeted training has therefore become an important way for staff members to improve their skills.

In order to find learning materials that are suitable for a staff member to learn, a user model has to be established to assess his/her skills on various topics [2]. In online systems, users' interaction records with the system are a handy source for user modeling, from which behavioral patterns can be extracted to map their interests/knowledge to a topic ontology [3]. The user model constructed can also be used for task generation in e-learning systems [4].

Extensive work has been done for personalized learning resource recommendation. Content-based filtering and collaborative filtering are widely used approaches [5]. Besides, folksonomy can also be used for community-based personalized recommendation and search [6].

In this paper, a personalized recommendation approach for staff training in complaint management systems in proposed. Complaint processing logs are extracted to form a

Z. Gong et al. (Eds.): ICWL 2015 Workshops, LNCS 9584, pp. 128–133, 2016.
DOI: 10.1007/978-3-319-32865-2_14

complaint space. Skills of staff members are assessed in terms of quantity, efficiency and quality on various topics. Similar staff members are clustered according to their behavioral characteristics. A learning material recommendation algorithm is presented to recommend complaint processing records for the staff members to learn.

The rest of the paper is organized as follows. Section 2 presents our resource recommendation method. Experiment results are described in Sect. 3. The conclusion is drawn in Sect. 4.

2 Personalized Resource Recommendation

The basic principle is that people are easy to learn from those who are highly skilled and are similar to them in terms of behavioral characteristics. Complaints in a company can be classified into various topics. Skills of customer service staff should be assessed for each topic, respectively. We define a topic ontology that represents the hierarchical structure of the topics. Each complaint is classified into a certain topic according to its content.

A complaint space is built from the historical complaint repository to describe the features of complaints. The complaint space is defined as a 5-tuple in (1).

$$CSpace = (PS, US, CS, f_u, f_s) \tag{1}$$

where $PS = \{p\}$ is the set of complaints in the company, $US = \{u\}$ is the set of customer service staff that handle complaints, CS is the set of complaint topics, $\forall c \in CS, c = \{p | topic(p) = c\}$, $f_u{:}PS \rightarrow US$ is a function from PS to US, $\forall p \in PS, f_u(p)$ is the customer service staff member that handles complaint p, f_s is a function, $\forall u \in US$ and $\forall c \in CS$, $f_s(u, c)$ is the skill assessment result of staff member u on complaint topic c.

With the complaint space $CSpace$ established, staff members' skills can be assessed using the accumulated historical data. For a particular topic c, a staff member's skills are assessed in 3 aspects, i.e., quantity (N), efficiency (E), and quality (Q). Each aspect is assessed according to several features extracted from $CSpace$. Formally, the assessment of staff member u on topic c is represented as a 3-tuple in (2).

$$f_s(u, c) = \left(f_N(u, c), f_E(u, c), f_Q(u, c)\right) \tag{2}$$

where f_N, f_E and f_Q are the assessment results in terms of quantity, efficiency and quality, respectively.

$$f_X(u, c) = \frac{1}{1 + e^{-\left(\sum_{i \in X}\left(R_i(u,c) - \overline{R_i}(c)\right)\right)}} \tag{3}$$

where $X \in \{N, E, Q\}$ is the set of aspects that are assessed, $R_i(u, c)$ is staff member u's rating for feature i on topic c, and $\overline{R_i}(c)$ represents the mean value of $R_i(u, c)$ for all staff members. All the feature ratings are normalized before used.

Staff members are clustered using the k-means algorithm. The feature vector of a staff member u that represents his/her behavioral characteristics is defined in (4).

$$BS(u) = (N, R_{E_1}, R_{E_2}, \cdots, R_{E_m}, R_{Q_1}, R_{Q_2}, \cdots, R_{Q_n}) \tag{4}$$

where N represents the number of complaints processed by staff member u, $R_{E_1}, R_{E_2}, \cdots, R_{E_m}$ are staff member u's ratings for features regarding processing efficiency, and $R_{Q_1}, R_{Q_2}, \cdots, R_{Q_n}$ are staff member u's ratings for features regarding processing quality.

The distance function used in the clustering algorithm is the squared Euclidean distance as shown in (5).

$$dist(u_1, u_2) = \left\| BS(u_1) - BS(u_2) \right\|_2^2 \tag{5}$$

After clustering similar staff members according to their behavioral characteristics, we can find highly skilled colleagues in the same cluster as the current staff member for whom we want to recommend learning materials. The learning material recommendation algorithm is shown in Algorithm 1.

Algorithm 1. Learning material recommendation
INPUT: $CSpace$, staff member u_0, number of recommended complaints num
OUTPUT: A set of complaints $PS_{recommend}(u_0) \subset PS$ to be recommended to u_0

$PS_{recommend}(u_0) \leftarrow \Phi$
Let $US(u_0) \subset US$ be the set of users that are in the same cluster as u_0
$N(u_0) \leftarrow \sum_c N(u_0, c)$ is the total number of complaints processed by u_0
for *each topic* $c \in CS$ **do**
  Get top-rated users $u \in US_E(u_0, c) \subset US(u_0)$ for $f_E(u, c)$
  Get top-rated users $u \in US_Q(u_0, c) \subset US(u_0)$ for $f_Q(u, c)$
  Get complaints $PS_E(u_0, c)$ and $PS_Q(u_0, c)$ processed by $US_E(u_0, c)$ and $US_Q(u_0, c)$ in c so that $|PS_E(u_0, c)|/|PS_Q(u_0, c)| = f_Q(u_0, c)/f_E(u_0, c)$
  $PS(u_0, c) \leftarrow PS_E(u_0, c) \cup PS_Q(u_0, c)$
  Randomly select $(N(u_0, c) \times num)/N(u_0)$ complaints from $PS(u_0, c)$ into $PS'(u_0, c)$
  $PS_{recommend}(u_0) \leftarrow PS_{recommend}(u_0) \cup PS'(u_0, c)$

3 Experiments

Preliminary experiments are conducted for the evaluation of the proposed method. The complaint management system in China Mobile Group Guangxi Company Limited is used as the complaint management platform in the experiment.

Historical complaint processing records of 1000 staff members are extracted from the system, which are classified into 10 topics, as shown in Table 1. The corresponding staff members are clustered according to their behavioral characteristics and their skills are assessed. Five staff members (A to E) are randomly selected from them and learning materials are recommended to them according to Algorithm 1. A survey is carried out

Table 1. Complaint topics in the system

No.	Name	Symbol
1	Service setup	B1
2	Website service	B2
3	3G service	B3
4	Refund not needed	B4
5	Refund needed	B5
6	Charges & billing	B6
7	Outbound calling	B7
8	Promotional SMS opt-out	B8
9	Supporting systems	B9
10	Internal feedback	B10

for the staff members to self-assess their skills on the topics, as well as their feedback to the recommended complaint records for them to learn from.

Figure 1 shows the overall characteristics of the topics in terms of feature ratings of staff members and the number of complaints. Among the feature ratings, *on-site solved rate* (E1) and *first contact solved rate* (E2) are those regarding processing efficiency, and *distribution accurate rate* (Q1) and *archive accurate rate* (Q2) are those regarding processing quality. From the figure we can see that the numbers of complaints vary between more than 500 and less than 5,000. Topic *service setup* (B1) gets the most complaints while *internal feedback* (B10) gets the least. For efficiency and quality related features, E2 consistently gets higher ratings than E1 for all the topics while Q2 gets higher ratings than Q1. Especially, the ratings of E1 for B3 and Q1 for B10 get rather low values compared to others.

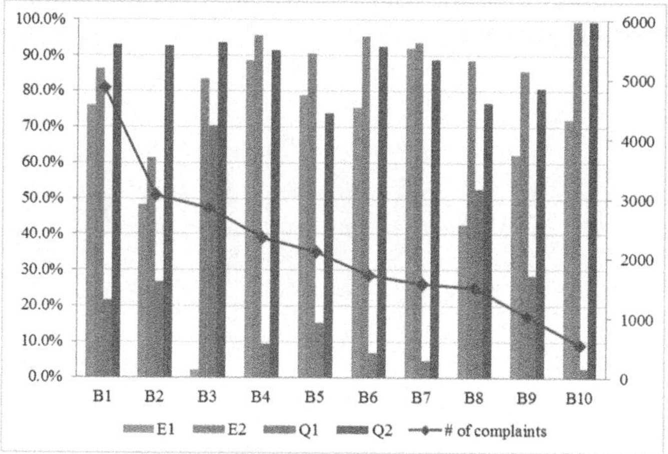

Fig. 1. Overall characteristics of the topics

Experiment results for skill assessment and learning material recommendation are as follows. Figure 2 shows the difference between computed and self-assessments. From the figure we can see that the differences of efficiency and quality skills both remain at a low level. The quality difference for staff member *D* and efficiency difference for *E* are a little higher, but are still reasonable. This indicates that the assessment of staff skills is accurate.

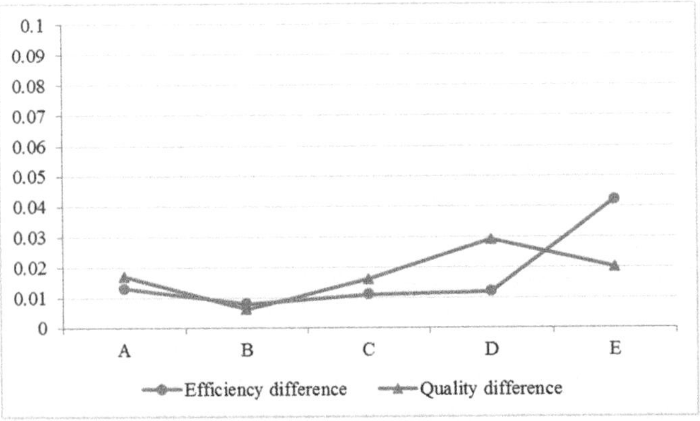

Fig. 2. Difference between computed and self-assessments

The staff members are asked in the survey to state whether they think the recommended learning materials are helpful to improve their skills. The results are shown in Fig. 3. From the figure we can see that staff members give positive feedback to the recommendations and think that the recommended materials are helpful to improve their skills. Among the topics, recommendations of *website service* (B2) and *outbound calling* (B7) are most helpful to them.

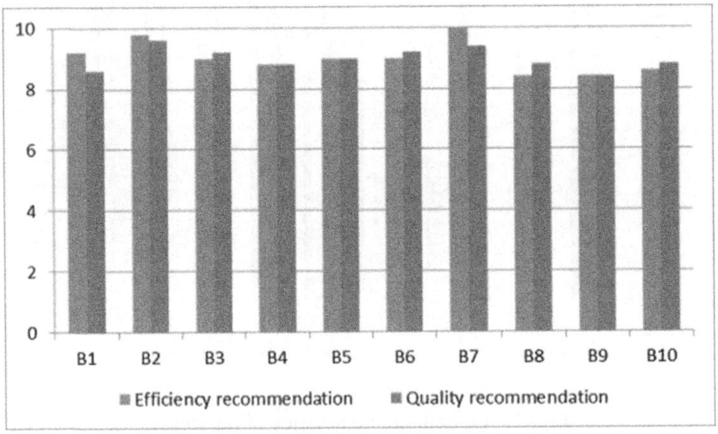

Fig. 3. Feedback of recommended learning materials

4 Conclusion

A personalized resource recommendation approach for staff training in complaint management systems is proposed in this paper. The idea is that people are easy to learn from those who are highly skilled and are similar to them in terms of behavioral characteristics. Skills of staff members are assessed and similar members are clustered. A learning material recommendation algorithm is presented to recommend complaint processing records. Experiments show good performance of the method.

References

1. Hunt, R.A., Killen, C.P., Bosch, V.G., Enriquez, F.T.: TQM and QFD: exploiting a customer complaint management system. Int. J. Qual. Reliab. Manage. **22**(1), 30–37 (2005)
2. Xie, H., Li, Q., Mao, X., Li, X., Cai, Y., Rao, Y.: Community-aware user profile enrichment in folksonomy. Neural Netw. **58**, 111–121 (2014)
3. Kim, H., Chan, P.K.: Learning implicit user interest hierarchy for context in personalization. Appl. Intell. **28**(2), 153–166 (2008)
4. Zou, D., Xie, H., Li, Q., Wang, F.L., Chen, W.: The load-based learner profile for incidental word learning task generation. In: Popescu, E., Lau, R.W., Pata, K., Leung, H., Laanpere, M. (eds.) ICWL 2014. LNCS, vol. 8613, pp. 190–200. Springer, Heidelberg (2014)
5. Adomavicius, G., Tuzhilin, A.: Toward the next generation of recommender systems: a survey of the state-of-the-art and possible extensions. IEEE Trans. Knowl. Data Eng. **17**(6), 734–749 (2005)
6. Xie, H., Li, Q., Cai, Y.: Community-aware resource profiling for personalized search in folksonomy. J. Comput. Sci. Technol. **27**(3), 599–610 (2012)

Social Network Application Development Based on Cloud Computing for Web-based Learning

Zhongyin Guo[1], Yanghui Rao[1(✉)], and Fu Lee Wang[2]

[1] School of Data and Computer Science, Sun Yat-sen University, Guangzhou, China
ericguowen@foxmail.com, raoyangh@mail.sysu.edu.cn
[2] Caritas Institute of Higher Education, Tseung Kwan O, Hong Kong
pwang@cihe.edu.hk

Abstract. Social network applications and Massive Online Open Course (MOOC) have been widely used in Web-based learning, which have generated large amounts of users and learning materials. Thus, it is useful to manage various learners and share the data efficiently. We here develop a social network application, V-share to facilitate the learner communication and share the learning data based on cloud computing. The V-share has achieved functions of sending and receiving instant voice messages, images and expressions, taking pictures, uploading learning materials instantly, and online voice call. To evaluate the effectiveness of the developed V-share, we compare it to the classical e-learning system on Web-based learning by various metrics. Experimental results based on the usage data of ten learners indicate that V-share could improve the activeness of learners in terms of the averaged browsing time, flow, learners' satisfaction, and frequency of data sharing.

Keywords: E-learning · Cloud computing · Social network software · Software development

1 Introduction

The rapid development of information technologies has been a great boon for the communication of users through instant-messaging tools, tweets, blogs and many other social network applications [1]. More and more people create and share their own content, ideas, and materials with millions of online users virtually. On the education side, e-learning or Web-based learning is becoming a trend gradually [2,3], which generates various users' information and a large volume of learning data [4]. According to a research on IOS, Android and Windows Phone platforms over 100,000 smart mobile phone users, the proportion of users who use social network applications to manage and share e-learning resources increased by 2.59 times yearly [5].

Y. Rao—The research work described in this article has been substantially supported by the Fundamental Research Funds for the Central Universities (Project Number: 46000-31610009).

Z. Gong et al. (Eds.): ICWL 2015 Workshops, LNCS 9584, pp. 134–139, 2016.
DOI: 10.1007/978-3-319-32865-2_15

In this article, we implement a social network application to share (i.e., upload and download) e-learning materials, in addition to facilitate the learner communication based on cloud computing. The process is comprehensive, including e-learning data management, user learning behavior modeling, and e-learning data sharing. Web-based learning evaluations based on the usage data of ten learners demonstrate the effectiveness of our application.

2 Related Work

In this section, we review two products directly relating to the development of our application.

Rongyun is one of the first professional instant-messaging providers of cloud services in China, which includes the instant communication and cloud services primarily. Through the cloud platform, developers do not have to set up the server-side hardware environment [6]. The instant communication and real-time network capacity can be rapidly integrated to the application. We thus employ it as our third-party host. It enables us to fulfill the design of online chat.

Sina App Engine (SAE) is a public cloud computing and distributed Web services platform in China [7]. It provides a series of distributed computing and storage services for developers, including distributed file storage, database clusters, cache and regular services, and these services could reduce the cost of software development largely.

3 Our Framework

The main framework of our application is shown in Fig. 1, which can be divided into the following three modules:

RongYun Server. The RongYun server acts as a transfer station. A user in our application first sends messages to the RongYun server through Internet, and then the server will transfer these messages to the other user.

Application Server. Application-side needs a token to access to the RongYun server, that is, an *Application Key* is necessary to request a token. However, it may generate many risks if the application-side requests a token by itself [8]. For instance, the *Application Key* may be revealed once the client code is decompiled. Thus, we create another application server, through which the application-side can get the token indirectly. Besides, we create a database to store the information of registers in the application server.

Application Design. After accomplishing the sign up and login functions on Android, we firstly get the user's username, nickname, password and email on the interface. Secondly, the program will encapsulate the above information into a string, which will be soon sent to the host in SAE. Thirdly, the host in SAE will judge the legality of username and password, i.e., check its correctness and existence. Based on the judge result, the host will send specific messages to the third-party host to get a specific token, which will be sent back to the Android

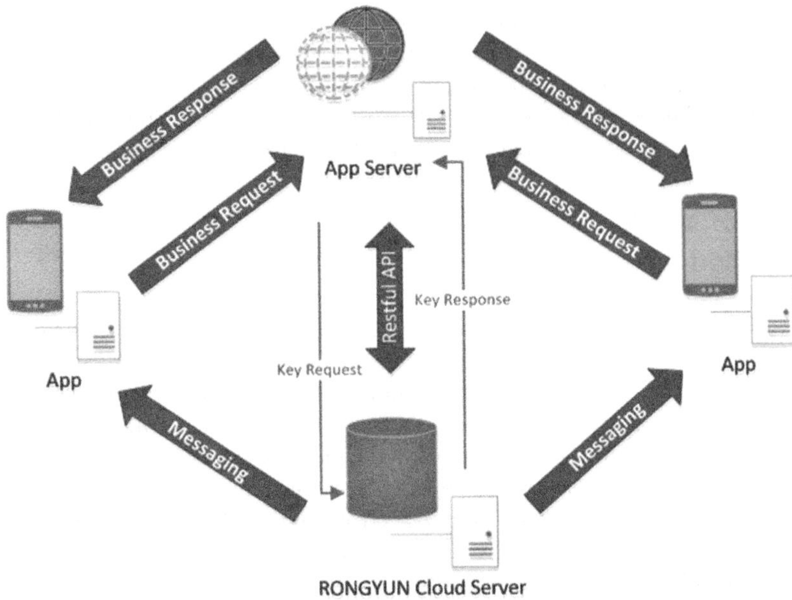

Fig. 1. System architecture

end system. Finally, the application can access RongYun server with this token, through which the instant communication is achieved. The detail of the host part in SAE is shown in Algorithm 1.

Sign Up. Application-side sends the register message, including the user identity, nickname, and password to the application server, and then the application server returns a token to it [9].

Login. With the above token, users can come back the login interface, and the user can input the user identity and the corresponding password. If matched, the application will be linked to the RongYun Server.

We implement the application by Java and Android 4.4.2 SDK. It consists of 5 class files and 4 activities. They can be divided into three major components: user interface, interaction with the server, and data processing. The interface of sign up and login is shown in Fig. 2(a).

After implementing the corresponding functions, we use two Android smart phones (SamSung S4 and Nexus 5) to test the application. The function of our application is as follows:

Single Chat: refers to two users chat one-on-one, in which the chat session is established and maintained by the third-party cloud platform (RongYun). The interface of our main menu and chat session is shown in Fig. 2(b). We have a rich library of emotional faces, which makes the chat more friendly. After exiting the chat session or off-line, users can also receive notifications.

Discussion Groups: chat among more than two users.

Algorithm 1. Procedure of sign up and login

```
if The mode is sign up then
    Get (email, username, password, nickname)
    Post-To-Host (email, username, password, nickname)
    Host-Check-Legality (repeated username? different password? used nickname?)
    if Legal then
        Return a specific token
    else if Illegal then
        Return error explanation
    end if
    Show the corresponding code
else if The mode is login then
    Get (email, password)
    Post-To-Host (email, password)
    Check the correctness
    Return the corresponding code
end if
```

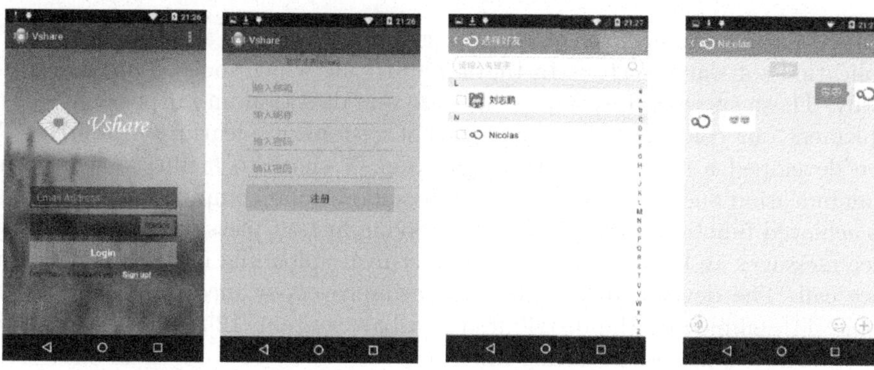

(a) Sign up and Login (b) Main menu and Chat session

Fig. 2. User interface

Session List: refers to the various sessions in accordance with the sequential order of the interface. The order of arrangement will depend on the top, the latest session, time and other factors.

4 Web-based Learning Evaluation

In this section, we evaluate the effectiveness of the developed V-share on Web-based learning. The usage data of ten learners was collected for the comparison between V-share and the classical e-learning system (baseline) [10].

Web-based learning evaluation on different applications is presented in Table 1, where p is the averaged speed of sharing (i.e., uploading and downloading) e-learning materials, t is the averaged browsing time per day, f is the

Table 1. Web-based learning evaluation on different applications

Applications	p (MB/s)	t $(hours)$	f (MB)	c	n
V-share	0.76	6.7	687	8.3	4.7
Baseline	0.89	1.2	34	4.4	1.3

averaged flow, c is the averaged value of learners' satisfaction, which ranges from 0 to 10, and n is the averaged frequency of data sharing. From which we can observe that V-share improved the activeness of learners in terms of the averaged browsing time, flow, learners' satisfaction, and frequency of data sharing. However, due to the extra module of encryption within cloud computing for our social network application, the averaged data sharing speed of V-share was slightly slower than that of the baseline.

5 Conclusion

With the rapid incremental of e-learning resources, there are many successful application softwares such as Instagram and Vine which focused on videos primarily. These successful examples indicate one direction and a possible way to implement our comprehensive management system of e-learning resources. We have developed a social network application, V-share to facilitate the learner communication and share learning data based on cloud computing. The V-share has achieved functions of sending and receiving instant messages such as instant voice messages and expressions, taking pictures, uploading instantly and online voice call. The developed V-share can be improved by incorporating the user profile [11], employing the distributed database system [12], and optimizing its e-learning teaching video sharing functions.

In the future, we plan to test our V-share in various mobile clients, such as Android smart phones and Android tablets. We will also collect and analyze the learners' data to conduct user modeling.

Acknowledgements. The research described in this paper has been supported by a grant from the Research Grants Council of the Hong Kong Special Administrative Region, China (UGC/FDS11/E06/14).

References

1. Yin, Z., Gupta, M., Weninger, T., Han, J.: LINKREC: a unified framework for link recommendation with user attributes and graph structure. In: Proceedings of the 19th International Conference on World Wide Web (WWW), pp. 1211–1212 (2010)
2. Li, Q., Lau, R.W.H., Wah, B., Ashman, H., Leung, E., Li, F., Lee, V.: Guest editors' introduction: emerging internet technologies for e-learning. IEEE Internet Comput. **13**(4), 11–17 (2009)

3. Zou, D., Xie, H., Li, Q., Wang, F.L., Chen, W.: The load-based learner profile for incidental word learning task generation. In: Popescu, E., Lau, R.W.H., Pata, K., Leung, H., Laanpere, M. (eds.) ICWL 2014. LNCS, vol. 8613, pp. 190–200. Springer, Heidelberg (2014)
4. DiMicco, J., Millen, D.R., Geyer, W., Dugan, C., Brownholtz, B., Muller, M.: Motivations for social networking at work. In: Proceedings of the 2008 ACM Conference on Computer Supported Cooperative Work (CSCW), pp. 711–720 (2008)
5. Yoshida, T.: Toward finding hidden communities based on user profiles. In: Proceedings of the IEEE International Conferences on Data Mining Workshops (ICDMW), pp. 380–387 (2010)
6. http://www.rongcloud.cn/
7. http://sae.sina.com.cn/
8. Wu, F., Huberman, B.A., Adamic, L.A., Tyler, J.R.: Information flow in social groups. Physica A Stat. Mech. Appl. **337**(1), 327–335 (2004)
9. Zaman, T.R., Herbrich, R., Gael, J., Stern, D.: Predicting information spreading in twitter. Proc. Neural Inf. Process. Syst. (NIPS) **104**(45), 598–601 (2010)
10. http://smie2.sysu.edu.cn/~xyz/mie311/
11. Xie, H.R., Li, Q., Mao, X.D., Li, X.D., Cai, Y., Rao, Y.H.: Community-aware user profile enrichment in folksonomy. Neural Netw. **58**, 111–121 (2014)
12. Hanandeh, F., Abdallah, E.E., Abdallah, A.E., Al-Daoud, E.: Simplified approach for generating integrity tests in distributed database systems. Int. J. Innov. Learn. **13**(4), 375–387 (2013)

Exploring Reviews and Ratings on Reviews for Personalized Search

Yang Yang[1], Shuyue Hu[1], Yi Cai[1(✉)], Qing Du[1], Ho-fung Leung[2], and Raymond Y.K. Lau[3]

[1] School of Software Engineering, South China University of Technology, Guangzhou, China
ycai@scut.edu.cn
[2] Department of Computer Science and Engineering, The Chinese University of Hong Kong, Hong Kong, China
[3] Department of Information System, City University of Hong Kong, Hong Kong, China

Abstract. With the development of e-commerce, e-commerce websites become very popular. People write reviews on products and rate the helpfulness of reviews in these websites. Reviews written by a user and reviews rated by a user actually reflect a user's interests and disinterest. Thus, they are very useful for user profiling. In this paper, we explore users' reviews and ratings on reviews for personalized search and propose a review-based user profiling method. And we also propose a priority-based result ranking strategy. For evaluation, we conduct experiments on a real-life data set. The experimental results show that our method can significantly improve the retrieval quality.

Keywords: Personalized search · User profiling · Review

1 Introduction

Currently, many academic works [1,2] have been done on utilizing users' data to construct user profiles for personalized search. Such data includes user's manually selected interests [3], browsing history [4], social annotations [5] and microblog behaviours [6], etc. However, few works have been done on leveraging users' reviews and ratings on reviews in e-commerce websites for personalized search.

In recent years, along with the flourish of e-commerce, e-commerce websites such as *Amazon*[1], *Epinions*[2] and *Ciao UK*[3] become widely popular. These websites allow users to write reviews on products and to rate the helpfulness of reviews. More specifically, a user may write a review on a product. We believe that users' reviews and ratings on reviews in e-commerce websites can reflect a

[1] www.amazon.com.
[2] www.epinions.com.
[3] www.ciao.co.uk.

Z. Gong et al. (Eds.): ICWL 2015 Workshops, LNCS 9584, pp. 140–150, 2016.
DOI: 10.1007/978-3-319-32865-2_16

user's concerns and unconcern. Therefore, they are very useful for user profiling and can improve the precision of user profiles. Previously, Moghaddam et al. [7] utilize them to achieve personalized review recommendation based on tensor factorization. However, existing research works do not make use of them for personalized search. To achieve personalized searching, a personalized search system ranks resources according to two guidelines: query relevance (relevance between a query and a resource profile) and user interest relevance (relevance between a user profile and a resource profile). In existing works on personalized search such as [5,8,9], a personalized search system aggregates the above relevance and return resources with highest aggregation values. To meet the basic requirement of a personalized search system, most researchers emphasize the effect of query relevance on aggregation values by assigning it with a larger weight. However, result ranking only based on aggregation values can not ensure that resources returned satisfy a user's basic information needs.

In our work, to construct a user profile, we propose a novel review-based user profiling method which can capture a user's concerns and unconcern. To ensure that resources returned satisfy a user's basic information needs, we propose a priority-based result ranking strategy. Resources should have different priority based on how well they satisfy a user's basic information needs, and they are ranked according to their aggregation values and priorities. The contributions of our work are listed as follows.

- To construct precise user profiles, we utilize them and propose a novel review-based user profiling method which can capture a user's both concerns and unconcern.
- We reveal the limitation of existing result ranking strategy which can not guarantee resources returned satisfy a user's basic information needs. To overcome the limitation, we introduce priority into result ranking strategy for personalized search.
- For evaluation, we conduct experiments on a real-life data set crawled from *Epinions*. The experimental results show that our method outperforms the stated-of-the-art methods in personalized search.

2 Related Works

Currently, many works have been done on personalized search, such as [1]. Current strategies of these works fall into two categories [10]: Automatic query expansion and result re-ranking. Automatic query expansion (AQE), such as [2,11], refers to modifying the original query by expanding it or assigning different weights to the terms in query. To re-rank the result list, Ma et al. [3] utilize users' selected interests and propose a framework that maps users' interests onto the categories of Open Directory Project(ODP). Xu et al. [5] take advantage of folksonomy and present a personalized search framework in which the rank of a web page is influenced by topic matching between user's interests and web page's topics.

3 Preliminary

In a personalized search system, there are a set of users denoted by U, a set of queries denoted by Q issued by users, and a set of resources available on web denoted by R. For each resource in R, they can be represented by some features. Thus, it is a common practice to adopt Vector Space Model (VSM) to represent a resource.

Definition 1. *A* ***resource profile*** *for a resource* j *denoted by* $\overrightarrow{R_j}$*, is a vector of* feature:value *pairs:*

$$\overrightarrow{R}_j = (f^r_{j,1} : w_{j,1}, f^r_{j,2} : w_{j,2}, ..., f^r_{j,n} : w_{j,n})$$

where n is the number of features in a resource profile, $f^r_{j,k}$ is the kth feature used for describing resource j and $w_{j,k}$ indicates to what degree the resource j possesses feature k. A higher value of the $w_{j,k}$ for the feature k indicates that to larger extent the resource j possesses feature k.

Definition 2. *A* ***user profile*** *for a user* i*, denoted by* $\overrightarrow{U}_i$*, is a vector of* feature:value *pairs, i.e.,*

$$\overrightarrow{U}_i = (f^u_{i,1} : v_{i,1}, f^u_{i,2} : v_{i,2}, ..., f^u_{i,n} : v_{i,n})$$

where n is the number of features in a user profile, $f^u_{i,k}$ is user i's k^{th} feature extracted from i's data and $v_{i,k}$ denotes user i's concern degree on feature k. The higher value of $v_{i,k}$ is, the user i is more concerned about the feature k.

Definition 3. *A* ***query*** *issued by user* i *denoted by* $\overrightarrow{q}_i$ *is a vector of terms as follows:*

$$\overrightarrow{q}_i = (t^q_{i,1}, t^q_{i,2}, ..., t^q_{i,m})$$

where $t_{u,k}$ is the kth term of the query issued by user i, and m is the total number of terms in a query. A personalized search system should return resources which not only satisfy a user's query, but also satisfy the user's personal interests. To achieve this goal, a personalized search system usually undergoes three processes.

The first one is query relevance, which is to find out to what extent resources satisfy a user's basic information needs. The query relevance of a resource can be measured by a **query relevance function** as follows:

$$\gamma : Q \times R \rightarrow [0, 1] \tag{1}$$

A higher result of γ function means that a resource is more relevant to a query.

The second process is user interest relevance, which is to determine to what degree a user is interested in resources. The user interest relevance of a resource can be measured by a **user interest relevance function** as follows:

$$\theta : U \times R \rightarrow [-1, 1] \tag{2}$$

where U is a set of users. A higher result of θ function suggests that the user is more interested in the resource. A positive result of θ implies that a user is interested in a resource, while a negative one implies that a user is disinterested in a resource.

The last process is result ranking. A personalized search system aggregates query relevance and user interest relevance for each resource, ranks resources with an appropriate strategy, and return resources in a result list to the user.

4 Review-Based User Profiling

4.1 Relationships Between Users' Reviews and Ratings on Reviews in E-Commerce Websites, and Users' Concerns and Unconcern

In an e-commerce website, a user can write a review on a product. Based on what a user mentions in an original review, we can identify what the user concerns about. Also, a user can give a helpfulness rating to a review in an e-commerce website. According to features appear in a user's high-score review, we can find out the user's concerns. By contrast, according to features appear in a user's low-score review, we can get to know what the user is disinterested in. Although most of the time, users just skip reviews they consider to be useless, for users who rate useless reviews with low scores, we consider that their low-score reviews still show what they are disinterested in.

4.2 Review-Based User Profiling Method

Based on the above illustrations, we believe that users' reviews and ratings on reviews can make a contribution to user profiling. We make the following assumptions.

Assumption 1. *For a user u, all the features mentioned in a review written by u are assumed as u's concerned features.*

Assumption 2. *For a user u, all the features mentioned in a review rated by u with a high score are assumed as u's concerned features.*

Assumption 3. *For a user u, all the features mentioned in a review rated by u with a low score are assumed as u's unconcerned features.*

According to Assumptions 1, 2 and 3, we propose a novel review-based user profiling method which can capture a user's concerns and unconcern. For each review-based user profile constructed by this method, it is composed of a user's concerned features and unconcerned features. These features are extracted from reviews written by the user or rated by the user. Formally, a review-based user profile can be defined as follows.

Definition 4. *A* ***review-based user profile (RUP)*** *for a user* i, *denoted by* $\overrightarrow{U}_i$, *is a vector of* feature:value *pairs, i.e.,*

$$\overrightarrow{U}_i = (f_{i,1}^u : v_{i,1}, f_{i,2}^u : v_{u,2}, ..., f_{i,n}^u : v_{u,n})$$

where $f_{i,k}$ is user i's k^{th} feature that occurs in reviews written by i, rated by i or both, $v_{i,k}$ represents user i's concern degree on feature k and n is the total number of features that occur in i's all kinds of reviews.

Since it is common for a feature to appear in several reviews and kinds of reviews, we make the following assumption on calculating users' concern degree on features.

Assumption 4. *For a user i and two given features x and y, if x appears in reviews written by i or reviews rated by i with a high score more frequently, we assume that i is more concerned about x than y.*

Assumption 4 illustrates that how much a user concerns about a feature is related to the feature's frequency in different kinds of reviews. A user's concern degree on a particular feature is positively correlated with the feature's frequency in the user's original reviews and high-score reviews, while it is negatively correlated with the feature's frequency in the user's low-score reviews. To be notice, a feature's concern degree is irrelevant to the sentiment words within reviews. Because sentiment words only show user's preference or detestation on a feature of a particular product, but not the user's concern degree on the feature. The following axioms in line with Assumption 4:

Axiom 1. *For a user i and a feature $k \in F_{i,w} \bigcup F_{i,h}, k \notin F_{i,l}$, if $f^w_{i,k} = 1, f^h_{i,k} = 1$ and $f^l_{i,k} = 0$, then $v_{i,k} = 1$.*

Axiom 2. *For a user i and a feature $k \notin F_{i,w} \bigcup F_{i,h}, k \in F_{i,l}$, if $f^w_{i,k} = 0, f^h_{i,k} = 0$ and $f^l_{i,k} = 1$, then $v_{i,k} = -1$.*

Axiom 3. *For a user i and two features $k_1, k_2 \in F_{i,w} \bigcup F_{i,h} \bigcup F_{i,l}$, if $f^w_{i,k_1} = f^w_{i,k_2}$, $f^h_{i,k_1} > f^h_{i,k_2}$ and $f^l_{i,k_1} = f^l_{i,k_2}$, then $v_{i,k_1} > v_{i,k_2}$.*

Axiom 4. *For a user i and two features $k_1, k_2 \in F_{i,w} \bigcup F_{i,h} \bigcup F_{i,l}$, if $f^w_{i,k_1} > f^w_{i,k_2}$, $f^h_{i,k_1} = f^h_{i,k_2}$ and $f^l_{i,k_1} = f^l_{i,k_2}$, then $v_{i,k_1} > v_{i,k_2}$.*

Axiom 5. *For a user i and two features $k_1, k_2 \in F_{i,w} \bigcup F_{i,h} \bigcup F_{i,l}$, if $f^w_{i,k_1} = f^w_{i,k_2}$, $f^h_{i,k_1} = f^h_{i,k_2}$ and $f^l_{i,k_1} > f^l_{i,k_2}$, then $v_{i,k_1} < v_{i,k_2}$.*

where $F_{i,w}$, $F_{i,h}$ and $F_{i,l}$ are sets of features appear in i's original reviews, high-score reviews and low-score reviews, $f^w_{i,k}$, $f^h_{i,k}$ and $f^l_{i,k}$ are frequencies of feature k appears in original reviews, high-score reviews and low-score reviews, respectively. Axioms 1 and 2 specify the boundary case of $v_{i,k}$. If a feature never occurs in a user's low-score reviews, but it appears in every high-score reviews and original reviews of the user, then this feature may be the user's concerned feature, hence $v_{i,k}$=1. On the contrary, if a feature never occurs in a user's original reviews or high-score reviews, but it occurs in every low-score reviews of the user, then this feature may be the user's most unconcerned feature, hence $v_{i,k}$=−1. Axioms 3, 4 and 5 specify the essence of calculating user's concerned degree for each features. The higher frequency of a feature occurs in a user's original reviews or high-score reviews is, the user is more concerned about the feature. By contrast, the higher frequency of a feature occurs in a user's low-score reviews is, the user is less concerned about the feature.

The following is a possible function to calculate concern degree of each feature, which satisfies Axioms 1–5.

$$v_{u,k} = \alpha \times \frac{|W_{i,k}|}{|W_i|} + (1-\alpha) \times \frac{\sum_{y=1, y \in H_{i,k}} \omega_{i,y}}{|H_i|} - \beta \times \frac{\sum_{y=1, y \in L_{i,k}} \omega_{i,y}}{|L_i|}, \alpha, \beta \in [0,1] \tag{3}$$

where α and β are free parameters to adjust the effects of different kinds of reviews on features' concern degree, W_i is a set of reviews written by i, H_i and L_i are sets of high-score and low-score reviews rated by i respectively, $W_{i,k}$, $H_{i,k}$ and $L_{i,k}$ are sets of i's original reviews, high-score reviews an low-score reviews containing feature k respectively, and ω helps to normalize the effects of reviews with different scores:

$$\omega_{i,y} = \begin{cases} \frac{r_{i,y} - r_{min}}{r_{max} - r_{min}} & r_{i,y} \geq \theta \\ -\frac{r_{max} - r_{i,y}}{r_{max} - r_{min}} & r_{i,y} < \theta \end{cases} \tag{4}$$

where $r_{i,y}$ indicates user i's rating on review y, r_{max} and r_{min} are the maximal and minimal helpfulness rating of a review respectively, and θ is a threshold to distinguish high-score reviews from the low-score reviews. A higher value of α implies a user's original reviews play more important roles in calculation of $v_{i,k}$. Besides, a higher value of β indicates that a user's low-score reviews have a greater impact on the calculation of a feature's concern degree. By utilizing users' reviews and ratings on reviews in e-commerce websites, our review-based user profiling method can construct user profiles which is able to reflect a user's concerns and unconcern.

5 Resource Profiling

To identify to what extent a feature in a resource profile can describe a resource, we adopt the normalized term frequency (NTF) [9] to measure the weight of feature as follows.

$$w_{j,x} = \frac{c_{j,x}}{|C_j|} \tag{5}$$

where $c_{j,x}$ is times of feature x used for describing resource j, C_j is the set of features of resource j, and $|C_j|$ indicates the total number of features of resource j.

6 Personalized Search

6.1 Query Relevance Measurement and User Interest Relevance Measurement

In our work, we adopt the Cosine Similarity measurement to realize the first two processes of personalized searching. The value of query relevance function γ in

Eq. 1 and user interest relevance function θ in Eq. 2 can be obtained by Eqs. 6 and 7 respectively.

$$\gamma(\overrightarrow{q}_i, \overrightarrow{R}_j) = \frac{\overrightarrow{R_j} \cdot \overrightarrow{q_i}}{|\overrightarrow{R_j}| \times |\overrightarrow{q_i}|} \tag{6}$$

$$\theta(\overrightarrow{U}_i, \overrightarrow{R}_j) = \frac{\overrightarrow{U_i} \cdot \overrightarrow{R_j}}{|\overrightarrow{U_i}| \times |\overrightarrow{R_j}|} \tag{7}$$

where $\overrightarrow{U}_i$ is user i's user profile, $\overrightarrow{R}_j$ is resource j's resource profile and $\overrightarrow{q}_i$ is a query issued by user i.

6.2 Limitations of Current Result Ranking Strategy

In current works on personalized search [8,9], to rank resources, most researchers first adopt one of the multiplication aggregation functions or the addition aggregation functions to aggregate resources' query relevance and user interest relevance. For example, Xu et al. [5] adopt Weighted Borda-Fuse as the aggregation function shown as follows:

$$Aggre(\overrightarrow{q}_i, \overrightarrow{U}_i, \overrightarrow{R}_j) = \delta \cdot \gamma(\overrightarrow{q}_i, \overrightarrow{R}_j) + (1-\delta) \cdot \theta(\overrightarrow{U}_i, \overrightarrow{R}_j) \tag{8}$$

where δ is a free parameter to adjust the effects of query relevance and user interest relevance on aggregation values, $\gamma(\overrightarrow{q}_i, \overrightarrow{R}_j)$ is query relevance and $\theta(\overrightarrow{U}_i, \overrightarrow{R}_j)$ is user interest relevance. Then they rank resources according to their aggregation values. A resource with a higher aggregation value gets a higher position in a result list.

To meet the basic requirement of a search system, they usually assume that query relevance is more important than user interest relevance in an aggregation function. Thus, they assign a larger weight to query relevance in an aggregation function. For example, δ in Eq. 8 may be assigned with a value in the range $[0.5, 1)$. However, no matter how large the weight of query relevance is, there is always a chance that resources which well match a user's interest but fails to satisfy a user's basic information needs are returned. Thus, assigning query relevance with a larger weight still can not ensure that resources returned by a personalized search system satisfy a user's basic information needs.

6.3 Priority-Based Result Ranking Strategy

To overcome the limitation and meet the basic requirement of a search system, we introduce priority into result ranking strategy. Instead of assuming that query relevance is more important than user's interest relevance, we assume that query relevance is prior to user interest relevance. Resources returned by a personalized search system should satisfy a user's basic information needs and had better satisfy a user's interests. More specifically, resources in a result list are assigned with different priorities according to how many keywords of a query they satisfy. Resources whose profiles contain all of the keywords of the query gain the highest priority, while resources whose profiles contain none of the keywords of the query gain the lowest priority. For resources with different priorities, resources with higher priority always get higher positions than resources with lower priority. For resources with the same priority, they are ranked according to their aggregation values of query relevance and user interest relevance. Even if a resource with lower priority gains a high aggregation value due to its matching with the user profile, the position of this resource in a result list will be lower than any of the resources with higher priority (satisfying more keywords of a query). By introducing priority into personalized search, our method ensure that resources returned satisfy a user's basic information needs.

7 Experiments

7.1 Data Set

The data set we use to evaluate our method is crawled from *Epinions*. We create a subset of 1345 users, who writes or rates 10–50 reviews about electronics or computer hardware from our data set, and the subset also contains 4430 reviews and 29395 user-review-rate tuples. On average, each user writes 3 reviews and rates 22 reviews. Among 29395 user-review-rate tuples in the subset, the ratings of almost 95 % of them is 5. We randomly split the data set into two parts, 80 percent of them are used as the training set and 20 percent of them are used as the test set. To test our method, we randomly extract two keywords from each review in the test set and take these keywords as input queries. In our experiments, we assume that relevant reviews for a query issued by user i are referred to reviews which not only satisfies all of the keywords of the query, but also written by i or rated by i with a high score.

7.2 Evaluation Metrics

We employ two metrics here to evaluate the effectiveness of our method.

The first metric we use is Mean Reciprocal Rank (MRR) which is a statistic for evaluating a ranking to a query. The reciprocal rank of a query result is the multiplicative inverse of the rank of the first correct answer. The mean reciprocal rank is the average of the reciprocal ranks of results for all the queries in the test set. It's defined as follows:

$$MRR = \frac{1}{m}\sum_{i=1}^{m}\frac{1}{rank_i} \quad (9)$$

where m is the number of queries in the test set, $rank_i$ is the position of the relevant resource in a result list for the query i. The larger the MRR is, the faster and easier for the user to find out the reviews he or she wants.

The second metric we use is Precision@n, which is used for measuring how often relevant resources are in the top-N result list. It's defined as follows:

$$Precision@n = \frac{M}{Q} \quad (10)$$

where Q is the number of all queries in the test set and M denotes the times of relevant resources returned in the top-N result list for each query in the test set. The larger the Precision@n is, the more effectiveness our method is.

7.3 Baseline Methods

Considering this is the first effort to apply users' reviews and ratings on reviews to personalized search, we compare our method with three most similar works [5,8,9] in collaborative tagging system. A review can be considered as a resource in an e-commerce website and features mentioned in a review can be considered as tags annotated on a resource (review). Xu et al. [5] (denoted by SIGIR'08) measure the weight of each tag in the user profile based on TF-IDF and BM25, and adopts the cosine similarity to measure the relevance. Vallet et al. [8] (denoted by ECIR'10) refine the measurement of tags in the user profile by using an aggregation of BM25 values. Cai et al. [9] (denoted by CIKM' 10) reveal the limitations of measuring tags' weights based on TF-IDF and BM25, and propose a novel personalized search framework.

7.4 Experimental Results

We compare our methods with the baseline methods. The experimental results of our methods and baseline methods are shown in Figs. 1 and 2. Figure 1 describes the comparison of our method and the baseline methods on MRR metric. According to it, the MRR value of RUP, CIKM'10, SIGIR'08 and ECIR'10 are 0.220, 0.199, 0.137 and 0.089 respectively. RUP significantly outperforms CIKM'10 by 10 %.

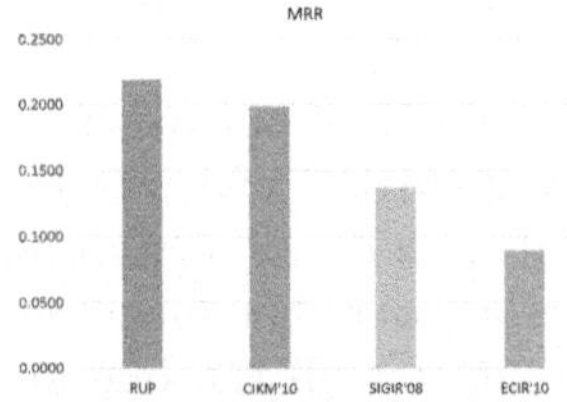

Fig. 1. Comparison between our method and baseline methods on *MRR*

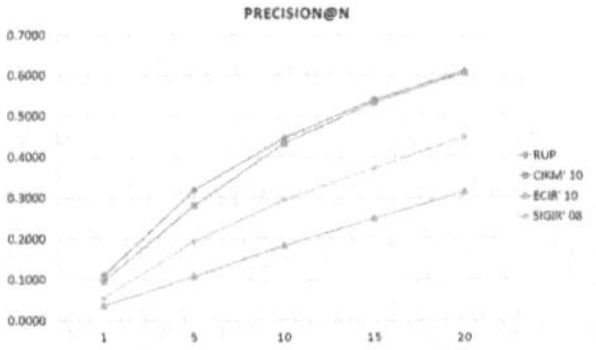

Fig. 2. Comparison between our method and baseline methods on *Precision@n*

Figure 2 depicts the trend of RUP, CIKM'10, SIGIR'08 and ECIR'10 on *Precision* metric with different n. The number of n denotes the size of a result list. From Fig. 2, with the increase of n, the *Precision* of all four methods increase. For all values of n (i.e., from 1 to 20), our method outperforms the baseline methods. When n=1 and n=5, the advantage of our method is obvious. When n=1, the *Precision*@1 value of RUP, CIKM'10, SIGIR'08 and ECIR'10 are 11 %, 9.5 %, 5.5 % and 3.5 %. When n=5, the *Precison*@5 of RUP, CIKM'10,

SIGIR'08 and ECIR'10 are 31.8 %, 28.1 %, 19.3 % and 10.7 %. Based on the comparison between our method and the baseline methods, we can conclude that our method which utilize both users' reviews and ratings on reviews to construct user profiles and introduce priority into the result ranking can significantly improve the personalized performance.

8 Conclusions

In this paper, we explore users' reviews and ratings on reviews for user profiling in personalized search. In order to improve the precision of user profiles, we propose a review-based user profiling method RUP, which can capture both a user's concerns and unconcern. Besides, to ensure a personalized system return resources that can satisfy a user's basic information needs, we introduce priority into personalized search. The experimental results show that our method can outperform the baseline methods.

Acknowledgement. This work is supported by National Natural Science Foundation of China (Grant NO. 61300137), the Guangdong Natural Science Foundation, China (NO. S2013010013836), Science and Technology Planning Project of Guangdong Province China NO. 2013B010406004, the Fundamental Research Funds for the Central Universities, SCUT.

References

1. Ghorab, M.R., Zhou, D., OConnor, A., Wade, V.: Personalised information retrieval: survey and classification. User Model. User-Adapt. Interact. **23**(4), 381–443 (2013)
2. Haiduc, S., De Rosa, G., Bavota, G., Oliveto, R., De Lucia, A., Marcus, A.: Query quality prediction and reformulation for source code search: the refoqus tool. In: Proceedings of the 2013 International Conference on Software Engineering, Series ICSE 2013, pp. 1307–1310. IEEE Press, Piscataway (2013). http://dl.acm.org/citation.cfm?id=2486788.2486991
3. Ma, Z., Pant, G., Sheng, O.R.L.: Interest-based personalized search. ACM Trans. Inf. Syst. (TOIS) **25**(1), 5 (2007)
4. Matthijs, N., Radlinski, F.: Personalizing web search using long term browsing history. In: Proceedings of the Fourth ACM International Conference on Web Search and Data Mining, Series WSDM 2011, pp. 25–34. ACM, New York (2011). http://doi.acm.org/10.1145/1935826.1935840
5. Xu, S., Bao, S., Fei, B., Su, Z., Yu, Y.: Exploring folksonomy for personalized search. In: Proceedings of the 31st Annual International ACM SIGIR Conference on Research and Development in Information Retrieval, Series SIGIR 2008, pp. 155–162. ACM, New York (2008). http://doi.acm.org/10.1145/1390334.1390363
6. Younus, A., O'Riordan, C., Pasi, G.: A language modeling approach to personalized search based on users' microblog behavior. In: Rijke, M., Kenter, T., Vries, A.P., Zhai, C.X., Jong, F., Radinsky, K., Hofmann, K. (eds.) ECIR 2014. LNCS, vol. 8416, pp. 727–732. Springer, Heidelberg (2014)

7. Moghaddam, S., Jamali, M., Ester, M.: Etf: extended tensor factorization model for personalizing prediction of review helpfulness. In: Proceedings of the Fifth ACM International Conference on Web Search and Data Mining, Series WSDM 2012, pp. 163–172. ACM, New York (2012). http://doi.acm.org/10.1145/2124295.2124316
8. Vallet, D., Cantador, I., Jose, J.M.: Personalizing web search with folksonomy-based user and document profiles. In: Gurrin, C., et al. (eds.) ECIR 2010. LNCS, vol. 5993, pp. 420–431. Springer, Heidelberg (2010). doi:10.1007/978-3-642-12275-0-37
9. Cai, Y., Li, Q.: Personalized search by tag-based user profile and resource profile in collaborative tagging systems. In: Proceedings of the 19th ACM International Conference on Information and Knowledge Management, pp. 969–978. ACM (2010)
10. Pitkow, J., Schütze, H., Cass, T., Cooley, R., Turnbull, D., Edmonds, A., Adar, E., Breuel, T.: Personalized search. Commun. ACM **45**(9), 50–55 (2002). doi:10.1145/567498.567526
11. Carpineto, C., Romano, G.: A survey of automatic query expansion in information retrieval. ACM Comput. Surv. (CSUR) **44**(1), 1 (2012)

Designing an Online Learning and Peer Feedback Platform for GRE Writing Test Preparation

Simon Ho Wang(✉)

Department of English, City University of Hong Kong,
83 Tat Chee Avenue, Kowloon, Hong Kong
simon.wang@my.cityu.edu.hk

Abstract. In this paper, an online platform for learning GRE writing and providing peer feedback is designed. The platform consists of 4 modules: the first module helps the users to get familiar with the rhetorical moves and linguistic features found in the model essays; the second module trains the users to recognise the problems with content and form and prepare the users for peer review; the third module simulates the test environment for the users to practice writing with time constraints; the final module allows the users to review other users' writing from module 3.

1 Introduction

Every year, thousands of Chinese students take GRE tests in order to apply for US graduate schools. In addition to verbal and math sections, they also need to take the GRE writing tests, which consist of two 30-min tasks. The writing test is very difficult for Chinese students as it is primarily designed to assess the critical thinking skills for American students who use English as their first language. Despite the challenges of GRE writing tests, neither English teachers in Chinese universities nor TESOL researchers in US universities pay much attention to these issues as the test is not part of the language teaching curriculum in Chinese and US universities. The tutorial schools such as New Oriental offer some training for GRE but most students still performed rather poorly in the writing tests.

In order to prepare for GRE tests and perform better in the writing tests, some Chinese students joined online communities to seek help from fellow test takers from all over the country and worldwide. GTER.net, one of the most prominent online communities for studying abroad, offers a forum for GRE test takers to discuss problems and difficulties related to the GRE writing tests. Also at GTER forum for GRE writing, students post their practice essays for the tests and offer peer feedback on one another's essays.

In this paper, some ideas about how to design and develop such a system are discussed. The main purpose of the system is to enable the students to write practice essays and offer peer feedback to their fellow test takers. The system would incorporate a number of technological elements commonly found in CALL and take into account some research

Z. Gong et al. (Eds.): ICWL 2015 Workshops, LNCS 9584, pp. 151–158, 2016.
DOI: 10.1007/978-3-319-32865-2_17

findings from the action research project of the author's PhD study. In particular, genre theory (Swales, 1990) will be drawn upon to inform the design of the system.

The rest of the paper is organised as follows. Section 2 reviews the related studies on teacher and peer feedback, computer assisted feedback system, genre theory and participatory genre analysis. Section 3 describes the action research project through which data about the GRE writing are collected. Section 4 discusses the main components of the online peer feedback system and a number of design considerations. The paper is concluded in Sect. 5 with some remarks on the contribution of the paper, the limitations and the direction for future studies.

2 Literature Review

2.1 Studies on Teacher and Peer Feedback

Researchers have been interested in how teacher and peer feedback help students improve their writing. Roughly speaking, feedback could be provided on the form and content of student writing (Ashwell, 2000). While peer feedback is considered a useful form of feedback for students to revise their writing (Y.-F. Yang, 2015), it is generally believed that students prefer teacher feedback as they place more trust on the advice from teachers (Paulus, 1999; Yang et al. 2006).

2.2 Computer Assisted Language Learning Tools

With the advent of inexpensive computing and the Internet, a variety of technologies have been developed to assist language teaching and learning. Recently, Golonka et al. (2014) have reviewed some of the technologies, a number of which are relevant to the design of the present system. Internet forum or message board, for example, offers an asynchronous communication platform for students and teachers to discuss different issues related to language learning and offer feedback not in real time. One of the major benefits of the system is that students may be engaged in an equal way without much anxiety. In addition, all the materials related to the discussion could be easily archived for future reference. A related technology-driven practice is for students to keep an e-portfolio, which is basically a collection of all the writing done by students over a period of time. Corpus is another useful tool as students may consult it as textual mentor to decide the appropriate usage of certain words and phrases. Corpus-based approaches have been taken to identify collocation errors found in the student essays and feedback on the miscollocation might be provided automatically (Futagi et al. 2008; Shei and Pain, 2000).

Also relevant is the e-rater and Criterion developed by ETS to automatically assess the quality of essays written by test candidates of TOEFL and GRE and to provide feedback to the test candidates preparing for the tests. While e-raters often take into account a number of different features including content and language forms (Attali and Burstein, 2006; Monaghan and Bridgeman, 2005; Powers et al. 2002), Criterion that is publicly available only provides limited feedback on the language forms of student essays (Attali, 2004).

While different technologies have been used in language learning, teaching and testing, there is no system that is publicly available for helping students preparing for standardized tests such as GRE and TOEFL. This paper attempts to explore some possible features that may be incorporated into such a system.

2.3 Genre Theory and Move Analysis

To introduce the design of the system, it is useful to discuss the genre-based approach to teaching writing. In the so-called post-process era of second language writing research (Atkinson, 2003), genre theory is particularly helpful in describing the rhetorical convention and the linguistic features of the texts written by expert writers who provide textual mentors for the novice writers. In the field of English for Research Publication Purposes (ERPP), numerous studies have been conducted to analyze the different sections of research articles and to identify the moves and steps that are usually found in the corpora made of published articles in order to adequately describe the genres (e.g. Brett, 1994; Bruce, 2009; Hirano, 2009; Hopkins and Dudley-Evans, 1988; Lim, 2006).

The moves identified in different sections of research articles from various disciplines could be used to describe the genre and to help novice writers to learn how to write in a way that may meet the expectations of the discourse community and the gate keepers, i.e. the reviewers and the editors of the journals. For example, based on a study of 252 research articles from 7 disciplines, Peacock (2002) found that the following 9 moves are frequently found in the corpus although the specific moves may vary in frequencies across disciplines:

1. information move
2. statement of result
3. finding
4. (un)expected outcome
5. reference to previous research
6. explanation
7. claim
8. limitation
9. recommendation

Pedagogically speaking, teaching students the concepts of moves and the generic features of the target genres can help students to develop a framework that may guide them in writing essays more effectively. This is one of the features of the system described in this paper.

3 Action Research on GRE Writing Tests

3.1 Keeping a Blog to Provide Model Essays and Outlines for the Entire Issue and Argument Pools

As I mentioned earlier, I have been helping Chinese students with their GRE writing tests at GTER, which is an asynchronous discussion forum. In the forum, I opened one thread as my blog on GRE writing, where I wrote full essays or detailed outlines on the issues and arguments disclosed by ETS. I have now finished writing full essays or outlines for all the 149 issues (31 outlines and 53 full essays, excluding 65 similar issues) and all the 174 arguments (44 full essays and 41 outlines, excluding 89 similar arguments). Students are encouraged to read and imitate the model essays or outlines I wrote before they wrote their own essays.

3.2 Provide Online Feedback on Content and Form

As a featured guest of the GRE writing sub-forum, I was granted the privileges to edit other members' posts in the sub-forum. Using these privileges, I provided feedback on both content and form issues by editing the posts of the practice essays written by the members. By reviewing over 300 practice essays by about 35 members, I have identified a number of recurrent issues related to content and form.

3.2.1 10 Issues Related to Content

1. Misunderstand the essay prompt: the student writers misunderstood the essay prompts in their essays;
2. Inappropriate thesis statement or topic sentences: the essay is seriously flawed as the thesis statement or the topic sentences that summarize the entire essays or the individual paragraphs have to be rewritten;
3. The proposed alternative situation is not appropriate: this is a problem more common in argument tasks where the student writers are expect to discuss alternative situations that may challenge the arguments;
4. Failure to address key words in the essay prompts: the essays missed some important issues or points that have to be addressed as shown in the keywords in the essay prompts;
5. Failure to follow the writing instructions: the writing instructions in GRE are specific and explicit, e.g. students may have to discuss the assumptions made in an argument.
6. Lack of supporting details: students may fail to provide supporting details to further elaborate their points or convince the readers;
7. Hedging: it is important to use hedging frequently in the argument tasks as the writers need to explore different possibilities;
8. Cohesion and transition: students may fail to focus on one point in a paragraph or do not pick up a point discussed in the previous sentence in the next.
9. Excessive contents: contents may have to be deleted to avoid confusion or wordiness;
10. Inappropriate examples: while examples are often used to support a point in issue tasks, students may choose examples that are not suitable or relevant.

3.2.2 10 Issues Related to Form

1. Errors of verb forms: verbs may be misused breaking the grammatical rules of tense or agreement;
2. Sentence structure: the sentence is not grammatically correct and needs to be revised;
3. Form of nouns: errors related to the use of nouns;
4. Vague or confusing meanings: the reader may not figure out the meaning of the whole sentences;
5. Unclear reference: it is not clear what the pronouns refer to in the sentences;
6. Diction and collocation: wrong words were selected or used with other words;
7. Part of speech: the words of different POS should have been used to be grammatically correct;
8. Insufficient information: the writers should provide further information to be more specific about the meaning of a phrase;
9. Run-on sentences: sentences should be broken into two to avoid confusion;
10. Direct translation from Chinese into English: the sentences were poorly written due to the negative transfer of L1 and attempts to translating Chinese thoughts into English.

3.3 The Needs for an Online Learning and Peer Feedback System

While the feedback on student writing has been useful in that 10 students have earned 4.0 or above in GRE writing tests after receiving such feedback, reviewing the student essays and giving feedback are too time-consuming to be sustainable. To help more students, it is useful to build an online platform that may guide the users to practice writing GRE essays and provide peer feedback. It is hoped that students may learn how to write effective GRE essays by imitating model essays first; they would then receive some training on recognizing the issues related to content and form; finally, they can use the system to provide peer review for one another.

4 Designing the Online Peer Feedback Platform

4.1 Overview of the Platform

The platform consists of 4 interrelated modules: in module 1, the users are guided to study some model essays and learn to recognize the moves and linguistic features found in the model essays; in module 2, the users receive some training for identifying the problems related to content and form in student essays; with some familiarity with model essays and problems in student essays, the users can then practice writing GRE essays in module 3; in module 4, the users review others' practice essays and provide peer feedback.

4.2 Module 1: Get Familiar with the Genre and Linguistic Features of Model Essays

In this module, the users will be presented with the model essays at sentence and paragraph levels. For each sentence, there will be labels indicating the rhetorical moves realized by the sentence and the linguistic features in the sentence that the users may imitate. For example, the system may present a paragraph highlighting the moves and linguistic features in Table 1.

Table 1. Rhetorical moves and linguistic features highlighted in a paragraph

Sentences	Rhetorical moves	Linguistic features
The first question we need to investigate is why shoppers came to the Central Plaza less often and spent less money here	Raise a question in the topic sentence	Complement clause
It is assumed in the argument that skateboarding was the main reason	Reiterate the original argument	Subject it-extraposition
But we need more information about shoppers' attitudes towards skateboarding and whether or not skateboarding had been a hassle to the shoppers and shop owners here	Point out other issues	Noun clause
Maybe the decline of popularity and business was due to the relatively high prices of the goods sold in Central Plaza or the opening of a fancier shopping mall in the region	Explore alternative scenario/causes	Parallel structure of noun phrases
If that was the case, prohibiting skateboarding would not improve the situation	Discuss the implication to the argument	-ing clause

It is important to note that the moves and linguistic features listed in the Table 1 are not exhaustive. By analysing a corpus of model essays in advance, a comprehensive list of moves and linguistic features will emerge and all the sentences would be tagged for the rhetorical moves and linguistic features. A list of recurrent rhetorical moves and linguistic features found in the corpus would be compiled along with their frequencies. The users will then be introduced such moves and linguistic features in context with examples from the corpus. Once they are familiar with the moves and linguistic features, they will be given some multiple choices to see if they could recognise the moves and linguistic features independently. Once they are fully aware of how model essays are written, they are ready to move on to the next step: training for peer review.

4.3 Module 2: Training for Recognising Problems Related to Content and Form

Similar to module 1, this module is based on a thorough analysis of a learner corpus composed of the practice essays written by students at GTER. As stated in Sect. 3.2,

20 issues related to content and form have been identified when I reviewed GRER students' practice essays. All the sentences are tagged with the specific content and form issues. The system would help the users to recognise these issues by first presenting them the examples and then giving them multiple choice questions.

4.4 Module 3: Timed Writing Practice with Keystroke Recording

Since students only have 30 min for issue and argument tasks, timed practices are essential part of test preparation. Students will not earn good scores if they have good ideas for the essay questions but could not finish writing the essays on time. This module will simulate the real tests by giving students a randomly selected essay questions from the issue or argument pool and allow only 30 min for writing. One feature of the module is that a keystroke recording program will be running in the background to record the details of when the writers paused and for how long. Data can be collected by asking students in retrospect what stopped them and efforts could be made to help students to deal with whatever problems they might have that affected their fluency. Another obvious benefit of this module is that students and teachers can easily track all the essays written by the students, which is essentially the management of e-Portfolio (Aydin, 2010).

4.5 Module 4: Peer Feedback on Student Writing

In this module, the users will be given other students' essays from module 3 and asked to identify problems related to content and form they have learned about in module 2. In addition to essays written by other users, they will also be given practice essays from the learner corpus to rate their accuracy in identifying the problems. Practice essays could be sent to multiple users as paragraphs or sentences so that the best answers could be selected based on the previous accuracy of the users as well as the consistency across the reviews of different users. Students may then revise their writing based on the peer feedback and their revised versions could be sent back to module 4 for further peer review.

5 Conclusion

In this paper, I describe how an online learning and peer feedback platform could be developed to help GRE test candidates prepare for the writing test, which has been widely regarded as the most challenging writing tests for Chinese students interested in US graduate schools. The proposed system incorporates some research findings generated from my action research projects focusing on how to help Chinese students perform better in GRE writing tests. Genre theory and research insights from feedback studies in second language writing have informed the design of the system.

References

Ashwell, T.: Patterns of teacher response to student writing in a multiple-draft composition classroom: is content feedback followed by form feedback the best method? J. Second Lang. Writ. **9**(3), 227–257 (2000)

Atkinson, D.: L2 writing in the post-process era: Introduction. J. Second Lang. Writ. **12**(1), 3–15 (2003)

Attali, Y.: Exploring the feedback and revision features of criterion. J. Second Lang. Writ. **14**, 191–205 (2004)

Attali, Y., Burstein, J.: Automated essay scoring with e-rater® V. 2. J. Technol. Learn. Assess. **4** (3) (2006). http://napoleon.bc.edu/ojs/index.php/jtla/article/view/1650

Aydin, S.: EFL writers' perceptions of portfolio keeping. Assessing Writ. **15**(3), 194–203 (2010). doi:10.1016/j.asw.2010.08.001

Brett, P.: A genre analysis of the results section of sociology articles. Engl. Specif. Purp. **13**(1), 47–59 (1994)

Bruce, I.: Results sections in sociology and organic chemistry articles: a genre analysis. Engl. Specif. Purp. **28**(2), 105–124 (2009)

Futagi, Y., Deane, P., Chodorow, M., Tetreault, J.: A computational approach to detecting collocation errors in the writing of non-native speakers of English. Comput. Assist. Lang. Learn. **21**(4), 353–367 (2008). doi:10.1080/09588220802343561

Golonka, E. M., Bowles, A. R., Frank, V. M., Richardson, D. L., Freynik, S.: Technologies for foreign language learning: a review of technology types and their effectiveness. Comput. Assist. Lang. Learn. 27(1), 70–105 (2014)

Hirano, E.: Research article introductions in English for specific purposes: a comparison between Brazilian Portuguese and English. Engl. Specif. Purp. **28**(4), 240–250 (2009)

Hopkins, A., Dudley-Evans, T.: A genre-based investigation of the discussion sections in articles and dissertations. Engl. Specif. Purp. **7**(2), 113–121 (1988)

Lim, J.M.H.: Method sections of management research articles: a pedagogically motivated qualitative study. Engl. Specif. Purp. **25**(3), 282–309 (2006)

Monaghan, W., Bridgeman, B.: e-rater as a Quality Control on Human Scores (2005)

Paulus, T.M.: The effect of peer and teacher feedback on student writing. J. Second Lang. Writ. **8** (3), 265–289 (1999)

Peacock, M.: Communicative moves in the discussion section of research articles. System **30**(4), 479–497 (2002)

Powers, D.E., Burstein, J.C., Chodorow, M., Fowles, M.E., Kukich, K.: Stumping e-rater: challenging the validity of automated essay scoring. Comput. Human Behav. **18**(2), 103–134 (2002)

Shei, C.-C., Pain, H.: An ESL writer's collocational aid. Comput. Assist. Lang. Learn. **13**(2), 167–182 (2000)

Swales, J.: Genre Analysis: English in Academic and Research Settings. Cambridge University Press, Cambridge (1990)

Yang, M., Badger, R., Yu, Z.: A comparative study of peer and teacher feedback in a Chinese EFL writing class. J. Second Lang. Writ. **15**(3), 179–200 (2006)

Yang, Y.-F.: Transforming and constructing academic knowledge through online peer feedback in summary writing. Comput. Assist. Lang. Learn. **29**, 1–20 (2015)

Individualization of Foreign Language Teaching Through Adaptive eLearning

Katerina Kostolanyova(✉) and Stepanka Nedbalova

Faculty of Education, University of Ostrava,
Fr. Sramka 3, 709 00 Ostrava, Czech Republic
katerina.kostolanyova@osu.cz,
stepanka.nedbalova@seznam.cz

Abstract. Lifelong learning has become an essential part of each profession. For this reason, personalized and adaptive learning has been drawing attention of professionals in the field of formal as well as informal education in the last few years. The effort has been made to design adaptive study supports regarding students' requirements, abilities and current knowledge. In the Czech Republic, particularly at the University of Ostrava, a team of educators, didactics professionals and IT professionals has been applying their mind to personalized learning in the electronic environment. They have been developing a suitable learning environment to fit students' learning styles. The paper describes a general model and a theory of adaptive eLearning from the perspective of the University of Ostrava professionals. It also demonstrates hard facts of the research in the field of language learning.

Keywords: eLearning · Personalization · Foreign language · Lifelong learning

1 Introduction

Individualization of education is a topic of current interest. With the use of the eLearning adaptive tools, the individualization of education could become very effective as the form of education could be adapted to a student's personal characteristics [1].

Undoubtedly, there is a way to make the education process in the classroom easier for students. However, it is more challenging to satisfy the needs of every student than to follow the individualized approach to education through information and communication technologies. Furthermore, a student can be provided with study materials according to their preferences. In contrast to the unified approach to a heterogeneous group of students in the classroom, the characteristic elements of these preferences can then be used more frequently in study materials.

As far as the heterogeneous group of students is concerned, the teacher tries to deliver the information to students in several ways in order to satisfy their educational preferences [2]. This reduces the time that can be spent on the particular curriculum and makes the education process less effective. Moreover, if a student is taught with respect to their personal characteristics, they are likely to achieve better study results (as far as the gain of knowledge is concerned). It is to be assumed that a student will be more motivated, which will result in the greater sustainability of gained knowledge.

Z. Gong et al. (Eds.): ICWL 2015 Workshops, LNCS 9584, pp. 159–170, 2016.
DOI: 10.1007/978-3-319-32865-2_18

2 Theoretical Background

If we look at the history of individualized education and cybernetic approaches, we learn that in the 1960s algorithmization started to be implemented to the education process, which laid the foundation of the so-called programmed learning. This theory was systematically elaborated by B. F. Skinner [3]. The curriculum is divided into small, content-compact units, which enable effective optimization of education according to a student's personal characteristics.

N. A. Crowder complemented Skinner's principle of linear program by a branched multiple answer program (a process of diagnosing errors with the possibility of individual correction). In order for the managed education systems to be effective, they need to meet three main requirements. The first is the input sensitivity. The second is output effectiveness of the control system. And the third is a program of the impact on the managed system. This program works as a connecting link between the system's "sensors and effectors" [3].

The combination of adaptive and adaptable systems offers an optimal solution for adaptive education through eLearning. The theory of adaptive eLearning is a topic that touches at least 3 areas – pedagogy, psychology and informatics [3].

As far as the Czech Republic is concerned, the Pedagogical Faculty of the University in Ostrava in cooperation with VŠB-Technical University of Ostrava deals with the theory of adaptive eLearning. The main idea of the theory is personalization of education, which consists in the education process being adapted and personally tailored to every student's personal characteristics. It is an adaptation, searching and compiling of the educational content [4]. The proposition of the complex adaptive model of education is based on finding a student's input characteristics, creation of a suitable adaptable study material and the formulation of adaptive algorithms. The theory of programmed learning has been included among pedagogical-algorithmic solutions of the adaptive eLearning principles.

The first generation of adaptive web systems was aimed at the adaptation of presentation and the support of adaptive navigation. The second generation of adaptive web systems expanded adaptive hypermedia by researching the adaptation of the content choice and adaptive recommendation based on the model of users' interest. The third "mobile" generation further expands it by the adaptation of added content models (place, time, computer platform, bandwidth of the classic user model) and examines the use of known technologies for adaptation to an individual user and the context of their work (Brusilovsky in [3]).

3 Basic Principles of Adaptive Education – General Model

A new model is based on a new paradigm – personalization of the educational environment, which takes into account students' personal characteristics, their abilities and current knowledge, their learning styles, etc.

In order for the education process to be adapted to a student's characteristics, it is necessary to know the characteristics (diagnostics of a student's static qualities) and to have a suitable study material. Then the process of managed education can begin. The

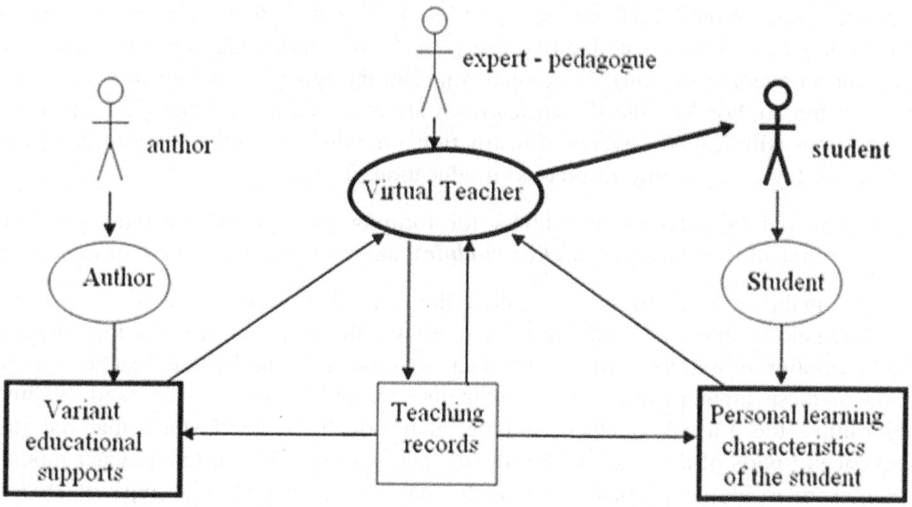

Fig. 1. Basic model of adaptive eLearning education management

entire system can be divided into three basic modules. In the education process these modules are represented by a student, a study material and the Virtual Teacher [4] (Fig. 1).

To solve the mentioned issue it is necessary to create a compact theory of individual education, including a definition of the set of a student's independent typical qualities (that influence the learning process), a definition of the set of teaching methods and styles (which enable the adequate reaction to a student's individual qualities) and the assignment of the optimal teaching method to every learning characteristic.

From a practical viewpoint, it was suitable to divide the system into 3 parts:

1. Preparation of the diagnostics of a student's learning characteristics, continuous instruction and testing of students (***the Student module***).

In the Student module, a questionnaire identifying each student's learning style is the main source of information. The priority is the value of each student's qualities (such as preferred sensory perception, motivation, etc.), which constitute a unique learning style of an individual. The student diagnostics is aimed at the following qualities: sensorimotor preferences, motivation to study, approach to study (depth, strategic, surface), way of study (in a group, on their own, with a teacher), self-regulation.

2. Structuralization of teaching aids, the creation of the methodology for the creation of adaptive study materials (the ***Author module***).

The Author module is the second basic part of the system. Basically, it is a database of modified variant study materials. The database contains not only study texts, images, or multimedia objects, but also detailed information about them – the so-called metadata. The metadata determine which part of the study material it is (whether it is a semantic, motivational, or theoretical part, etc.), for which preferred sensory type of student it is indented (visual, auditive, etc.), and of which difficulty level the content is (e.g. for an average student). In comparison with the typical structure of study materials, in the Author Module the structure of study materials is being developed that corresponds with Gagné's events of instruction – the division of the study material into individual layers according to phases of education (Table 1).

3. Proposition of adaptive algorithms for forming the optimal personalized study environment (the ***Virtual Teacher module***) and recording the course of education.

The main control program is called the Virtual Teacher. Students' individual characteristic features (i.e. their learning style) and the structure of study material (i.e. the description of it in the form of metadata) are crucial for the Virtual Teacher. On the basis of these input parameters and with the use of elementary rules and adaptive algorithms, the Virtual Teacher compiles a personally tailored study material (the sequence of parts of the study material) for each student. The Virtual Teacher module contains rules of the adaptation of study materials to a particular type of student according to their qualities, which is enabled by the flexible structure of study materials.

4 Individualization of Education in Foreign Languages Area

Teaching of a foreign language, compared to other subjects, requires a different approach as emphasis is placed on the ability to use the language rather than the theoretical knowledge. Therefore, it is necessary to prepare for a student such a way through the education process that would help them master the foreign language and actively use it. It means that the education process needs to be adapted to a student's personal characteristics.

As for the teaching of foreign languages, so far (2012) the issue of individualization of education in the electronic environment has been dealt with only at the level of concepts, "Computer Assisted Language Learning" (CALL), "Mobile Assisted Language Learning" (MALL) and "Intelligent Computer Assisted Language Instruction" (ICALI). As for the testing of language knowledge, it is "Computer Assisted Language Testing" (CALT) or "Computer Based Language Assessment" (CBLA). In the area of language competence testing one can come across the term "adaptive tests", which determine a student's language level by assigning either easier or more difficult tasks according to their answers [5].

For creating adaptive study materials in eLearning I used the theoretical principles for the creation of multimedia language projects. The basis for the creation of adaptive study materials is the SLA (Second Language Acquisition) model based on Krashen's concept (1982), which tries to define input characteristics of the target language and in which way a student should work with the input in order for it to influence the development of their linguistic skills in a positive way [6]. The basic SLA components in the interactive research [7] are:

- INPUT;
- APPERCEPTION (pick up on previous knowledge);
- COMPREHENSION (understanding the meaning of words and sentences);
- INTAKE;
- INTEGRATION (into a student's linguistic system);
- OUTPUT (productive).

5 Integration of Foreign Language Teaching into Adaptive Education General Model

As has already been mentioned, the content of the curriculum is the subject of both adaptation and personalization of education, the basis for which is a quality and elaborate study material, which will undergo adaptation [8].

When creating teaching aids in the general model of adaptive education, generally known pedagogical and didactic principles are respected. The following are the individual steps of the teaching process: beginning of a class, instruction, exercises, examination and conclusion. To realize the principle in the area of adaptable education, the education process has been divided into parts according to Gagné (in [3]). The implementation of Gagné's principles into adaptive teaching aids can be seen in Table 1.

Table 1. Implementation of Gagné's principles in the structure of adaptive study materials

Event (according to Gagné's theory)	Use of a particular part in an adaptive teaching aid
Draw attention	Motivational part
Inform students about the goals	Formulation of goals
Evoke the already learned information	Input testing of knowledge
Present the material	Theoretical part
Guide students through the study process	Explanatory part
Initiate and encourage the performance	Examples from practice
Provide feedback	Self-testing – questions and examples
Evaluate the performance	Test results, answer key to unresolved tasks
Improve the remembering process and enable the transfer	Fixation, repetition, practice part

The structure of adaptive study material for the area of adaptive teaching of foreign languages is divided in a different manner. The structure of the instruction frame in the Author module had to be proposed in a way so it would meet the requirements for the teaching of a foreign language. It means that it had to take into account the principles of the SLA (Second Language Acquisition) and ESA (Engage – Study – Activate) models. These principles are listed in Table 3. The selected models are the basis for the teaching of a foreign language and penetrate all the other models, which secure the logical sequence of the teaching of a foreign language – these are the ARC model

(Scrivener), the PPP model (Lewis), the OHE model (Lewis) and the TBLT model (Lewis). The SLA model was chosen in this research as it is closely related to several disciplines including linguistics, sociolinguistics, psychology, neuroscience, and education, and consequently most theories of second-language acquisition can be identified as having roots in one of them. In comparison, involvement load hypothesis (ILH) is mainly connected with vocabulary acquisition research [9], the same for cognitive – based models [10] (Table 2).

Table 2. Interconnection of ESA and SLA models

ESA model phases	SLA model phases
ENGAGE (abb. E) (introducing the curriculum to students)	INPUT (phase of exposing a student to a target language)
STUDY (abb. S) (presentation and practicing of the new curriculum)	APPERCEPTION (Phase of perception according to previous experience), COMPREHENSION (understanding phase), INTAKE (knowledge acquisition phase)
ACTIVATE (abb. A)	INTEGRATION (phase of using the information and remembering it), OUTPUT (productive output phase)

The universal structure of adaptive study materials (divided into individual layers according to Gagne's events of instruction) is adapted to the didactic principles of the teaching of foreign languages.

Table 3. Change in the order of layers in the basic frame for the teaching of a foreign language

ESA model = SLA model	Types of layers in the basic frame for the teaching of general subjects
Engage (initial)	Other layers (motivational)
Study (study)	Instructional layer (theoretical)
Activate (activation)	Instructional layer (fixation)
Recess	Instructional layer (semantic)
Testing layer	Testing layer (questions, exercises, practical tasks)

6 Realization of Teaching in Adaptive eLearning Environment

Nowadays, the individualization of education is an oft-discussed topic. With the use of adaptive tools in eLearning the individualization of education can become so effective that the transfer of knowledge will be adapted to the student's personal characteristics.

Undoubtedly, there is a way to make the education process in the classroom less difficult for the student. However, it is more demanding to satisfy all the students' needs than to choose the individualized approach to education through information and communication technologies. Moreover, the student can be presented with study materials according to their learning preferences. Compared to the uniform approach to the heterogeneous group of students, the characteristic elements of those preferences then can be used to a greater extent in study materials.

As far as this group of students is concerned, the teacher tries to present the information to students in different manners so that the preferences of all students in the classroom are satisfied. However, this also shortens the time spent on the presentation of the curriculum. As a result, it can be expected that, as far as the long-term point of view is concerned, the teacher will lag behind and thus the requirements of the teaching plan will not be met.

Moreover, if a student is taught in accordance with their personal characteristics, they will probably achieve better results as far as knowledge gain is concerned [11].

As far as the individualization of education is concerned, the issue of learning styles and their contribution to the education process is being dealt with. The use of the individual model was tested on the English language. The individual model, which is a part of adaptive eLearning, was designed for the purpose of study of foreign languages in the distance learning study programs of secondary, higher vocational and university education. All these study programs share a common link – sporadic contact with the teacher, which results from the nature of the study. This kind of teaching can also be used as a tool for tutoring students who have unsatisfactory study results.

The pedagogical research – an experiment – was carried out to verify the assumption that the students who learn according to the compiled model will achieve better results. In this case, knowledge tested immediately after the conclusion of the instruction and then again after three months is considered better study results. This kind of research was chosen because its nature corresponds to the nature of determining the intended results.

The aim of the experiment was to confirm/disprove the hypothesis that, compared to the traditional approach to education (i.e. without the preference of study materials), the approach that takes the students' preferred sensorimotor qualities into account has a positive impact on their knowledge gain.

6.1 Determining Target Group

For the purposes of this experiment 120 students were selected. When selecting the students, emphasis was placed on the B1 language level as it was the level at which the adaptive teaching aids, which were used to determine knowledge gain, were compiled. To determine the actual language level the placement tests of UCLES – the internationally recognized Cambridge testing center – were used.

6.2 Expected Results

It was expected that the students, who – besides the standard instruction, experienced the instruction in adaptive eLearning – would achieve better results. Knowledge gain was being determined by comparing the pretest and posttest results (listening, reading, writing). In each language area students had to fill out one pretest (at the beginning of the course) and one posttest (at the end of the course).

6.3 Preparation of Experiment

The preparation of the experiment consisted of the following steps:

- Every student took the UCLES placement test through which a student's entry language level was determined;
- Every student took the VARK psychological test through which a student's sensory preference was determined;
- Every student received their own username and password for access to adaptive eLearning. Every student was also assigned study materials that corresponded to their sensory preference;
- 30 adaptive study materials in .pdf format, which represented 1 topic – equivalent to 1 unit – were inserted into the system. Besides the worksheets, 12 relaxation components, which followed all the partial contents of the curriculum, were inserted into the system. These components were to help students relax after the session so they could then return rested and focused. The 42 worksheets covered one subject with its listening, reading and writing parts;
- "Google Forms" and "Google Drive" were the tools used for data collection and subsequent determination of knowledge gain in adaptive eLearning;
- The content of the pretests and posttests in individual units was taken from the CERMAT testing tasks and the online testing tasks of the California Distance Learning Project for the teaching of the English language (www.cdlponline.org).

6.4 Experiment

The experiment was carried out in the form of comparison of study results within the experimental group and comparison of study results of the experimental and control groups.

The experimental group consisted of 70 students who were divided into two sub-groups according to sensory preferences (44 Aural-Verbal students and 26 Read/Write – Visual students). Study materials were assigned to them according to the following chart:

Table 4. Assignment of adaptive study materials in the experimental group

Group	Student type	Type of the assigned study materials
1	Aural/Verbal (22 students)	Audial (in accordance with preferences)
2	Aural/Verbal (22 students)	Visual (not in accordance with preferences)
3	Read/Write – Visual (13 students)	Visual (in accordance with preferences)
4	Read/Write – Visual (13 students)	Audial (not in accordance with preferences)

Table 4 shows that in the experimental group study results in the "Aural/Verbal" sub-group were being compared. Half of the students were assigned adaptive study materials that were in accordance with their sensory preferences and half of the students were assigned study materials that were not in accordance with their sensory preferences. A similar approach was used in the "Read/Write – Visual" sub-group. The control group consisted of 38 students. This group did not have access to adaptive study materials.

On the basis of the two defined groups of students and with the use of methodical principles – "AURAL/VERBAL and "READ/WRITE – VISUAL" – worksheets were created focusing on the student's sensorimotor preferences. As far as the "A/V" students are concerned, worksheets with audial and verbal educational elements were created. As far as the "R/W-V" students are concerned, worksheets with visual and text educational elements were created.

7 Interpretation of Experiment Results

The evaluation of study results according to the proposed process (see Table 5) was conducted through the SPSS statistical tool (Statistical Package for the Social Sciences) with the $\alpha = 0.05$ level of importance (commonly used in pedagogical research) being determined for all the tests.

The one-sample Kolmogorov-Smirnov test was used to verify the normality of data division in the selected files. The following hypotheses were being verified:

> *H0: As far as the statistical difference is concerned, the distribution of the reading and listening results in the group of visual and audial students does not differ from the standard distribution.*
> *H1: As far as the statistical difference is concerned, the distribution of the reading and listening results in the group of visual and audial students significantly differs from the standard distribution.*

Since in both cases the significance is less than 5 % (0.13 = 1.3 %) and (0.18 = 1.8 %), we disprove H0 in favor of H1. Therefore, we can claim that since the distribution of the reading and listening results from the statistical viewpoint significantly differs, non-parametric tests need to be used for further processing of the results. The following non-parametric tests were used for further processing of the results: Median test and Wilcoxon test; a box plot was used for the graphic representation of the results.

The main hypothesis was formulated:

The students studying the English language according to the individual model in eLearning, with regard to their sensorimotor preferences, will achieve better results than those who do not study in this manner. Before the pedagogical experiment began, it was necessary to find out whether or not the language level structure in groups A, B, C was comparable in order to prevent the possible incomparability of groups having adverse effect on the subsequent results that would be determined by further statistical measuring. Using the good agreement test, in which the distribution of language levels in groups A/B, B/C and A/C was being compared, the following hypotheses were being verified:

> *H0: The structure of language levels in groups A, B, C is comparable.*
> *H1: The structure of language levels in groups A, B, C is not comparable.*

The evaluation had several phases. Firstly, the difference of the test score between pre-test and post-test 1 and between pre-test and post-test 2 concerning listening and reading in groups A, B, C was statistically evaluated. This was followed by the statistical evaluation of the difference of the test score between pre-test and post-test 1 and between pre-test and post-test 2 concerning writing in groups A, B, C – particular attention was paid to listening in individual groups.

In each of the phases several hypotheses were being tested. "The comparison of the pre-test and post-test listening and reading results in group A" will serve as an example:

Table 5. The comparison of the pre-test and post-test listening and reading results in group A

Group A				
	Listening PRETEST-listening POSTEST 1	Listening PRETEST-listening POSTEST 2	Reading PRETEST-reading POSTEST 1	Reading PRETEST-reading POSTEST 2
N	−4.701[c]	−4.381[c]	−1.427[c]	−.236[d]
Wilcoxon test significance	.000	.000	.154	.813

Firstly, the difference of the test score between pre-test and post-test 1 and between pre-test and post-test 2 concerning listening and reading in groups A, B, C was statistically evaluated.

This was followed by the statistical evaluation of the difference of the test score between pre-test and post-test 1 and between pre-test and post-test 2 concerning writing in groups A, B, C.

This part contains data which show deterioration of students' test score concerning listening and partly reading in groups A, B, C. The data were processed using the non-parametric Wilcoxon test. The data are presented by groups (A, B, C).

Table 5 shows negative differences between listening and reading paired values (the N line in the table) in group A. This means that the test score of students has decreased. The testing of the following hypotheses will show whether or not the deterioration was statistically significant.

Groups B and C were tested in a similar manner. In both groups (B and C) the test score of students concerning both reading and listening decreased. The listening and reading progress of the tested students was made by difference between listening pretest score and listening postest score. The same approach was applied for reading area. The score of listening pretest was higher than the score of listening postest 1 and postest 2.

The aim was to verify the hypothesis that the students studying the English language according to the individual model through ICT, with regard to their sensorimotor preferences, will achieve better results than those who do not study in this manner.

As far as the conclusions made and research claims are concerned, it cannot be said that the students studying according to the created model (listening and reading) will achieve better study results. The presupposition concerning these language areas was not fulfilled – either immediately following the course or after 3 months. The possible results of why the presupposition was not fulfilled are mentioned below.

As far as writing is concerned, the presupposition was fulfilled. The group A students studying according to the created model, with regard to their sensomotoric preferences, achieved better results than those who did not study in this manner.

How can worse listening results be explained?

Students' lack of motivation to spend more time completing the assignments than necessary could be one of the reasons. In spite of the fact that the students had study materials in both adaptive and non-adaptive forms for 3 months, the majority of them started to study in the exam period, which lasts 3 weeks.

Another reason could be the limited number of worksheets which the students were supposed to go through before taking the post-test, which was aimed at the detailed testing of the understanding of the recording (compared to the listening pre-test).

These adverse effects could be eliminated by the measuring of the study results through open answers. This way, the activity of students, which is necessary to pass the control tests, would be guaranteed.

8 Conclusion

The need for the knowledge of one or more foreign languages in professional life is increasing. In the paper we introduced a new possibility of teaching a foreign language according to a student's preferred sensory characteristics. The described concept of foreign language teaching through eLearning and on the basis of the preference of a student's particular quality can be considered a significant contribution in the field of controlled individualization of education. It was proved that the education process can be personalized through ICT. The research results can be used for the improvement of the process of implementation of modern information and communication technologies in education and also for the linguistic-didactic aspects of foreign language teaching.

References

1. Sak, P.: Man and education in the information society: education and life in the computerized world (2007)
2. Gregorc, A.F.: Learning/teaching styles: potent forces behind them. Educ. Leadersh. **36**(1), 234–238 (1979)
3. Kostolányová, K.: Teorie adaptivního e-learningu (The Theory of Adaptive e-Learning). University of Ostrava, Ostrava (2012)
4. Kostolányová, K., Šarmanová, J.: Methodology for Creating Adaptive Study Material (2013)
5. Fulcher, G.: Practical Language Testing. Hodder Education, London (2010)
6. Long, M.H.: The Role of Linguistic Environment in Second Language Acquisition: Handbook of Second Language Acquisition. San Diego (1996)
7. Chapelle, C.A.: Multimedia CALL: lessons to be learned from research on instructed SLA. Lang. Learn. Technol. (1998). http://llt.msu.edu/vol2num1/article1/index.html
8. Turčáni, M., Magdin, M.: The Impact of Interactivity on Students′ Results When Passing Through an E-learning Course (2012)

9. Zou, D., Xie, H., Li, Q., Wang, F.L., Chen, W.: The load-based learner profile for incidental word learning task generation. In: Popescu, E., Lau, R.W.H., Pata, K., Leung, H., Laanpere, M. (eds.) ICWL 2014. LNCS, vol. 8613, pp. 190–200. Springer, Heidelberg (2014)
10. Chen, C.M., Chung, C.J.: Personalized mobile English vocabulary learning system based on item response theory and learning memory cycle. Comput. Educ. **51**(2), 624–645 (2008)
11. Kostolanyova, K., Jurickova, R., Simonova, I., Poulova, P.: Flexible hybrid learning: comparative study. In: Cheung, S.K.S., Kwok, L.-F., Yang, H., Fong, J., Kwan, R. (eds.) ICHL 2015. LNCS, vol. 9167, pp. 70–81. Springer, Heidelberg (2015)

Learning Analytics

Research on Visualized Design for Role-Based Online Learning Analytics

Lamei Wang(✉), Jun Xiao, Yuanyi Qi, and Ye Yu

Shanghai Engineering Research Center of Open Distance Education,
Shanghai Open University, Shanghai, China
{wanglamei, xiaoj, qiyy, yuy}@shtvu.edu.cn

Abstract. The in-depth application of new technologies have brought about an explosion of educational data and people are placing more and more emphasis on learning analytics. Against this background, how to make better use of these data and display them in a visualized manner has become an urgent issue in applying learning analytics to education and learning process. This paper introduced the current research status and relevant cases of learning analytics visualization, brought forward learning analytics visualization model, and then displayed the design connotation of learning analytics visualization from the perspectives of different stakeholders (students, teachers and administrators).

Keywords: Learning analytics · Learning analytics visualization · Educational big data · Online learning

1 Introduction

The application of technology in education has witnessed constant progress and development with the continuous development of information technology. The educational informatization has gone through transformations at both learning management system and Web2.0 application levels. Although the conventional teaching process also involves student achievement evaluation and teaching process analysis for the purpose of improving teaching quality, there are limited data acquired from these activities and the analysis results are comparatively less effective. With the popularization of network-based learning method, more data in respect of learning behaviors and learning results can be obtained and the in-depth application of new technologies also brings about an explosion of educational data. How to make better use of these data and display them in a visualized manner has become an urgent issue in the educational and learning process. This issue has also gradually become a research hotspot.

With more attention geared to learning analytics, the international conferences themed learning analytics and knowledge have been held for many times. The *Horizon Report* of New Media Consortium (NMC) has referred to learning analytics technology for years successively. Learning analytics represents the analytics and application of "big data" in education. As big-data-based analytical technology, the learning analytics technology has become an indispensable core factor in powering online learning development. By revealing, understanding and effectively utilizing (e.g., teaching

Z. Gong et al. (Eds.): ICWL 2015 Workshops, LNCS 9584, pp. 173–185, 2016.
DOI: 10.1007/978-3-319-32865-2_19

intervention and learning prediction) the information hidden behind the data, we can maximize the educational benefit.

2 Definition of Core Concept

The definition of learning analytics evolves with the progress of relevant studies, the EDUCAUSE gives the definition of "new-generation of learning challenge": Learning analytics technology is to predict learners' learning progress and performance as well as their future performance and detect potential problems by means of data and model [1]. Siemens, analyst of learning analytics field (2010) held that learning analytics makes use of intelligent data and data generated by learners and analytical model to explore information and social connection for the purpose of offering learning predictions and suggestions [2]. The annual conference on "learning analytics and knowledge" (LAK, 2011) deemed that learning analytics aims to comprehend and optimize learning and learning context, and measures, collects, analyzes and reports the data about learners and their contexts [3]. It lays emphasis on comprehending and optimizing learners and their contexts. NMC (2012) carried that learning analytics is a process of evaluating learners' academic results, predicting future performance, detecting potential problems and expounding the collected massive data generated by students [4], with emphasis placed on evaluating academic results, predicting future performance and detecting potential problems.

Although these definitions vary in terms of wording and focus, they basically reflect the nature of learning analytics, i.e., various technical methods are utilized to acquire comprehensive data information related to learners' learning, and different analytical methods and data models are used for analyzing these data. Then, according to the results of analysis, efforts will be made to explore the learners' learning process, reveal their learning pattern, expound their learning performance and give corresponding feedback to learners, teachers, educational administrators, teaching designers or researchers so as to facilitate more effective learning.

Learning analytics visualization refers to that, by means of information tracking technology, mirroring technology and data mining technology and other technological means, the learners' learning behaviors and history are traced during the whole process, and the massive learning information are recorded, integrated and displayed in the form of digits, charts and graphics on the basis of data mining and analysis so as to provide learners, teachers, administrators and other stakeholders with learning analytics. Learning analytics visualization can provide multi-level learning support for different users so as to facilitate learners to realize self-examination, self-recognition and meaning construction, and provide support for teachers and researchers to achieve instant cognition, real-time monitoring and early warning. Relying on these data, the educational administrators can make timelier and wiser decisions on education and teaching. Learning analytics visualization can, according to different needs of users, display learning analysis data in different dimensions, such as the use of interactive learning tool, cognition and usage of files, social interaction data and learning results, to provide support for users.

3 Current Situation Analysis

3.1 Research Status

According to modern theory of learning evaluation, the analysis and evaluation of learning process are more important than the evaluation of learning results. George Siemens [5], professor of Athabasca University in Canada gave a systematic exposition of the system regarding the aspects such as the source of learning analytics technology, the key technology that influences learning analytics, the prevailing learning analytics tool, technology and application as well as knowledge modeling, and brought forward learning analytics model. Wu et al. analyzed and summarized the foreign and domestic literatures about learning analytics, and defined the concept and traced the origin of learning analytics. On this basis, they systematically expounded the research, development, technical strategy and other aspects of learning analytics, and finally summarized the challenge and prospect of learning analytics [6]. Wei et al. introduced the current technical research on learning analytics both at home and abroad, summarized the key technology and analysis models involved in learning analytics technology, and displayed the application of learning analytics technology in network-based learning process analysis from different user perspectives, such as administrators, teachers and learners [7]. Some domestic researchers have also given comprehensive and systematic introduction to the tools of learning analytics, e.g., Meng et al., in an effort to provide technical support for learning analytics, categorized the tools of learning analytics from multiple perspectives, compared in detail different tools from multiple dimensions such as using environment, data support format and virtualization, and discussed the characteristics of 24 learning and analysis tools [8]. In addition, some scholars also carried out learning platform development and application study based on "learning analytics" technology, e.g., Zhu et al. utilized the learning analytics technology to develop a self-adaptive learning system framework and integrated the data analysis tools by carrying out secondary development of the Sakai learning platform in a bid to realize various functions of the self-adaptive learning system [9].

Through literature analysis, we can find that the current study on learning analytics is mainly epitomized in the following aspects: The study on the data model of learning analytics, mainly including data acquisition mode, behavior analysis factors model and analysis application model, etc. The study on the learning analytics data acquisition technology and system implementation, including network sniffing and acquisition technology, mobile intelligent agent technology and e-portfolio technology, etc. The study on learning analytics technology, including business intelligence, network analysis, educational data mining and academic analysis, etc. The study on the behavior index of learning analytics, including three-dimensional analysis and evaluation targets in the aspects of learning results evaluation, collaborative learning and platform usage. The study on learning analytics framework, e.g., M.A. Chatti put forward that learning analysis reference model was consisted of four dimensions: data and environment, technology, stakeholders, objectives. Greller and Drachsler presented a framework for learning analysis, which was composed of six key dimensions: stakeholders, objectives, data, tools, internal constraints and external constraints [10]. The study on the learning analytics visualization, e.g., many network-based educational platforms (Khan Academy,

Duolingo and Noodle, etc.) have designed display dimensions and display forms of learning visualization according to their service targets and learning scenarios, including learners' learning activities, learners' time spent on each learning link, learners' completion rate, inter-learner interaction and display of learning results, etc.

3.2 Case Analysis

Comparatively, foreign countries have a long history of study on learning analytics. Therefore, they have carried out a great amount of empirical studies and accumulated much research data besides theoretical study. In the meanwhile, they have also developed the tools, technologies and application processes applicable to learning analytics.

In terms of the development and research of learning analytics tools, the "learning network visualization and evaluation project" [11] undertaken by Wollongong of Australia and participated by several colleges and universities, developed the visualized evaluation tool SNAAP for learning network based on the concept of learning analytics. University of Maryland, Baltimore County, developed a tool of "Check my activity", which is used in combination with BlackBaord, is capable of checking the learners' activities, time online and using frequency. The GPS (Grade Performance Status) of Northern Arizona University is an online student performance evaluation system developed by Northern Arizona University, and it is mainly used for evaluating the classroom learning performance of the full-time students in the school. The system can collect the performance rating of the learners in classroom and offer corresponding suggestions which are sent to learners via e-mail. The e-mail of the GPS system mainly includes the learners' attendance, academic performance and academic problems, and the students will respond after receiving the e-mail [12].

In terms of learning analytics visualization, Khan Academy launched learning instrument panel which covers the whole learning process. All the knowledge to be learned is finely divided into nearly one hundred knowledge points and made into a visual "task schedule" chart comprising 549 small lattices. The "happy learning" online intelligent English question tank provides different visual pages of learning analytics for students, teachers and parents, e.g., the type and quantity of learners' wrong answers to questions will be displayed during the practicing process and then individualized test will be generated by analyzing these wrong answers [13].

4 Visualized Design for Role-Based Learning Analytics

The core of the learning analytics is to collect and analyze the learning data, including data collection, analysis, student learning, the benefit and intervention. We propose the visualization model design for learning analytics (Fig. 1), which mainly includes the following elements: Data acquisition for learning analytics visualization, visualization methods and techniques of learning analytics, visualization target of learning analytics (data application), and stakeholders of learning analytics visualization.

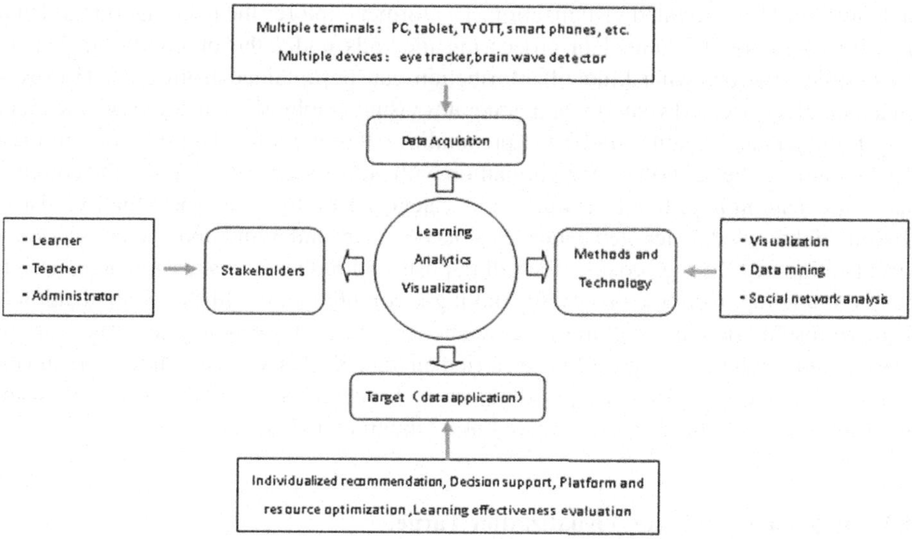

Fig. 1. Visualization model of learning analytics

4.1 Data Acquisition for Learning Analytics Visualization

Based on the online learning feature of "teachers and students separating from each other", a wide selection of data resources are included, which are data from different learning terminals (PC, tablet, TV OTT, smart phones, etc.) and a third party data platform. Techniques used are not only the common ways of obtaining virtual data, namely Web blogs, database, etc., instruments like eye tracker and brain wave detector are also adopted to get data of learners' physical sign, all of which contribute to a comprehensive and objective data. This has set up a basis for the following in-depth analysis.

The main data of learning analytics visualization are sourced from four aspects, firstly, students' behavioral data coming from their performance during the learning process, including test, assignment, resource browsing, discussion participation, attendance and time allocation, etc. Secondly, learners' learning results, including test scores and assignment scores, etc. Thirdly, learners' characteristics, including psychological characteristics, temperamental characteristics and background information, etc. Fourthly, course attributes, including the essential attributes of course, such as course content, course resources and course activities, etc.

4.2 Methods and Technology of Learning Analytics Visualization

The methods and technology of learning analytics mainly include statistical method, visualization, individualized recommendation, data mining and social network analysis method, etc. Among them, visualization is an approach that displays the data or data analysis results in a graphic form, and it is an effective means in exploring massive and complex data. Generally speaking, data visualization comprises exploratory visualization and understanding-oriented visualization. The former explores the information hidden in data by means of different data processing methods under the precondition that it's impossible to know what kind of information can be obtained from data. However, understanding-oriented visualization generates visual graphics in a most vivid, clear and easy-to-understand manner under the precondition that the information hidden in these data has already been known. In combination with online learning behavior, the common data visualization in online learning can be categorized into three types: Firstly, visualization of knowledge learned, such as concept map and mind map, etc.; secondly, visualization of learning process, including posts and replies in discussion area, assignment completion, resource browsing, and login condition, etc.; thirdly, visualization of learning results, such as assignment score and test score, etc. Among them, the learning process and result visualization can be carried on trend analysis (such as line chart and bar chart), ratio analysis (such as pie diagram and stacked area chart) and relationship analysis (such as bubble chart, scattered point diagram and spider diagram).

4.3 Learning Analytics Visualization Target

Learning analytics is of great value to the stakeholders—students, teachers and administrators. Learning analysis visualization mainly provides them with various services and supports, including identifying potential dropouts, establishing behavior patterns of learners, providing individualized recommendation service for students, offering decision support for educational administrators, rendering support for platform and resource optimization and enabling learning effectiveness evaluation, etc. Learning analytics visualization provides students with real-time feedback on behaviors and activities, and recommends social networking information as well as other analysis reports. Students can customize personalized and self-adaptive learning process and content that will be pushed to them in a timely manner. The feedback and suggestions come from not only teachers but also anonymous companions [14]. For teachers, learning analytics visualization will help them to trace students' academic performance, understand how to make teaching more effective and offer students pertinent teaching intervention. In the meanwhile, teachers also undertake the task of teaching designers, and learning analytics will facilitate them to provide students with individualized resources and services and to help students choose more appropriate and effective learning modes [15]. Learning analytics also provides decisions-making basis for administrators to a certain extent. From the perspective of school administration departments, various levels of tracing and analysis for learning-related activities will influence their decision-making regarding the tool and learning space resource allocation.

4.4 Stakeholders of Learning Analytics Visualization

Learners, teachers and administrators are direct benefiters of learning analytics. Learning analytics visualization varies in the aspect of display content depending on different roles. Learners focus on individual data, pay attention to the mastery of knowledge points, their behavioral expression as well as individualized content recommendation, etc. Teachers focus on the whole class performance, the knowledge mastery of individual students as well as the whole class, students' learning progress, their active level as well as quality of course content, etc. Administrators focus on the overall academic performance of the whole school, course usage, website traffic, etc. and they also compare the conditions of different classes and grades.

(1) *Learner-oriented learning analytics visualization design*

Learner-oriented visualization mainly displays three aspects: Firstly, mastery of knowledge points, which are obtained according to assignment and test data. Secondly, learners' performance, including learning engagement, etc. Thirdly, individualized content recommendation, where learning resources and learning approaches are recommended according to the learner information collected from different sources and pertinent learning activities. The main concerns of learners are as shown in Table 1.

Table 1. Categorization of learner-oriented visualization concerns

Categorization	Visualized content
Learning statistics	Credit statistics (linked to degree certification)
	Learning engagement (time management)
	Learning progress (course learning progress and independent learning progress)
	Learning task (course task, assignment and activity participation)
Learning test and recommendation	Learning result feedback (results and test reports)
	Individualized content recommendation

Personal report mainly features the comparison between the student's personal learning activities and the average level of the class, including the total number of student's course visits, time spent on learning, interaction degree and learning task completion as well as learning result feedback (score). As shown in Fig. 2, the blue (darker color) line represents the performance of a certain student while the yellow (lighter color) line represents the average level of the whole class.

Figure 3 displays the number of courses subscribed by part of students of Shanghai Open University, the average visits of the courses as well as the visits of the specific resources of the courses. Users can also learn about the visits of a certain student to different type of resources (file, text and url, etc.) in terms of the course of lifelong learning and occupational development.

(2) *Visualized design of teacher-oriented learning analytics*

Visualization of teacher-oriented learning analytics mainly comprises five aspects: Firstly, mastery of knowledge points of an individual student and the whole class. This function can enable the discovery of mistakes commonly made by students as well as the difficult points for the whole class so that pertinent support and help can be rendered for relevant students. Secondly, students' learning progress. This function can

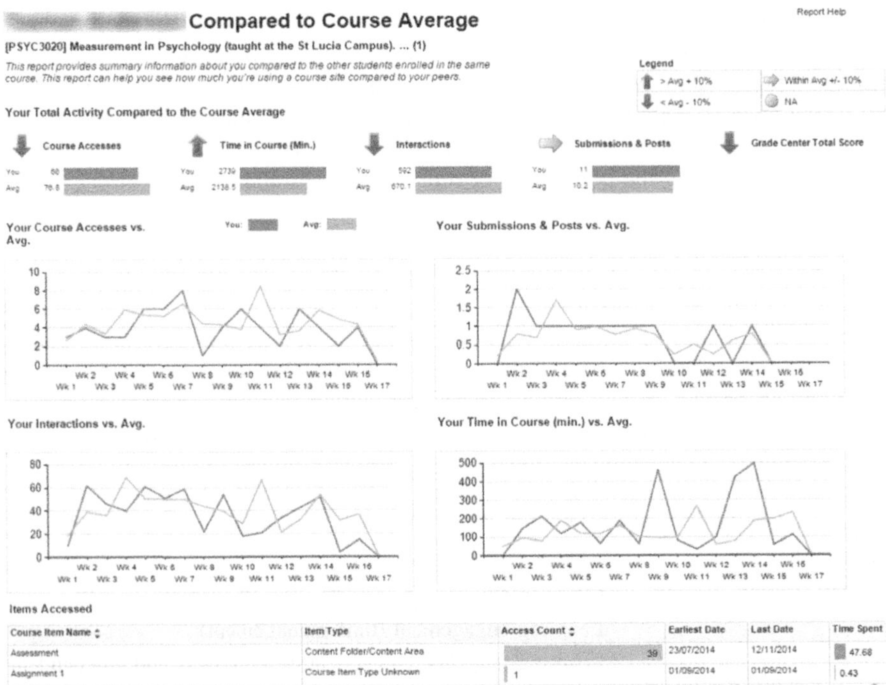

Fig. 2. Visualization of personal learning report [16] (Color figure online)

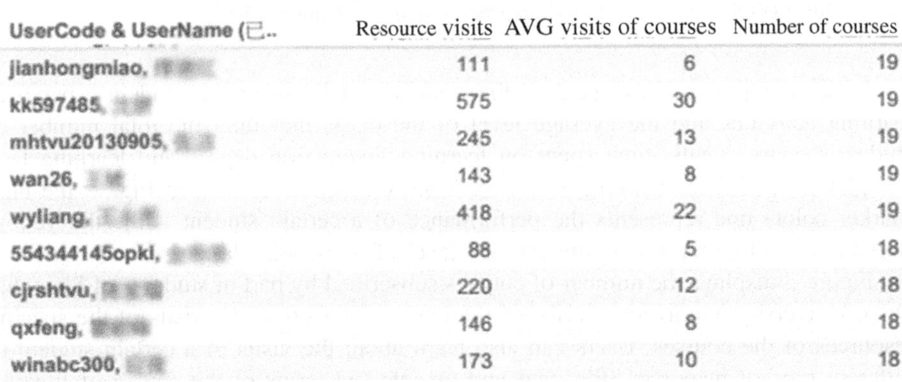

UserCode & UserName (E..	Resource visits	AVG visits of courses	Number of courses
jianhongmiao, [illegible]	111	6	19
kk597485, [illegible]	575	30	19
mhtvu20130905, [illegible]	245	13	19
wan26, [illegible]	143	8	19
wyliang, [illegible]	418	22	19
554344145opkl, [illegible]	88	5	18
cjrshtvu, [illegible]	220	12	18
qxfeng, [illegible]	146	8	18
winabc300, [illegible]	173	10	18

Fig. 3. Visualization of an individual student's learning report of Shanghai Open University

enable the direct observation of which students are left behind and to what degree they are left behind so that intervention can be carried out for them. Thirdly, students' active degree. The data mainly come from forum performance, login condition and assignment submission, etc. Fourthly, learning about students' interest, i.e., what content or what type of resources are the students interested in. Fifthly, quality of course content.

On one hand, it is manifested in the architecture of the course content, connection between knowledge points, connection between knowledge points and learning objects, etc. On the other, it is manifested in the effectiveness of course resources, which is obtained by evaluating the relationship between the utilization of course resources and academic performance. See Table 2 for the main concerns of teachers.

Table 2. Categorization of teacher-oriented visualization concerns

Type	Visualized content
Group—individual characteristic visualization	Mastery of knowledge points
	Course learning progress
	Course score and learning time
	Learner's interest
	Active degree
Course application visualization	Access to course resources
	Quality of course resources
	Popularity of course resources

Figure 4 displays the visualization of the course content access statistics report. Teachers can learn about the specific content of the course (individual resource or task). The report lists all the individual resources or individual tasks that are included in the course. The main content of statistics includes the total number of students' visits to single component resource or task (item), date of visiting as well as the time spent on each resource. Specifically, the content includes the number of visits by a certain student to a certain resource (pdf file, short video or resource link), number of visits by all students, beginning and end of learning time, average time spent by students on this resource as well as the male/female ratio of the students accessing the resource.

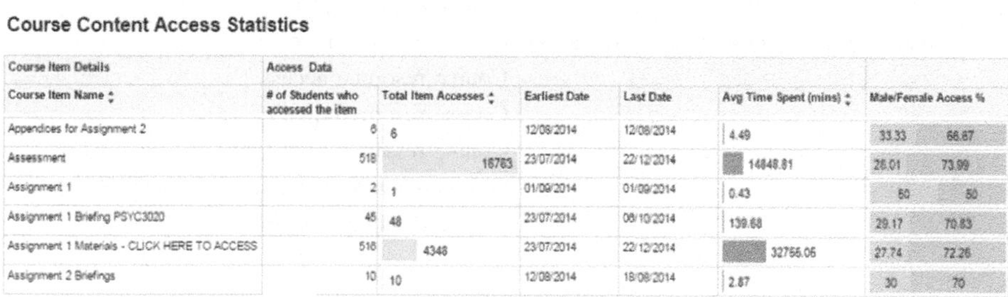
Course Content Access Statistics

Course Item Details	Access Data					
Course Item Name	# of Students who accessed the item	Total Item Accesses	Earliest Date	Last Date	Avg Time Spent (mins)	Male/Female Access %
Appendices for Assignment 2	6	6	12/08/2014	12/08/2014	4.49	33.33 66.67
Assessment	518	16783	23/07/2014	22/12/2014	14848.81	26.01 73.99
Assignment 1	2	1	01/09/2014	01/09/2014	0.43	50 50
Assignment 1 Briefing PSYC3020	45	48	23/07/2014	08/10/2014	139.68	29.17 70.83
Assignment 1 Materials - CLICK HERE TO ACCESS	516	4348	23/07/2014	22/12/2014	32765.05	27.74 72.26
Assignment 2 Briefings	10	10	12/08/2014	18/08/2014	2.87	30 70

Fig. 4. Visualization of statistical report for course content visits [17]

In actual application at Shanghai Open University, we selected part of courses as examples to acquire students' visits to each chapter and each knowledge point of these courses. The size of the lattices shows clearly which resource of a specific chapter is most popular and frequently visited. The lower part of Fig. 5 displays the specific

Fig. 5. Visualization of the number of course visits by students of Shanghai Open University

number of visits to the course by all the students that have selected this course, according to which, the teachers can better grasp the students' learning status.

(3) *Visualized design of administrator-oriented learning analytics*

Administrators are mainly concerned about the overall teaching conditions from the school level. The visualization of learning analytics needs to display two aspects: Firstly, the overall academic performance of the school, the number of teachers and students, the total and average number of various activities of learners as well as the total and average number of various activities of teachers, etc. They also compare the conditions of different classes and grades. Secondly, visualization of teacher administration. Administrators can adjust the overall strategy to make it more adaptive to both teaching and learning according to data from various sources. See Table 3 for the main concerns of administrators.

Table 3. Categorization of administrator-oriented visualization concerns

Type	Visualized content
Visualization of school administration	Report on overall conditions of school
	Course learning progress
Visualization of teacher administration	Course establishment
	Course resource access
	Course resource quality
	Course resource popularity
	Online teaching behaviors of teachers
	Online teaching performance of teachers

Figure 6 presents the analysis data of a certain course. By comparing the data of a certain course (including visits, visiting date, number of resources and course tools, etc.) with the average value of all the courses that adopt the same teaching method in the same semester, the relevant courses can be evaluated.

In actual application, Shanghai Open University made survey of the hits of part of the courses. The total hits of courses within 24 h, the 24-h online user distribution as well as 24-h hits per course are calculated to analyze the most active period of course access as well as the more frequently accessed courses, as shown in Fig. 7.

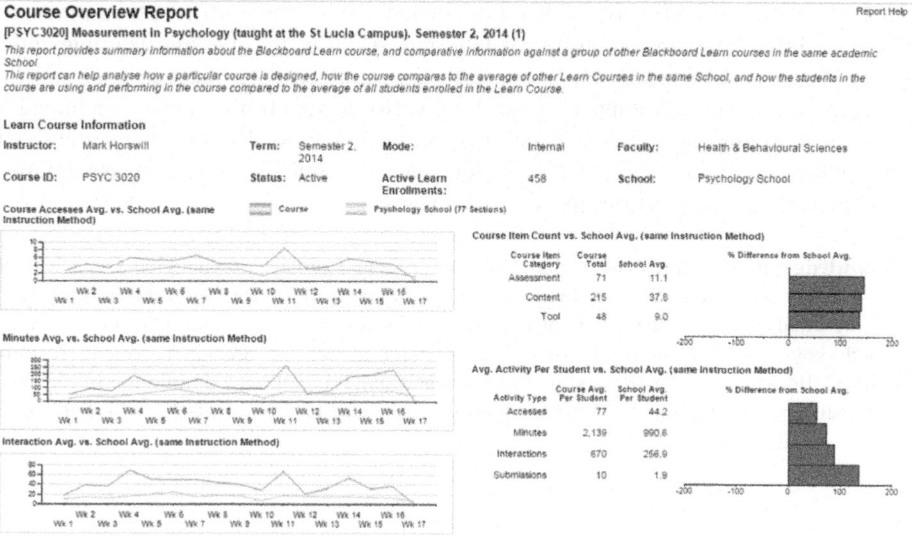

Fig. 6. Visualization of data analysis on a single course and the average value of all courses [18] (Color figure online)

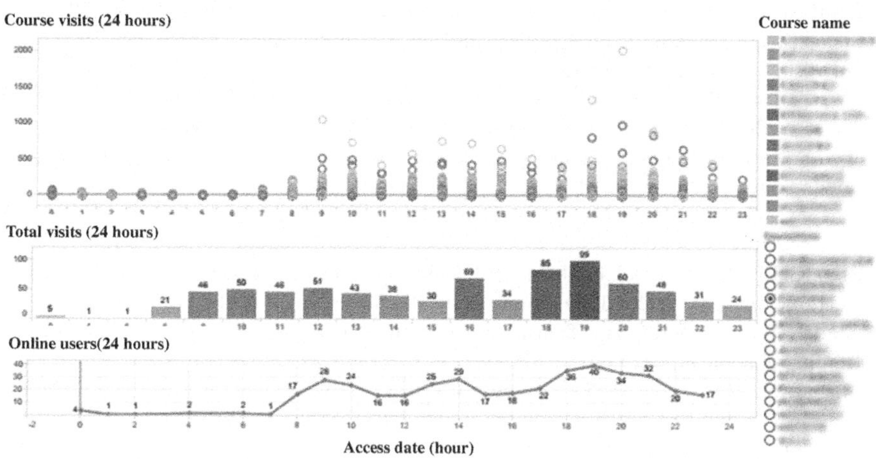

Fig. 7. Visualization of course hits survey of Shanghai Open University (Color figure online)

5 Conclusion

Learning analytics technology plays a great role in teaching, scientific research and administration. In this paper, based on the study of learning analysis of other digital learning system, we brought forward learning analytics visualization model, and analyzed some data from our e-learning system. With the further development of education informatization, to fully explore and visualize the massive learning information stored in the educational software system is of great significance in optimizing the learning process and improving teaching performance. In the future, we intend to study the learning analysis visualization specification. Visualization of learning analytics will pay more attention to the efficiency and dynamics of data analysis and meet individualized learning requirements in real sense.

Acknowledgement. This paper is funded by the research project of Shanghai Open University —"Research on Classification Model of Online Learning Behaviors from the Perspective of Learning Analytics" (JF1508). It is also supported by the 2014 Shanghai education scientific research key project "The Study of online learning model for Shanghai lifelong learning (A1403)". Besides, thanks for the support of Science and Technology Commission of Shanghai Municipality research project "Shanghai Engineering Research Centre of Open Distance Education (13DZ2252200)".

References

1. Brown, M.: Learning analytics: the coming third wave, 31 May 2015
2. Siemens, G.: What are learning analytics, **10** (2011). Accessed March 2010
3. Siemens G.: 1st International Conference on Learning Analytics and Knowledge (2011)
4. Consortium TNM. Learning Analytics. The Horizon Report 2011 Edition, pp. 28–30
5. Siemens, G.: Learning analytics: the emergence of a discipline. Am. Behav. Sci. (2013). doi:10.1177/0002764213498851
6. Wu, Y., Chen, D., Ma, X., Cao, P., Feng, X., Zhu, Z.: Learning analytics: the new coming wave of education information. J. Distance Educ. (04), 11–19 (2013)
7. Wei, S.: Learning analytics: mining the value of education data under the big data era. Mod. Educ. Technol. (02), 5–11 (2013)
8. Meng, L., Gu, X., Li, Z.: The comparison of learning analytics tools. Open Educ. Res. (04), 66–75 (2014)
9. Zhu, K., Liu, Q.: Research on the development and application of learning platform based on "learning analysis" technology. China Educ. Technol. (09), 127–132 (2013)
10. Greller, W., Drachsler, H.: Translating learning into numbers: a generic framework for learning analytics (2012)
11. Macfadyen, L.P., Dawson, S.: Mining LMS data to develop an "early warning system" for educators: a proof of concept. Comput. Educ. **54**(2), 588–599 (2010)
12. Ling, Q., Wang, T.: Review of research and application of learning analysis technology. China Educ. Technol. (08), 129–133 (2012)
13. Zhang, Z., Liu, W., Han, Z.: Learning dashboard: a novel learning support tool in the big data era. Mod. Distance Educ. Res. (03), 100–107 (2014)
14. Siemens, G., Gasevic, D., Haythornthwaite, C., Dawson, S., Shum, S.B., Ferguson, R., et al.: Open Learning Analytics: An Integrated & Modularized Platform. Open University Press, Maidenhead (2011)
15. Retalis, S., Papasalouros, A., Psaromiligkos, Y., Siscos, S., Kargidis, T. (eds.): Towards networked learning analytics–a concept and a tool. In: Proceedings of the Fifth International Conference on Networked Learning (2006)

16. Activity and Grade Scatter Plot report. https://www.elearning.uq.edu.au/content/activity-grade-scatter-plot-report
17. Course Content Access Statistics report. https://www.elearning.uq.edu.au/content/course-content-access-statistics-report
18. Course Overview report. https://www.elearning.uq.edu.au/content/course-overview-report

Construction on Learning Analytics Object for Sharing and Interoperation of Educational Big Data

Yonghe Wu[1(✉)], Wei Zhong[1], Chun Zhou[2], and Xiaoling Ma[2]

[1] East China Normal University, 3663 Zhongshan Road (N.), Shanghai, China
yhwu@dec.ecnu.edu.cn, xzw0706@163.com

[2] East China Normal University, 500 Dongchuan Road, Shanghai, China
czhou@vc.ecnu.edu.cn, xlma@dec.ecnu.edu.cn

Abstract. Educational Big Data (EBD) come from various types of Educational Systems such as LMS, CMS, ITS, SLS, and MOOCs. How to share and interoperate Educational Big Data for Learning Analytics (LA) has garnered a lot of research attention. In the paper, we probe into the process of Learning Analytics, outline the dataflow of EBD, define the Learning Analytics Object, and propose a new data format model for the Learning Analytics object to actualize the sharing and interoperability of Learning Analytics.

Keywords: Educational Big Data · Learning Analytics Object · Data Format Model of Learning Analytics · Dataflow

1 Introduction

The utilization of "Big Data" in the world of business have achieved great success so far, which inevitably sparks the enthusiasm in experimentation and application of Big Data in the field of education. Educational Big Data (EBD) generally fall into two categories: one is student identity data, and the other is activity-based data sets with the potential to improve learning outcomes, including user interactive data, inferred content data, system-wide data and inferred student data [1].

Learning Analytics (LA), as an innovative approach to educational application of Big Data, is an emerging field of research that aspires to use data analysis to make informed decisions on every tier of educational systems. LA is the measurement, collection, analysis and reporting of data about learners and their contexts, for purposes of understanding and optimizing learning and the environments in which it occurs according to the first International Conference on Learning Analytics and Knowledge [2].

LA, now, is still in its early phase of development, faced with both opportunities and challenges. We have collected structured data in the education sector for years, typically in the form of attendance records or test scores. Recent advances in educational technology have capacitated researchers to amass large volumes of unstructured data from different environments for the further analysis. Meanwhile, a wide range of data structures have been generated by various learning platforms or educational systems, such as Web-based System (WBS), Learning Management System (LMS),

Z. Gong et al. (Eds.): ICWL 2015 Workshops, LNCS 9584, pp. 186–195, 2016.
DOI: 10.1007/978-3-319-32865-2_20

Social Learning System (SLS) and Live Teaching System (LTS). All these enable efficient collection of much richer data sets than previously possible, thus creating new research challenges and opportunities for developing desirable learning environments. One of the biggest challenges is how to standardize the data on the front end, which does not only mean converting unstructured to structured data, but also constructing a unified Learning Analytics Object.

Attempts to record Educational Big Data from different educational systems are abundant. Adam Cooper proposed the framework of characteristics for analytics [3]. Under IEEE Standard for Learning Technology, data exchange model (IEEE 1484.11.1) and communication specification (IEEE 1484.11.2) are employed for Learning Analytics [4, 5], while Experience API stipulated the structure of data statements [6]. IMS introduced IMS Caliper - Learning Measurement Framework, which features IMS Learning Sensor API and Learning Events [7]. However, these broadly defined frameworks are not easy to handle when it comes to capturing and recording EBD. Therefore, to facilitate sharing and interoperability of EBD from various systems, we propose a new data format model for the Learning Analytics Object, refining and integrating the above several frameworks with use cases from real-life scenarios.

2 Related Research

2.1 Definition and Terminology

Educational Big Data are generated by and collected from various types of educational systems, including LMS (Learning Management System), CMS (Content Management System), EPS (e-Portfolio System), ITS (Intelligent Training System), SLS (Social Learning System), LTS (Live Teaching System Based on Classroom), LDS (Learning Design System) and SIS (Student Information System), etc. EBD, as the data for Learning Analytics, are the learning log data generated through real-time or non-real-time interoperation between various stakeholders and the aforesaid educational systems. The following definitions are formulated and discussed first to facilitate understanding of this paper.

(1) *Learning Data*

Definition 1. Learning Data (LD) are the data obtained by analyzing, cleaning and pretreating learning log data generated by educational systems.

Learning log data encompass all the situational data related to user, content, operation (action), time and location. User covers all the relevant information about stakeholders such as students, teachers, administrators, resource developers, and policy makers. Content refers to the learning content, i.e., learning resources, which can be expressed by the Learning Object Meta data. Operation (action) here refers to the user operational behaviors, which can be either general or private. Time refers to the time when tracking logs are generated, which can be indicated by the universal Internet time. Location, as well, refers to where tracking logs are generated, including both virtual and physical address spaces.

(2) *Learning Analytics Data*

Definition 2. Learning Analytics Data (LAD) are data obtained by mining and analyzing masses of learning data.

LAD can be displayed in the dashboard, outputted to a third party data-analysis tool by means of LAD exchanging, or fed back to relevant educational systems. LAD, processed by LAS (Learning Analytics System) engines, are of great value for learning Analysis.

(3) *Learning Analytics System*

Definition 3. Learning Analytics System (LAS) is a subsystem of a digital educational system, collecting learning log data, processing learning data, and generating Learning Analytics data.

In addition, LAS outputs analysis results to the dashboard and provides feedback and intervention for the educational system. LAS is designed to improve the service quality of educational systems and meet the demands of various stakeholders.

2.2 Object and Learning Object

An object is an entity that has state, behavior and identity [8]. The state of an object refers to the current context and properties of the object. Behavior is the action and reaction of the object in terms of its state change. Identity is that property of an object which distinguishes it from all other objects. These three characteristics are interconnected and interacting with each other. Objects can be either concrete or abstract entities, for example, a student or a student's learning process.

The term "learning object" was first popularized by Wayne Hodgins in 1994 (Polsani 2002) [9]. According to the definition of the IEEE Learning Technology Standards Committee, a learning object is "any entity, digital or non-digital, which can be used, re-used and referenced during technology-supported learning" (IEEE 2001) [10]. Narrower, Wiley (2002) defined learning objects as "any digital resource that can be reused to support learning" [11]. It is integral to computer-based instruction, relying on object-oriented computer science and coalesced with sophisticated instructional theories.

2.3 Capturing and Recording EBD

The research community in Learning Analytics domain has long recognized, for the sake of academic research, the importance of collecting data from public, open-access sources. Only with shared data sources can their research results be verified, reproduced and compared [12]. An array of frameworks have been proposed by research institutions and organizations worldwide to capture and record Big Data efficiently. Some of the most influential ones are explored here below.

(1) *DataShop*
DataShop [13] by PSLC (Pittsburgh Science of Learning Center) provides interactive learning datasets between students and Intelligent Tutor System, featuring web-based analysis and visualization tools [14]. The data format for DataShop is Tutor Message format, designed to capture the details of the interaction between students and Tutor to represent a guided session. There are four types of information involved: contextual information, tool information, guidance information and other miscellaneous information.
(2) *IMS Caliper - Learning Measurement Framework*
IMS Caliper - Learning Measurement Framework presents the general procedure about representing, capturing and marshaling the learning-related data, which include IMS Learning Activity Metric Profiles, IMS Learning Sensor API and Learning Events, Learning Tools Interoperability and Learning Information Services Extensions. Based on the Learning Tools Interoperability and other related specifications, IMS Learning Activity Metric Profiles aims to define a standardized and structured collection of Learning Activity Metrics that specific to actions and relevant context about each learning activity. The IMS Learning Sensor API and Learning Events support the transmission of Learning Activity/Content data to the Analytics Store. Particularly, Learning Events are represented in the form of a data triple - **"LearningContext"** - **"Action"** - **"ActivityContext"** [7].
(3) *IEEE 1484.11 and Experience API*
Under IEEE Standard for Learning Technology, data exchange model (IEEE 1484.11.1) and communication specification (IEEE 1484.11.2) are used for Learning Analytics. Experience API statements follow the structure: *<actor> <verb> <object>, with <result>, in <context>*, but it is flexible that allows the extension of some elements. The actor element usually represents a learner. The verb element describes the action performed by the student. The object element indicates "who" or "what" experienced the action which defined in the verb. The result element means an outcome to the statement and the context field adds additional information to the statement, such as the relationship and position of the activities [4–6].

In general, the prevailing frameworks as discussed above are far from sufficient for concrete interpretation of student profile information. Besides, they are not consistent in data format for LA, which impairs interoperability and increases costs. Thus, there is an urgent need to formulate specific standard structures for LAD.

3 Learning Analytics System Data-Flow and Learning Analytics Object

3.1 Learning Analytics System Data Flow

When it comes to the process of Learning Analytics, Siemens (2010) believes that Learning Analytics undergoes such stages as data collection, data analysis, data prediction and data adjustment [15]. According to Elias (2011), Learning Analytics goes through three stages, namely, collection, processing and application, which form a continuous cycle. Learning Analytics involves six activities, which are acquirement, selection, gathering, prediction, use, and optimization [16]. As we see it, Learning Analytics entails data collection, data processing, data analysis and data application.

Considering the state of data throughout the Learning Analytics process, we depict the data flow in Learning Analysis System as shown in Fig. 1. Data flow involves recording learning log data, producing Learning Data, LAS Engine processing, producing Learning Analytics Data and using Learning Analytics Data. In this sense, EBD comprises learning log data, Learning Data and Learning Analytics Data.

EBD = {LLD, LD, LAD}

① Recording learning log data: Learning Log Data (LLD) are recorded when educational systems are running.

② Producing Learning Data: Learning Data are produced after Learning Log Data are cleaned and preprocessed.

③ Producing Learning Analytics Data: Learning Analytics Data are generated after Learning Data are processed with LAS Engines.

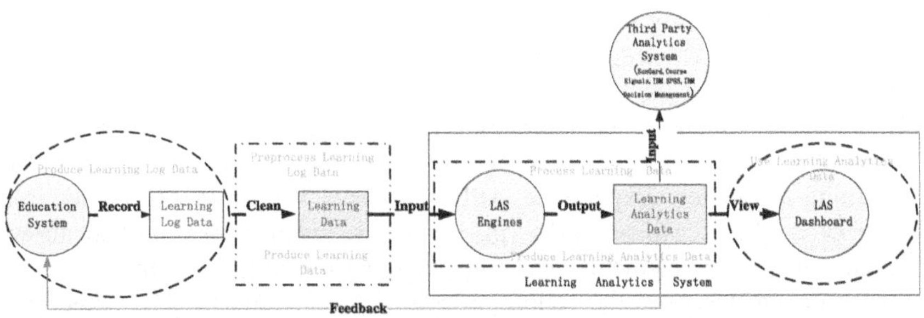

Fig. 1. Dataflow of Educational Big Data in a learning analytics system

④ Using Learning Analytics Data: when Learning Analytics Data are generated, a variety of analytical charts and diagrams can be displayed on the LAS Dashboard. Apart from offering valuable feedback to monitor educational systems, Learning Analytics Data can be outputted to a third-party analysis system.

3.2 Learning Analytics Object

As the research focus of LA is on the data generated in the process of learning, we intend to define LAO from the perspective of dataflow in Learning Analysis System.

Definition 4. Learning Analytics Object (LAO) is any EBD from the educational system that can be reused to support learning, and LAO is composed of Learning Data and Learning Analytics Data.

The exact meaning of LAO is clearly shown in Fig. 2.

$LAO = \{LD\}^m + \{LAD\}^n$, $m, n \in \{0,1,2\ldots\}$, When $m = 0$, $n \neq 0$; and while $n = 0$, $m \neq 0$. In this sense, LAO has at least one LD or LAD.

LAD derives from LD by means of tools and algorithm, such as SPSS, R Program, Bayesian algorithm and so on.

So $LAD = f(LD)$, and $LAO = \{LD, f(LD)\}$

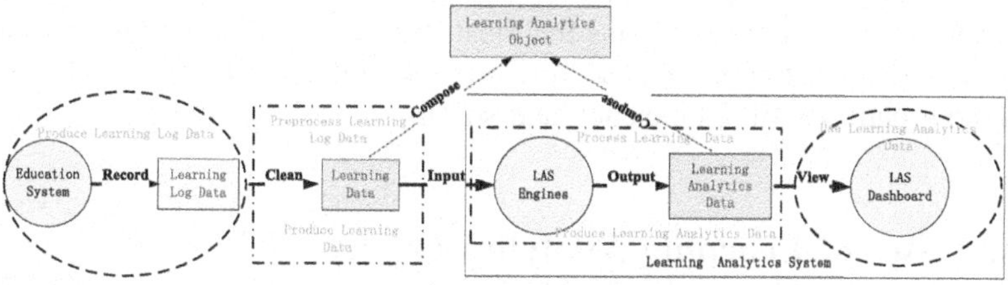

Fig. 2. Learning Analytics Object

3.3 Data Format Model of Learning Analytics Object

Based on DataShop, xAPI, IMS and other data recording modes, as well as its concept and characteristics, we develop five modules for Learning Analytics Object: Students/Teachers, Resource, Context, Result and Action. We also incorporate such features as learners' specific behavioral types and operating objects from the Learner Action Model by Katrien Verbert et al. [12] into our corresponding modules when we construct our Data Format Model of Learning Analytics Object, as indicated in Fig. 3.

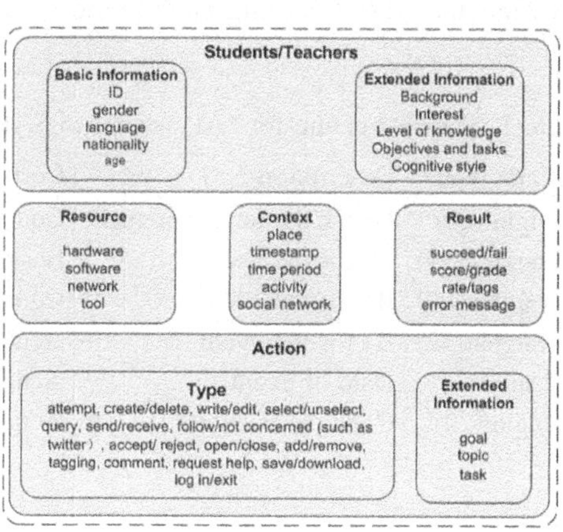

Fig. 3. Data Format Model of Learning Analytics Object

(1) Students/Teachers: They are major participants in online learning settings. This module covers their basic profile information and extended information such as their competence level and learning objective.

(2) Resource: Resource module mainly describes the characteristics of educational resources. By educational resources, we mean the objects to be operated by platform users, including hardware, software and other instruments.
(3) Context: Context module refers to the actual learning situations where learners are involved in, including where the platform users are, what activities they are engaged with, when learning occurs, etc.
(4) Result: Result module is about what learners achieve in summative evaluations such as tests or exercises.
(5) Action: Action module contains the most important data in LAO. The operations conducted by learners on platform resources reflect a learner's learning style, learning path, learning efficiency and so on.

4 Use Cases of Learning Analytics Object

Sakai and MOODLE are open source LMSs featuring Learning Analytics capabilities. A systematic analysis of their datasets reveals that their LA capabilities are mainly with their learning event database. Therefore we export the event table structures from data-storing MySQL for further study. Apart from Sakai and MOODLE, we probe into edX-based MOOCs from Harvard University and MIT, datasets of which give us more insight into Learning Analytics Object as well.

4.1 Sakai System

Table 1 demonstrates the table structure for 'sst_events', which is used to store learning events. Data from sst_events table are Learning Data in the Learning Analytics Object.

Table 1. Table structure for "sst_events" in SAKAI

Data	Data type	Description	Corresponding modules
ID	bigint(20)	ID for the auto increment	Context
USER_ID	varchar(99)	ID for the user	Basic information
SITE_ID	varchar(99)	ID for the site	Context
EVENT_ID	varchar(32)	ID for the event	Action
EVENT_DATE	Date	Date of event	Action
EVENT_COUNT	bigint(20)	Count of events	Action

4.2 MOODLE System

In the Moodle system, three table structures - "mdl_stats_daily", "mdl_stats_weekly" and "mdl_stats_monthly", are used to store learning events, and they are of the same structure, as shown in Table 2. Data from these three tables are labeled as Learning Analytics Data in the Learning Analytics Object.

Table 2. Table structure for 'Mdl_Stats_Daily' in Moodle

Data	Data type	Description	Corresponding modules
Id	bigint(10)	ID for the auto increment	Context
courseid	bigint(10)	ID for the course	Resource
Timeend	bigint(10)	End time of the course	Context
roleid	bigint(10)	ID for different roles	Basic information
stattype	varchar(20)	Statistics type	Action
stat1	bigint(10)	Statistics1	Action
stat2	bigint(10)	Statistics2	Action

For Moodle users, there are three tables: "mdl_stats_user_daily", "mdl_stats_user_weekly" and "mdl_stats_user_monthly". The structures of the three tables are the same, as shown in Table 3. Data from the three tables are categorized as Learning Data in Learning Analytics Object.

Table 3. Table structure for 'Mdl_Stats_User_Daily' in Moodle

Data	Data type	Description	Corresponding modules
Id	bigint(10)	ID for the auto increment	Context
courseid	bigint(10)	ID for the course	Resource
Userid	bigint(10)	ID for the users	Basic information
Roleid	bigint(10)	ID for different roles	Basic information
Timeend	bigint(10)	End time of the course	Context
Statsreads	bigint(10)	View the post	Action
Statswrites	bigint(10)	Post to the discussion forum	Action
Stattype	varchar(30)	Statistics type	Action

4.3 edX-Based MOOCs

The use case for edX-based MOOCs from Harvard University and MIT [14] illustrates how Learning Event is recorded in MOOCs system. The data are structured with one student per row for each course taken (taking multiple courses results in multiple rows of data). And they fall under the category of Learning Data in Learning Analytics Object. The data columns (taken from the Person Course Documentation file) are shown below (Table 4):

Table 4. Use case for edX-based MOOCs from Harvard University and MIT

Data	Description	Corresponding modules
course_id	ID for the course	Resource
userid_DI	De-identified unique identifier of student	Basic information
registered	Registered for this course	Context

(*Continued*)

Table 4. (*Continued*)

Data	Description	Corresponding modules
viewed	Anyone who accessed the 'courseware' tab	Context
explored	Anyone who accessed at least half of the chapters in the courseware	Context
certified	Anyone who earned a certificate	Result
final_cc_name_DI	De-identified geographic information	Basic information
LoE	User-provided highest level of education completed	Extended information
YoB	Year of birth	Basic information
gender	Self-explanatory	Basic information
grade	Final grade in course	Result
start_time_DI	Date of course registration	Action
last_event_DI	Date of last interaction with course	Action
nevents	Number of interactions with the course	Action
ndays_act	Number of unique days student interacted with course	Action
nplay_video	Number of play video events	Action
nchapters	Number of courseware chapters with which the student interacted	Action
nforum_posts	Number of posts to the discussion forum	Action
roles	Identifies staff and instructors	Basic information

5 Conclusion and Future Work

To standardize Learning Analytics Object will facilitate sharing and interoperability of data from different learning platforms. In this study, EBD's dataflow in Learning Analytics System is analyzed. Then, Learning Analytics Object and Data Format Model of Learning Analytics Object are defined and illustrated. And Use Case from Sakai, MOODLE, and edX-based MOOCs from Harvard University and MIT are used to support Learning Analytics research efforts. The Data Format Model of Learning Analytics Object proposed in the paper is only a preliminary data model coalescing relevant data elements. More efforts are needed from the whole community to test, revise and further improve the current model.

For future work, our team will focus on the research for metadata of Learning Analytics Object, and set up LAO metadata. And then LAO ontology will be studied.

Acknowledgments. This work was supported by the 2014 Shanghai Pujiang Program (Grant 14PJC034) and the 2014 Shanghai "Technology Innovation Action Plan" Project (Grant 14511109300).

References

1. Ferreira, J.: Big Data in Education: The 5 Types That Matter [Blog post] (2013). https://www.knewton.com/resources/blog/ceo-jose-ferreira/big-data-in-education/. Accessed 12 Sept 2015
2. Siemens, G.: Knewton-the future of education?. http://www.learninganalytics.net. Accessed 28 Aug 2015
3. Adam Cooper, A.: CETIS Analytics Series: A Framework of Characteristics for Analytics, vol. 1, no. 7 (2012). http://publications.cetis.org.uk/2012/524
4. IEEE: 1484.11.1, IEEE Standard for Learning Technology - Data Model for Content Object Communication (2004). http://www.ieee.org/index.html. Accessed 10 Aug 2015
5. IEEE: 1484.11.2, IEEE Standard for Learning Technology - ECMAScript Application Programming Interface for Content to Runtime Services Communication (2003). http://www.ieee.org/index.html. Accessed 10 Aug 2015
6. Advanced Distributed Learning. Experience API Version 1.0.1. https://github.com/adlnet/xAPI-Spec/blob/master/xAPI.md. Accessed 10 Aug 2015
7. Learning Measurement for Analytics Whitepaper, IMS Global Learning Consortium. http://www.imsglobal.org/IMSLearningAnalyticsWP.pdf. Accessed 10 Aug 2015
8. Booch, G., Maksimchuk, R.A., Engle, M.W., Young, B.J., Conallen, J., Housyon, K.A.: Object-Oriented Analysis and Design with Applications, 3rd edn. Pearson Education India, Chennai (2006)
9. Polsani, P.R.: Use and abuse of reusable learning objects. J. Digit. Inf. **3**(4) (2003). https://journals.tdl.org/jodi/index.php/jodi/article/view/89
10. IEEE: IEEE Learning Technology Standards Committee (LTSC) IEEE P1484.12 Learning Object Metadata Working Group; WG12 Home page (2001). http://ltsc.ieee.org/wg12/s_p.html
11. Wiley, D.A.: Connecting learning objects to instructional design theory: a definition, a metaphor, and a taxonomy (2002). http://www.reusability.org/read/chapters/wiley.doc. Accessed 10 Aug 2015
12. Verbert, K., Manouselis, N., Drachsler, H., Duval, E.: Dataset-driven research to support learning and knowledge analytics. Educ. Technol. Soc. **15**(3), 133–148 (2012)
13. TEL Europe: DataShop. https://pslcdatashop.web.cmu.edu/index.jsp?datasets=public. Accessed 10 Aug 2015
14. Koedinger, K.R., Baker, R.S.J.d., Cunningham, K., Skogsholm, A., Leber, B., Stamper, J.: A data repository for the EDM community: the PSLC DataShop. In: Handbook of Educational Data Mining, vol. 2011, pp. 43–55. CRC Press (2010)
15. Siemens, G.: What Are Learning Analytics. http://www.elearnspace.org/blog/2010/08/25/what-are-learning-analytics/. Accessed 16 Jan 2011
16. Elias, T.: Learning Analytics: Definitions, Processes and Potential. http://learninganalytics.net/LearningAnalyticsDefinitionsxProcessesPotential.pdf. Accessed 16 Jan 2011

Using Learning Analytics to Support Personalized Learning and Quality Education: A Case Study of China's "Everyone Connected" Project

Xiaohua Yu[1(✉)], Jueqi Guan[2], and Jing Leng[1]

[1] Department of Education Information Technology, East China Normal University, Shanghai, China
{xhyu,jleng}@deit.ecnu.edu.cn

[2] School of Open Learning and Education, East China Normal University, Shanghai, China
jqguan@dec.ecnu.edu.cn

Abstract. The "Everyone Connected" project plays a very important role in the construction of the twelfth Five-year Plan of Educational Informatization in China. The project serves personal learning level, and expresses the real implementation of the needs of personalized learning and quality education. By using learning analytics through the organic interactive mechanism between personal learning space via the "Everyone Connected" project and "Two Platforms", personalized push of resources and services and customized report of learning can be effectively realized.

Keywords: The "Everyone Connected" project · Personal learning space · Learning analytics · Personalized learning

1 Background and Objectives

In recent years, the research and development of digital learning environment has been a focus in academic fields. With the rapid development of cloud technology and mobile internet and the rise of smart education, individual service-oriented learning environment has become a new focus. In China, the "Everyone Connected" project in the "Three Connected and Two Platforms" initiative is put forward to meet the development trend of the times. The "Three Connected" refers to the "School Connected" project (means school-to-school network), the "Class Connected" project (means class-to-class quality resources sharing) and the "Everyone Connected" project (means person-to-person connected learning cyberspace) [1]. And the "Two Platforms" are the educational resource public service platform and the educational management public service platform [1]. "Three Connected and Two Platforms" is the iconic program of the twelfth Five-year Plan of Educational Informatization in China and the "Everyone Connected" project is the ultimate goal of this program. It reflects the strategic thought of China's educational informatization stepping into individual learning service level, and expresses the vision of the implementation of learner-oriented, personalized learning and quality education. To achieve this goal, this paper proposes that learning analytics

Z. Gong et al. (Eds.): ICWL 2015 Workshops, LNCS 9584, pp. 196–201, 2016.
DOI: 10.1007/978-3-319-32865-2_21

(LA) could be potentially effective. Thus, two core problems of using LA in the "Everyone Connected" project will be discussed in the following. One problem is how to apply LA in the construction of individual learning cyberspace. The other is how learners carry out personalized learning effectively in learning cyberspace with the support of LA.

2 Theoretical Framework

2.1 The "Everyone Connected" Project and Personal Learning Space

The main objective of the "Everyone Connected" project is to let everyone to own a real-name network space in which individuals can conduct learning, communicate and share information. It also enables the resources and services in the space to be utilized to really promote individual development. To achieve this goal, there is no doubt that the construction of learners' individual learning space should be personalized and dynamic. At present, the most popular concept about the construction of a personalized learning space is personal learning environment (PLE). The core idea of PLE is the personal control and freely configuration of the environment. As a result, we assume that personal learning space (PLS) via the "Everyone Connected" project should be an integrated learning environment which is controlled by individuals. It can provide personalization and diversity of individual learning by supporting data and resource services, learning Scaffolding and management tools, with the help of learning analytics. It is a learning cyberspace which coordinates teaching and learning activities controlled by individuals, building a bridge for connecting and sharing information among individuals, institutes and other cyberspaces conveniently [2]. But unlike PLE, PLS emphasizes the connections between formal and informal learning spaces.

2.2 Personalized Learning and Learning Analytics

Personalized learning becomes increasingly prominent in policy discussions on the future of education. And the development of technologies makes the concept of personalized learning become widely adopted in all kinds of education [3]. The central trait of personalized learning is customization, the necessary premise of which is to fully understand and grasp of learners and their learning activities. The aim of LA is to design and optimize learning process and environment, by which data about learner and learning situation is measured, collected, analyzed and reported [4]. Data analytics from microscopic service level is proposed, and individual differences among learners and procedure problems during learning processes are focused. Therefore, using information revealed by LA (including learner preferences, current knowledge structure, learning task confronted and so on), the learning system can effectively support learners' personalized learning effectively by providing them with appropriate learning resources, tools and construct the best fit learning environment.

3 Method

3.1 Construction of Personal Learning Space Based on Learning Analytics

The construction of PLS is based on the idea of PLE. Downes [5] describes PLE as a "loose collection of tools, services, people and resources, as a way of harnessing the power of the network". Gillet [6] considers PLS as "a set of devices, tools, applications, and physical or virtual spaces associated by learners at a specific time, for a specific purpose, and in a given context". In short, the concept centers on the idea of "small pieces and loosely joined". As shown in Fig. 1, PLS can be decomposed into five elements, including e-Portfolio, resources, tools, activities and relationships. In the view of the "Everyone Connected" project, the operation of PLS depends on the services provided by the educational resource public service platform and the educational management public service platform, so PLS is regarded as a personal portal build by the two platforms.

- E-portfolio. The electronic portfolio contains the basic information and learning records of learners.
- Resources. The educational resource public service platform is the primary resource provider of PLS. The resources can also be from other places other than the platform. These resources can be classified as document, picture, video, program, link and so on according to the media type.
- Tools. Tool is the foundation to implement teaching, learning and management, part of the management tools come from the educational resource public service platform, such as information perception tools, learning process tracker tool.
- Activities. In order to realize the specific learning activities, resources and tools can be chosen freely in PLS by learners. Learners can also connect external learning activities through the ways of widget or link to collect different sources of learning activities, such as the elective course in Moodle.
- Relationships. The role and the social networks of learners in different learning activities are organized and managed by the form of relationship circle, such as class, family, group, friends and so on. In general, we think the degree of relationship in formal learning is closer than in informal learning.

Resources, tools and activities and relationship are the main constitutional elements for learning analytics data, which play an important role in making the learning analysis results act on the PLS. The learning process of learners was reflected in the electronics file, their behavior and data was also delivered to the educational resource public service platform and the educational management public service platform. By LA, the two platforms will trace the learning situation, diagnose conditions to give suggestions for pushing resources, recommending activities and evaluating learning process. Thus, personalized learning can be realized by equipment adaptation and situation adaptation.

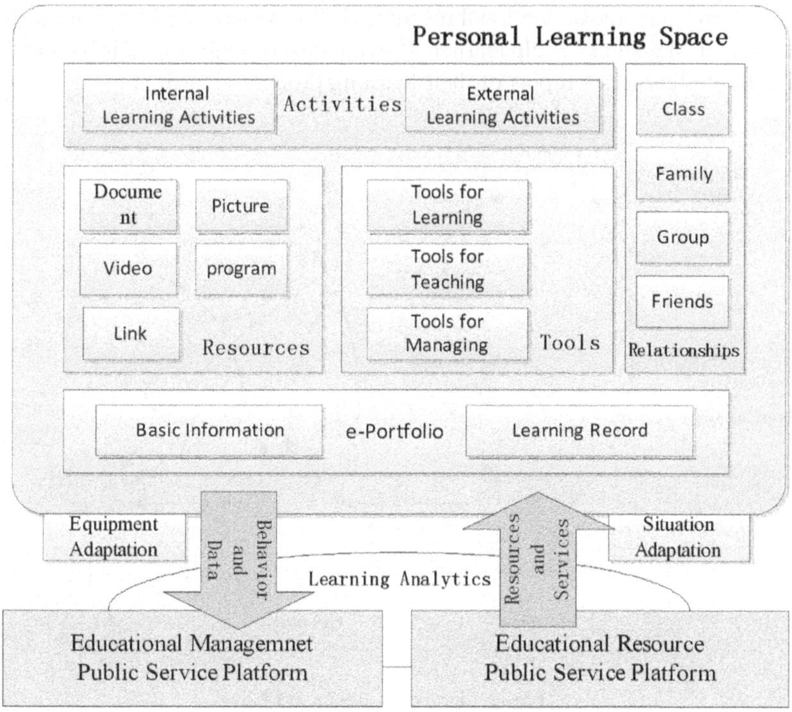

Fig. 1. Construction of PLS

3.2 Development of Personalized Learning Under the Support of Learning Analytics

In PLS, learners control and manage their learning, which means learning development depends on the learners' autonomy. Based on Zimmerman's three-stage model of self-regulated learning [7], universal learning activities can be divided into plan phase, performance phase and reflection phase. In the personalized learning of the "Everyone Connected" project, LA is applied in the push of resources and services, and the provision of learning report. The core characteristics of personalized learning are to reflect individual differences and meet individual needs.

- In plan stage, the educational management public service platform provides its historical study report for learners by LA, to assist learners to choose and arrange activities on the basis of fully understanding their learning situations. At the same time, the educational resource public service platform restructures learning resources in a personalized way and pushes them to learners under the support of LA.
- The core content of performance stage is learners' interactive learning. Based on the analysis of current distribution and state of entire learning space, the educational management public service platform pushes suitable learning companions, thematic learning communities timely and effectively and management tools to help learners to manage their spaces.

- In reflection stage, the educational resource public service platform will push appropriate level test gauges to help learners to evaluate and diagnose their learning results, while giving learners a report of their learning process records (Fig. 2).

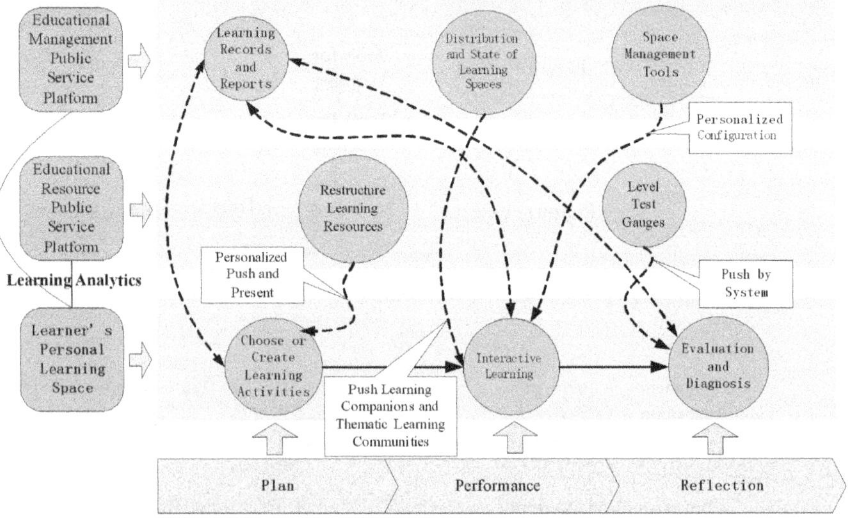

Fig. 2. Learning stages in PLS

4 Significance of the Study

LA shows that technologies can be integrated into teaching and learning in an insightful and smart way. It can greatly promote the implementation of personalized learning in "Everyone Connected" project in China. A PLS with five elements in the project is proposed. The organic interactive mechanism of "Two Platform" and PLS based on LA is also discussed in realizing personalized learning. The design idea can provide some references for the practices of applying LA to the "Everyone Connected" project in China. The implementation method needs to be refined in future research, including the problems of uniform format and secure interaction of learning behavior data from different sources, coordination and integration of cross-platform application services and so on.

Acknowledgements. This study was supported by grants from the project of construction specification development of the "Everyone Connected" project and the advantage discipline innovation platform principal investigator construction project in teacher education at East China Normal University.

References

1. Liu, Y.: Speech in the National Educational Informatization Work Video Conferences (2012) (in Chinese). http://www.moe.gov.cn/publicfiles/business/htmlfiles/moe/s3342/201211/144240.html
2. Poot, A., Learning, P., Austin, L.: The personal learning space – technology enabling engaging pedagogy. In: Proceedings of ASCILITE - Australian Society for Computers in Learning in Tertiary Education Annual Conference 2011, pp. 1015–1020. ASCILITE (2011)
3. UNESCO. Personalized Learning: A New ICT-Enabled Education Approach (2012). http://iite.unesco.org/publications/3214716/
4. Ferguson, R.: The state of learning analytics in 2012: a review and future challenges. Technical report KMI-12-01, Knowledge Media Institute, The Open University, UK (2012). http://kmi.open.ac.uk/publications/techreport/kmi-12-01
5. Downes, S.: Learning networks in practice. Emerg. Technol. Learn. **2**, 19–27 (2007)
6. Gillet, D., Law, E.L.C., Chatterjee, A.: Personal learning environments in a global higher engineering education Web 2.0 realm. In: IEEE EDUCON Education Engineering 2010 Conference, Madrid, Spain, pp. 897–906. IEEE (2010)
7. Zimmerman, B.J.: Becoming a self-regulated learner: an overview. Theor. Pract. **41**(2), 64–70 (2002)
8. Davis, F.D.: Perceived usefulness, perceived ease of use, and user acceptance of information technology. MIS Q. **13**(3), 319–340 (1989)

Author Index

The manufacturer's authorised representative in the EU is Springer Nature Customer Service Centre GmbH, Europaplatz 3, 69115 Heidelberg, Germany. If you have any concerns regarding our products, please contact ProductSafety@springernature.com

Printed and bound by CPI Group (UK) Ltd, Croydon, CR0 4YY
24/09/2026
02222124-0003